Geraldene Holt's
COMPLETE BOOK OF
HERBS

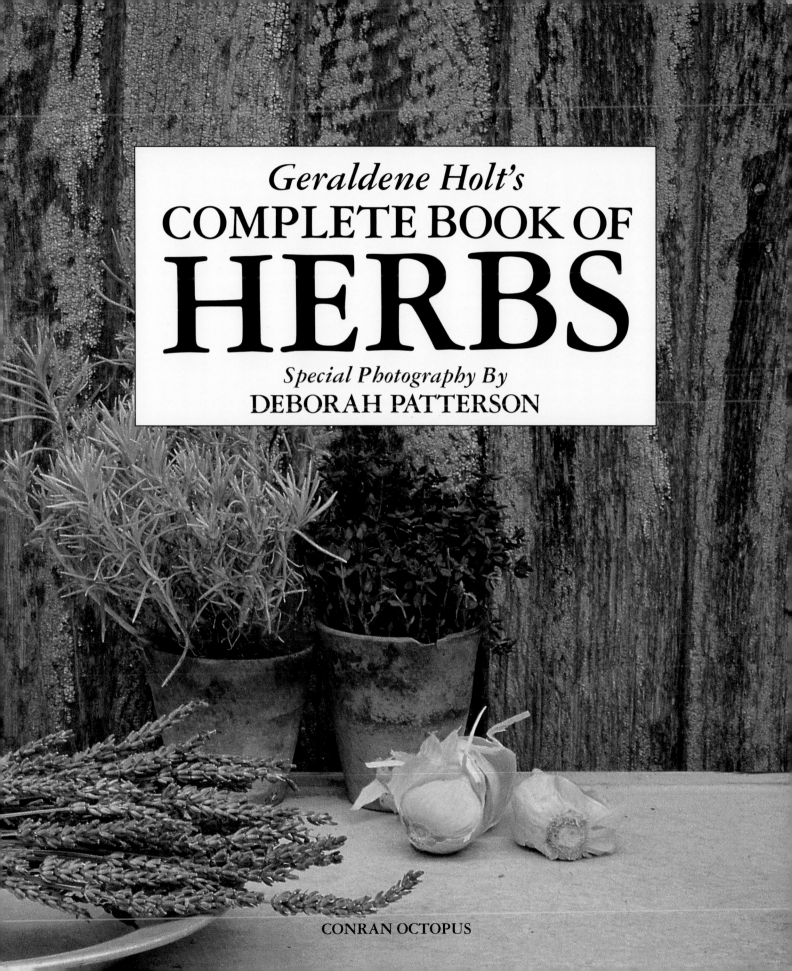

Geraldene Holt's
COMPLETE BOOK OF
HERBS

Special Photography By
DEBORAH PATTERSON

CONRAN OCTOPUS

For my mother, gifted gardener and cook, with my love

First published in 1991 by
Conran Octopus Limited
37 Shelton Street
London WC2H 9HN

Reprinted 1992

British Library Cataloguing in Publication Data
Holt, Geraldene
  Geraldene Holt's Complete Book of Herbs
  1. Herbs
  I. Title
  581.63

  ISBN 1-85029-325-2

PROJECT EDITOR **JOANNA COPESTICK**
EDITORS **MICHELLE CLARKE, NORMA MACMILLAN,**
        BARBARA MELLOR
EDITORIAL ASSISTANT **ROD MACKENZIE**
ART EDITOR **KAREN BOWEN**
PICTURE RESEARCH **JESSICA WALTON**
PRODUCTION **JULIA GOLDING**
HOME ECONOMIST **JANE SUTHERING**
ASSISTED BY **MEG JANSZ**
SPECIAL PHOTOGRAPHY **DEBORAH PATTERSON**

Printed and bound in Singapore
Typeset by Servis Filmsetting Limited
Colour separation by Chroma Graphics (Overseas) Pty
Limited

IMPORTANT NOTE
This book is intended as a reference volume only. It is not
a medical manual or a guide to self-treatment.

Herbs are powerful plants. It is dangerous to use them as
a treatment for serious or chronic medical conditions
without consulting a medical herbalist. Before trying any
herbal remedy, sample a small quantity first in case you
suffer an allergic reaction. Do not take herbal remedies if
you are undergoing any other course of medical
treatment without seeking professional advice.

Both metric and imperial quantities are given in the
recipes. Use either all metric or all imperial, as the two are
not interchangeable.

CONTENTS

Part 1

HERB GARDENING

Gardeners, like plants, invariably grow from small beginnings. Carrot tops afloat in a saucer of water, a plate of mustard and cress seed sprouting on pink blotting paper, or a handful of mint leaves carefully plucked, one by one, from one's own patch of garden – from such ventures, lifelong gardeners are born.

On Sundays, when I was young, I was allowed to chop mint leaves in a suitably child-sized metal mill with a smooth wooden handle that you turned like a musical box. Next, I spooned the brownish-green mint mixture into a little dish and stirred in honey or sugar, some hot water and a few drops of vinegar. Then the best part; tasting it to check the flavour. Finally I would carry it very slowly to the table for serving with roast lamb.

And so for me, growing herbs and cooking with them became as one. I remain a gardening cook and still value herbs principally for their culinary virtues. Yet, as the years pass, one begins to appreciate these fascinating plants for their other equally timeless qualities.

We all know the evocative nature of scent and smell, how instantly we are transported to a time, a place or a person, at the merest hint of a remembered fragrance. Perfumed plants do this superbly and it contributes greatly to their charm.

It may be that for this reason alone, the first herb gardens were created.

Happily, for those of us enamoured of these fascinating plants, a herb garden is one of the simplest and easiest kinds of garden to create. Even a window box or a collection of flowerpots filled with your favourite plants is a herb garden in miniature form.

Establishing a herb garden on a slightly larger scale is one of the most enjoyable garden projects you can undertake. For, knowingly or otherwise, one follows in the footsteps of many distinguished herb gardeners of the past. Pliny the Elder, who tended the box hedges and scented violets in the garden of his Laurentian villa; Sir Thomas More, who introduced a rosemary bush into his garden in Chelsea; and Vita Sackville-West, who planted her rare white-flowered borage in the herb garden at Sissinghurst Castle in Kent.

Some garden historians now believe that many of today's rosemary bushes found in Chelsea gardens are descended from Sir Thomas More's original plant. Indeed, Geoffrey Grigson, the poet and gardener, described plants as 'vehicles of life' and noted how they have been grown in the same place for centuries; as if in response to some memory of our shared garden heritage.

The herb garden at Eyhorne Manor in Kent is laid out in the medieval manner: long rectangular beds filled with a single species of herb. In front is a bed overflowing with varieties of sage.

Perhaps it is their instinct for survival, even in a hostile climate, that so endears these plants to one. For me, their historical significance and ancient value in medicine and food only add to their horticultural attraction.

Herb gardening illustrates perfectly this continuity of ideas in gardening, for the plants that have been grown since before Christian times are mercifully little changed today. Moreover, many contemporary designs for herb gardens draw directly on the past, when herbs were revered as plants with special powers.

There is no doubt that herbs have a power to charm. Of course, they make the most delightful presents, both to give and to receive: a pot of basil, a wreath of bay leaves or a bouquet of freshly-picked herbs please me far more than the most luxurious chocolates. And where is the cook who does not warm to a window box planted with tarragon, chervil and chive plants?

One of the most inspired herb presents that I know was given to a friend of mine by her husband. Early one Christmas morning, working quietly beneath the bedroom window, he constructed a tiny parterre herb garden, marked out with scroll-edge tiles and filled with her favourite herbs. Although difficult to wrap, unveiling it must have been a fabulous surprise.

Yet, the pleasure of planning and constructing your own herb garden is hardly less keen. When I think back over herb gardens that I've planted, I fondly remember my chequerboard herb garden in Hertfordshire where I uncovered a worn silver coin from the time of Edward I. And, in Oxfordshire, where I grew my herbs in a large island border set in the lawn. And now, in Devon, where I decided to move my herbs nearer the house and create a simple rectangular herb garden inspired by my wild herb garden in Provence.

In my own herb garden I am always captivated by the changing appearance of the garden as the seasons unfold. In late February and early March the bright green shoots of spring appear: the fine tendrils of the first chives, the folded, felted leaves of mint and the lacey sprigs of sweet cicely all signal the end of winter. I hasten to protect these welcome omens with a small cloche or even a jam jar, to prevent damage to the herbs from an unforeseen late frost which is a constant threat at this time of year.

By April the garden begins to look furnished, with its burgeoning clumps of marjoram and thyme, hyssop and lavender, their bushy new growth jostling for space. Scented purple violets, mauve and yellow heart's-ease pansies and sky-blue violas light up the spaces between the clumps with colour.

In midsummer the herb garden is a riot of growth, resembling a diminutive landscape with its tall trees of fennel and angelica, its hedges of parsley and hyssop and its low fields of chamomile and lemon thyme. Edible flowers bedeck the garden as if it were a medieval mead – roses and dianthus combine with soft blue sage flowers, mauve lavender spikes and the scarlet mop-head monarda or bee balm. Imperceptibly, late summer arrives with the hot, bright sunshine hues created by marigolds and nasturtiums, the yellow-flowering curry plant, and ruby-red blooms of marjoram bursting forth.

The autumn is heralded by softer tones, offset by the grey foliage of rosemary, lavender and cottage pinks whose clove-scented gillyflowers glow among the quiet greens. Gradually the garden slows, the tarragon begins to look tired, there are fewer fresh spikes of chives and I harvest my last handfuls of tender herbs to preserve them for winter use. Some time in November a light powdering of snow or a severe frost marks the resting time for many herbs. Yet some valiant plants such as sage, sweet bay and thyme accompany one through the winter and every cook is glad of them. Even in deep winter a well-planned herb garden is still beautiful, a geometric abstract pattern of grey and white.

I designed my herb garden with simplicity in mind: four beds are divided by gravel paths leading to a central sundial, and another gravel path leads round the outside of the whole garden. Wandering round the garden picking a sprig here and there is one of my greatest pleasures and inspirations when I am thinking about cooking, so it was important to me to be able to reach all the herbs fairly easily. And as any cook who uses herbs a lot will want to be able to dash out to the herb garden at any time, winter or summer, in fair weather or foul, cobbles, bricks or any other quick-draining surface is essential for paths.

Still with practicality as well as aesthetics in mind, I planted each bed from the centre outwards. In the middle went the tallest herbs – angelica, fennel, lovage and bay – to be surrounded by ones of medium height, such as sage, rosemary, borage, dill, tarragon and lavender. Marjoram, basil and other low-growing herbs went in next, beside the paths, and then I edged the beds with herbs that form neat cushions, such as chives and parsley, sorrel and hyssop. Finally I planted the circular area round the sundial with many different forms of low creeping thyme to form an aromatic evergreen carpet.

These, then, were my priorities. Other people's will naturally be different. You may long for a scented retreat full of soft colour and shady bowers, a haven for wildlife where you will be tempted to linger on drowsy summer afternoons. You may seek the restful qualities of a formal garden, large or small, where the cool symmetry of uncluttered lines and restrained compositions of green on green are somehow soothing to both the senses and the intellect. You may feel inspired to re-create a Tudor or Renaissance knot, or to make a garden to complement a particular architectural style, be it classical Georgian or flamboyant high-Victorian, Arts and Crafts Edwardian or thirties Metroland. Or you may simply want to throw caution to the winds and make a garden with pots and containers in glorious defiance of limitations of space or exposure. Or of course you may, like me, be a gardener cook, with the pleasures of the table in mind.

All these different styles of gardens – and infinitely more – are possible with herbs. Yet, despite their variety, herb gardens tend to be highly personal places, invariably planted and designed with special care. They allow for creative experiments with colour, scent and design on a manageable scale, and they yield pleasures and satisfactions for all the senses.

Although my own preference is for the small, intimate style of herb garden, there is no doubt that the large formal garden makes a fine spectacle. What matters is that your own herb garden reflects your own choice of style and plants. The individuality of herb gardens and how they reflect their owners is one of their most outstanding qualities. For me, the herb garden is ultimately a personal garden, created for one's own purposes and delight, close by one's home and truly, the perfect pleasure garden.

One of the pleasures of herb gardens is their versatility: they can be adapted to suit virtually any soil, exposure, size of plot or style of building. Whether small or large, formal or informal, they have a way of settling in and billowing out which very quickly gives them an air of maturity. In a cottage garden (left), plump cushions of lavender form a softly natural complement to spiky iris leaves and the tall spires of hollyhocks. In a more formal design (above), feathery santolina and thyme are used to edge the neat individual beds set among old, worn brick paths.

HERBS AND THEIR HISTORY

A page from a medieval herbal. Borage was used to allay 'hot complaints' and to make cooling cordials, but it was valued chiefly for the flavour it imparted to wine and cider.

The study of plants has been of absorbing interest to mankind since the earliest times. It is, moreover, one of his oldest and most fascinating fields of intellectual enquiry. During the prehistoric era, when still a nomadic hunter-gatherer, man began to discover which plants were of particular value. In time, as he settled and farmed, it became necessary to organize and codify this learning so that it could be passed on to succeeding generations and hence this essential wisdom was recorded for reference.

We know that over 5,000 years ago the ancient Assyrians, Chaldeans, Chinese and Egyptians each had their own schools of herbalists. Some of the earliest written evidence dates from the time of the ancient Egyptians who inscribed recipes for herbal remedies on clay tablets and on rolls of papyrus. The Ebers papyrus which is thought to date from around 2000 BC, contains over 700 herbal remedies recorded and annotated by the priest who compiled it.

During the fifth century BC, Hippocrates, and later Aristotle and Theophrastus, documented the existing knowledge of herbs. These herbals and that of Dioscorides in the second century AD became the foundation of European herbal scholarship. Dioscorides was a contemporary of Pliny. Although Greek – he was born in Asia Minor – he became an army doctor with the Roman legions. The original of his magnificent herbal, written in Greek, though widely known by its Latin title, *De Materia Medica*, has been lost. However, quite miraculously, an illustrated sixth-century copy, which contains details of over 500 plants, has survived to become an inspiration to every herbalist since.

In Britain the popular herbals of the seventeenth century, written by Gerard and Culpeper, drew heavily upon the classical herbals, but, although correct in many respects, they repeated the same myths and mistakes. Gradually, however, the Greek theory of humours, the medieval Doctrine of Signatures and the astrological symbolism of herbs were discarded. In fact, up until only a century ago, the close link between medicine and herbs in Britain was maintained by the inclusion of the *Materia Medica* in the examination syllabus of medical students.

Plants have been man's principal source of medication since recorded history. Although herbal medicine in the Western world is often seen as a lowly alternative to chemically manufactured drugs, the herbalists of India and the 'barefoot doctors' of China continue the tradition of treating illness with the extracts and tinctures of plants. Increasingly, the rest of the world is regarding the healing power of herbs, or 'green medicine', favourably. And many people, despairing of conventional medicine, are seeking help from homeopaths and herbalists.

Some herbs have, of course, always been used in cooking. The Roman cookery book written by Apicius contains many recipes for dishes flavoured with culinary herbs. And to judge from English cookery books of the sixteenth and seventeenth centuries, herbs were regarded as an important ingredient in cooking. John Evelyn's *Acetaria*, published in 1664 and subtitled, *A Discourse on Sallets*, not only stressed the unique contribution of fresh vegetables and herbs to man's diet but also shared with the reader the author's enthusiasm for growing them. Like every author on herbs before him, John Evelyn regarded a plant's culinary and medical properties as of equal interest. Yet, the practice of treating illness with culinary herbs and special foods, which has effectively died out in the West, continues in China, where health restaurants serve special diets devised to alleviate particular disorders and afflictions.

The magical powers attributed to many herbs in medieval Britain were, unknowingly, partly founded upon what have since been discovered to be sound principles of chemistry. For instance, the practice of carrying garlic to ward off evil spirits and infection does have a scientific basis because the high sulphur content of the herb acts as a bactericide. Herbal pomanders carried to protect the owner from the plague worked in a similar way. And tussie-mussies and nosegays of herbs containing rue and rosemary, carried by dignitaries when visiting their poor subjects, repelled insects.

Every herb has its own history: a herb is defined as 'a plant useful to man either by its leaf, flower, stem or root', and a little research into those uses makes fascinating reading and yields intriguing insights into little-known byways of social history. Sweet violets, for instance, among all their many other uses down the ages, were used by the ancient Greeks as a cure for hangovers. Paracelsus is supposed to have sold an extravagantly expensive elixir based on balm to royal customers, on the promise that it would restore their virility. Woad, used by the ancient Britons to paint themselves sky blue according to Julius Caesar, was also used to dye policemen's uniforms until the advent of chemical dyes. Laurel used to be thought to attract the muse, and poets and writers would keep a bay leaf in their pocket or under their pillow – hence, eventually, the title 'poet laureate'. Rosemary was burned in the streets of London to ward off disease, and in times of plague the price of a sprig would increase by up to thirty times. The list is endless.

The present-day interest in the ecology and

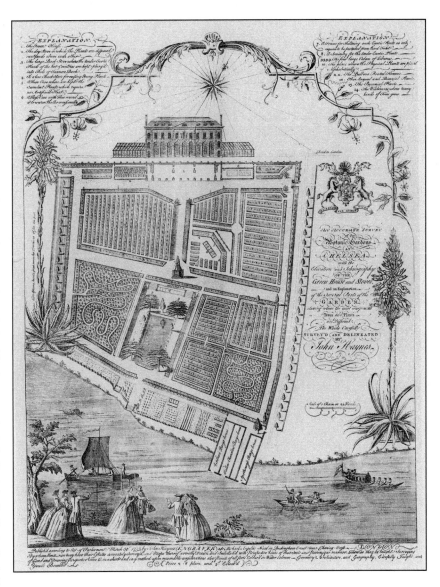

future of our planet has encouraged scientific enquiry into the efficacy of herbs. Some of the results are heartening. Feverfew, for example, has been prescribed by herbalists for centuries as a treatment for headaches. Sir John Hill in *The British Herbal*, published in 1772, writes of feverfew, 'In the worst headaches this Herb exceeds whatever else is known'.

Although the Vatican had founded a physic garden for the study of plants in 1277, it was not

The first physic garden in Britain for the systematic study of medicinal herbs was founded at Oxford in 1621. In 1673 the Chelsea Physic Garden followed, established by the Worshipful Society of Apothecaries for the 'manifestation of the glory, power and wisdom of God, in the works of creation.'

until the seventeenth century that Britain's most famous physic garden was started on the bank of the river Thames in London. During the eighteenth century, Philip Miller, working with the Society of Apothecaries, established a fine, walled garden of specimen beds planted with different plant families to facilitate formal botanical study. Due to the foresight of Miller's patron, Sir Hans Sloane, the Chelsea Physic Garden exists today in hardly altered form and is well worth visiting.

Considerable advances in the botanical and chemical classification of herbs were made during the eighteenth and nineteenth centuries. However, it was not until 1931 that Mrs M Grieve, FRHS, produced her comprehensive *Modern Herbal*, which assembles the horticultural, medical and culinary properties of over 1,000 English and American herbs.

Mrs Grieve influenced many people – mainly women – who began to grow and write about the cultivation and use of herbs. Mrs Hilda Leyel had founded the Society of Herbalists in 1926 and later opened a herb shop named after Nicholas Culpeper, the seventeenth-century herbalist, and contributed, too, to the literature on herbs. The prolific writer Mrs Eleanour Sinclair Rohde helped to popularize herbs and herb gardening in Britain and North America. In 1933 the Herb Society of America was founded.

Many new herb gardens and herb farms were established by the pioneers of the herb movement. Consequently, even though there are some historic gardens in Britain, it has been estimated that the great majority of today's herb gardens are under 50 years old.

During the last 40 years, increased foreign travel has developed our appetite for food from countries where herbs are still considered of culinary value. As a result, cooks have been keen to grow their own supply of fresh herbs. Indeed, it could be said that in their long history there has never been more active interest in the virtues of herbs than there is now. A few years ago, the distinguished gardening writer Rosemary Verey wrote, 'I do not think that there has been a period in garden history when the herb garden has played a more important role both in garden design and in the use of herbs for cooking than it does today'. The enthusiasm of gardeners, cooks and herbalists continues apace.

The Renaissance was the heyday of domestic herb gardens: the mistress of any house of substance would cultivate aromatic plants and fragrant flowers in a secluded formal garden, walled or hedged around with arbors of roses, vines or pleached fruit trees. She would then carefully pick and sort the leaves and flowers, as shown in Lucas van Valkenbosch's meticulously detailed painting Spring (1595), before putting them to innumerable different uses: scenting rooms and stuffing pillows, strewing floors and weaving garlands, making healing potions and flavouring dishes to name but a few.

MEDICINAL AND MONASTIC HERB GARDENS

Though a life of retreat offers various joys,
None, I think, will compare with the time
*   one employs,*
In the study of herbs, or in striving to gain
Some practical knowledge of nature's domain.
Get a garden!
WALAFRID STRABO, 'HORTULUS' OR
'THE LITTLE GARDEN', 900AD

In Europe, the Christian church adopted a small enclosed garden style known as the 'paradise' from the Middle East, and built them to their own design, either round or semi-circular, adjoining their monastic churches and cathedrals. Although the garden itself has disappeared, the fifteenth-century doorway to the paradise garden at Winchester Cathedral is still standing. Normally, the paradise garden was in the care of the sacrist who grew sacred flowers and plants there for decorating the altar and the church on feast days.

In contrast to the small, private paradise, the 'cloister' garden was a larger, enclosed space, usually built against the nave of the church and surrounded by colonnaded cloisters where monks could study and write. Many magnificent examples remain: the cloister garden of the church of St Trophime in Arles, France, and a similar form at Ely Cathedral, England immediately come to mind. This style of garden was known in medieval England as the 'cloister garth' and it contained aromatic plants and herbs that perfumed the air and offered solace to the monks during their long meditation.

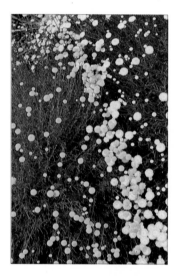

As well as being one of the most popular and useful plants for edging in the herb garden, being both decorative and evergreen, santolina is also pungently aromatic. Traditionally, when winter clothes were put away, sprays of santolina would be laid in chests and wardrobes to guard against moths and insects.

OPPOSITE *This design for a cloister garden by Tim Martin for the Chelsea Flower Show in 1987 includes a mixture of vegetables, flowers and traditional medicinal and culinary herbs, rather like a French* potager.

For over a thousand years after the Roman occupation, medical knowledge resided in the monasteries and religious houses of Britain. These became the principal seats of learning where the texts of classical herbals, usually derived from the work of Dioscorides in the second century, were copied out and amended.

Each religious community aimed to be self-sufficient and, most notably in the case of the Benedictines, the practical art of gardening became highly skilled. A monastery endeavoured to grow all its own food and also a special area was devoted to growing the plants that were valued for their medicinal properties. Usually the medicinal herbs were grown separately, in the physic garden, and they constituted the only form of medicine administered to the sick and infirm.

The earliest known plan of a medicinal herb garden dates from the time of Abbot Walafrid Strabo, in the ninth century, and was discovered at the Benedictine monastery of St Gall in Switzerland. The detailed map of the monastery shows a cloister garth built on the protected south side of the church and the medicinal, or physic, garden sited by the physician's house and the infirmary.

The square garden, or 'herbularius', was divided into 16 parallel beds with a different herb 'both beautiful and health-giving' grown in each. These included cumin, fennel, fenugreek, lovage, mint, pennyroyal, rose, rosemary, rue, sage, savory and tansy.

It is thought that each herb was grown in a separate bed to make harvesting and identifi-

cation easier. The raised beds were edged with pegged wooden boards to keep the soil in place. Whether the St Gall garden was ever constructed is unknown, though its pattern is echoed in the garden design that followed for several centuries. Indeed, the design of the twelfth-century herb garden at Canterbury Cathedral is remarkably similar to the St Gall plan. And, although no longer a herb garden, the little cloister garden at Westminster Abbey formed part of the infirmary garden in medieval times.

The earliest English herbal that has survived dates from the second half of the ninth century. It was written in Anglo-Saxon under the direction of a monk called Bald who lived at the time of King Alfred. The manuscript gives prescriptions for a wide range of herbal remedies and medicines. 'The Saxons had a much wider knowledge of herbs than the doctors of Salerno, the oldest school of medicine in Europe', claimed Dr J C Payne in a lecture delivered to the Royal College of Physicians in 1903. Bald's herbal describes the monastic herb garden of the time, known as the 'wyrttun', in which, among other herbs, gillyflowers, peonies, marigolds, violets and periwinkles were cultivated.

Medicinal herb gardens continued in use up until the latter half of the nineteenth century. As late as 1862 the famous gardener, William Robinson, complained that medical students who were required to collect examples of the plants in the *Materia Medica*, gathered the flowers and buds from his rare plants, making propagation difficult.

At about the same time in North America, the Shaker communities, who had used herbal medicine since they had founded their settlements, established a series of flourishing medicinal herb gardens from which they operated a very successful seed business, even exporting to Britain.

Although most of the historic medicinal herb gardens have now disappeared, the restored herb garden at Acorn Bank in Cumbria (owned by the National Trust) displays much of its former glory and includes many of the plants listed by Thomas Tusser in 1580 as 'necessaire herbes to growe in the garden for physick'.

As far as I've been able to discover, most of the monasteries in Britain today have allowed their herb gardens to decay, though there are a number of very fine modern gardens based on medieval

physic gardens. Westminster Abbey has a little garden of medicinal herbs growing on what was probably the site of the original infirmary garden. At Michelham Priory another modern physic garden contains a large and carefully researched range of medicinal plants that would have been known in the sixteenth century. And Brother Robert at Caldy Abbey near Tenby tells me that he is planning a new herb garden for the abbey. He is a keen cook and so the garden will include culinary as well as medicinal herbs, and will, indeed, embody the advice given in Ecclesiasticus, 'The Lord hath created medicines out of the earth; and he that is wise will not abhor them'.

Many of the herbs that most of us now grow for cooking, or simply for the enjoyment of their fragrant leaves and flowers, have for centuries also been prized for their healing qualities. The physic garden would also contain many plants which are now mainstays of the flower garden, such as roses, foxgloves, pinks and irises. Here they are grown in raised beds edged with wooden boards, in medieval monastic style.

A carpet of creeping thyme, releasing its heady Mediterranean scent as you pass, is one of the pleasures of the herb garden. An infusion of the leaves of both thyme and sage (here the purple-leaved variety) is a traditional remedy for colds and sore throats, while a tisane of lovage leaves (behind) used to be drunk for a wide range of illnesses. Today its spiciness makes it a useful addition to salt-free diets.

CULINARY HERB GARDENS

Gardening cooks have, I imagine, always preferred to gather their own fresh culinary herbs rather than depend upon the vagaries of the market. Even in Hellenic Egypt, where vegetables were usually grown in the fields and sold in markets and shops, herbs such as coriander, mint and parsley were more often cultivated closer to hand in the garden.

During the first century BC, Columella sang the praises of home-grown produce and gave detailed advice on how to grow vegetables and herbs. He listed garlic, mint, mustard and parsley as essential herbs for cooking.

Hardly 100 years later, Pliny the Elder made a similar plea: 'That quarter of the garden serveth our house with poignant herbs instead of sauce, to give a commendable taste and seasoning to our meat, showeth plainly that the master and mistress thereof were not wont to run in the Merchants' books for Spicerie, but changed the Grocer or Apothecaries' shop, for the garden'.

The history of culinary herbs naturally follows the development of cooking fairly closely. Furthermore, until 200 years ago culinary herbs were also considered in terms of their medicinal properties, which may, at times, have led to their overuse. A character in the play, Pseudolus, by Plautus, comments:

'I don't season a dinner the way other cooks do, who serve up whole pickled meadows in their patinae – men who . . . thrust herbs at you, then proceed to season these herbs with other herbs.'

Mint has enjoyed a place of honour in herb gardens and cooking pots since ancient Egyptian times at least. Hardy, attractive and tolerant to the point of invasiveness, it occurs in a dozen or so varieties, with nuances in flavour ranging from apple, ginger and lemon to refreshing spearmint and peppermint.

OPPOSITE *There are so many culinary herbs to choose from, with such a variety of heights and shapes and different colours and textures of leaves and flowers, that it is not difficult to make a garden that is useful as well as pretty throughout the year.*

Early English writers usually refer to 'greenstuff' and pot herbs, meaning both vegetables and culinary herbs. They talk of 'herbes grown in a herber', a small plot or garden containing a mixture of herbs and vegetables and sometimes fruit and flowers, grown together almost in the style of a traditional English cottage garden or a French *potager*.

In the latter half of the fourteenth century, the number of small gardens in England increased considerably. The great plague had left many landowners short of labour to steward their grounds and so they leased it to tenants to use as cottage gardens.

More specialized than the cottage garden was the cultivated plot of ground in every monastery known as the 'hortus'. Here both pot herbs and vegetables were grown together in a rectangular garden enclosed by walls or wattle fencing and divided into 20 or more long, narrow beds, separated by gravel or grassed paths.

Depending on the nature of the soil, the beds or 'floores' were raised or left level. Sometimes the raised beds were surrounded by wooden boards and even painted rails. Even by today's standards the variety of culinary herbs grown in a hortus was impressive. The ninth-century garden at the monastery of St Gall contained a selection of herbs that would delight any cook: black cumin, chervil, coriander, chives, dill, garlic and parsley.

Of course, the wealthy also gardened at home on a grand scale, often inspired by redoubtable female enthusiasts. In the early years of the

seventeenth century, Lucy Russell, Countess of Bedford and a keen gardener, encouraged Giacomo Castelvetro to write his treatise on Italian vegetables, herbs and fruit, intended to encourage the English to enliven their diet. Interestingly, although his book is a gem of culinary literature, all the herbs he discusses also appear in the 1580 edition of Thomas Tusser's *Five Hundred Points of Good Husbandry*, though their use sometimes varies. Tusser, for instance, recommends growing basil as a strewing herb whereas Castelvetro includes it as one of the 13 herbs that constitute his Excellent Mixed Salad.

Similarly, Lady Elinor Fettiplace showed a deep interest in the growing and cooking of greenstuff in her kitchen garden. In Hilary Spurling's absorbing book about Elizabethan country-house cooking she writes, 'Elinor Fettiplace devoted a whole page of her book, *To Set or Sow All Manner of Herbs*, to the question of successive plantings, pricking out, earthing-up, feeding, pruning, cutting and harvesting, so as to be able to pick something fresh all the year round'.

An Elizabethan herb garden was indeed a glorious sight, a treasury of plants of value to the kitchen and the stillroom, usually bounded by a hedge of fruiting and flowering bushes. Dr John Hall, a botanist and surgeon, described his enclosed garden in 1563:

> *'It hedged was with honeysuckles,*
> *Or periclimenum;*
> *Well mixed with small cornus trees,*
> *Sweet briar and ligustrum.*
>
> *The white thorn, and the blackthorn both,*
> *With box and maple fine:*
> *In which branched the briony,*
> *The ivy and wild vine.'*

In some gardens the fruit trees and rose bushes were prettily trained against trellises, and it was fashionable to have a vine-covered arbor on one side of the garden to provide a shaded area for sitting and resting.

Thomas Tusser tells us of the wide variety of herbs – culinary, medicinal and strewing – that were cultivated in an Elizabethan garden. Although we still grow most of the herbs, we appear to have forgotten that some of them are edible. The twenty-one 'herbs and roots for sallets

FAR LEFT *As well as the more familiar culinary herbs, the herb garden at Gunby Hall in Lincolnshire contains an evocative catalogue of names which recall traditional British recipes and remedies of former centuries: including tansy, lovage, camphor and balm.*

LEFT *With its sweetly scented purple-blue flowers and aromatic deep-green foliage, hyssop (flanked here by mint and an airy stand of fennel) makes a delightfully informal edging to a path. Gascon cooks use the spicy leaves to flavour rich meat dishes and tomato preserves, while in Britain they are traditionally added to the syrup of cooked peaches.*

and sauce' contain one or two surprises, including the 'blessed thistle' and sea holly. Violets are also included, and are only one of the many flowers that used to be eaten much more freely than they are today. In Elizabethan cooking, flowers were strewn over sweet and savoury dishes and they were candied and conserved. In Sir Hugh Plat's *Delightes for Ladies*, published in 1602, the many flower recipes include preparations for primroses, cowslips, gillyflowers, marigolds and nasturtiums. Above all, the rose and the violet figure most prominently in cookery and household books of the time.

Herb flowers such as rosemary, lavender, hyssop, thyme and marjoram were added to salads and were steeped in a sugar syrup to make sweetmeats. Fennel seeds were made into candied comfits and every sweetly scented herb was distilled with water to make a perfumed potion or spirit. The Elizabethan fondness for scented food seemed to know no bounds and gardeners and cooks were adventurous in their search for unusual herbs and flowers. It would seem that during the reign of Elizabeth I there was a spirit of delicious enquiry in both the herb garden

and the kitchen which would be well worth recapturing today.

The most celebrated gardening cook of the seventeenth century was John Evelyn whose work of 1664, *Acetaria: A Discourse on Sallets*, lists 73 different culinary herbs with their medicinal virtues. In his splendid kitchen garden at Sayes Court in Deptford, London, where he even designed an early glasshouse, Evelyn advised growing chervil as an edging herb because it 'is handsome and proper', and took pains to grow vegetables and herbs that would enable him to serve a salad every day of the year. He produced a special calendar listing the plants to incorporate into salads. These included many herbs with interesting varieties such as Greenland sorrel and Indian nasturtium. He approached the making of salads as an art, emphasizing the importance both of suiting the salad to the person who was going to eat it and of finely tuning the ingredients: 'In the Composure of a Salid, every plant came in to bear its part, without being over-power'd by some Herb of a stronger taste, so as to endanger the native Sapor and Vertue of the vert; but fall into their places, like the Notes of Music in which there

Here horseradish grows next to a clump of lemon balm, whose lemon-scented leaves can be used to add a delicate lemon flavour to a host of dishes, including soups and salads, custards and ice creams, teas and sponge cakes, stuffings and vinegars. Bees love it too.

shall be nothing harsh or grating.'

Evelyn's gardening contemporary in France was Olivier de Serres, described as the Father of French Agriculture, and famous for some important horticultural innovations. His unusual herb garden design was built on a mound or small hillock with a long, spiralling path to the summit, lined each side with herbs.

Olivier de Serres lived in the moderate climate of the Ardèche region of France. Yet, even the comparatively discouraging climate of Scotland spurred on one avid seventeenth-century garden-

er. In his book, *The Scots Gard'ner*, published in 1683, John Reid advised:

'Of sweet herbes: as, Clary by seeds and offsets in Aprile; at which time you may slip and set Tansie, Sage, Cost, Mint, Balme, Winter Savory, Thyme, Penniroyall, Wild Marjorum, Maudlin, Fennell, etc. Prune their tops and fibres, and plant in garden soil, 8 rowes in the bed; they all continue long: but cutting their tops in growing time makes them more durable: and cut them all within a handful of the ground at August, that they may recover against the winter'.

John Reid dedicates his book 'To all the Ingenious Planters in Scotland' and proceeds to give sound advice on how to cultivate tender herbs such as basil, dill and rosemary, that in ideal circumstances prefer to grow in a much warmer Mediterranean climate.

During the heyday of kitchen gardening, in Victorian England, herbs regained some of their earlier importance. The most familiar and often-used English herbs, mint, parsley and sage, were to be found in almost every garden. In the walled kitchen gardens of grand houses, more unusual culinary herbs, such as tarragon and fennel, were planted in the protected south- and west-facing borders at the foot of the wall; and glass cloches and leaded lights enabled the gardener to extend the season of many culinary herbs in order to satisfy the needs of the country-house kitchen.

From the 1880s onwards a more naturalistic style of garden design was introduced under the influence of William Robinson and Gertrude Jekyll. Herbs began to be reassessed as attractive plants in their own right. The few herb gardens that Gertrude Jekyll designed contained a mixture of culinary and medicinal plants. She had an exciting approach to planting, and created great swathes of foliage by planting a dozen or more plants at a time, thereby increasing their impact and producing a more natural effect.

The great revival of interest in growing herbs that began between World Wars I and II has led to many new herb gardens being established. Shortages of patent medicines based on chemical products during both wars prompted a return to traditional herbal remedies. This trend for natural medicine continues today.

Some of the most handsome culinary herb gardens in the British Isles have been created by talented cooks. In the Northamptonshire village of Farthinghoe, Nicola Cox and her husband, Simon, run a flourishing wine and food school in the former rectory. They have gradually restored the magnificent walled kitchen garden where Nicola has planted a charming culinary herb garden. Large enough to provide plenty of herbs for both her cooking classes and her family's meals, the design is based on a series of diagonal borders separated by gravel paths. The narrow beds, from which it is easy to gather the herbs, are edged with Cotswold stone. The wide variety of culinary plants includes bronze fennel and Egyptian onions, angelica and lemon thyme, heart's-ease pansies and horseradish, and they are planted with a fine regard for contrast of leaf and colour and so form a most attractive area of the garden. A similar, though more extensive, culinary herb garden has recently been created by Dorinna Allen at Ballymaloe House, near Cork, in southern Ireland. Once again, the garden is intended to supply the needs of a cooking school and a family, plus, in this case, the requirements of her parents-in-law's beautiful hotel. Starting with a quarter of an acre of virgin meadow, sheltered by a belt of mature trees on one side and a high hedge on another, Dorinna has created a classic, symmetrical design of twenty geometrically shaped herb

beds surrounded by low, clipped box hedging and separated by gravel paths. A summer house at one end of the garden is balanced by an antique wrought iron seat and a sundial placed at the other. Here, on a summer's day, a cook can sit in quiet contemplation, dreaming of dishes inspired by this sumptuous display of herbal beauty. A bed of crimson-red orache stands next to a tower of flowering fennel, a tapestry of orange and yellow nasturtiums is backed by a froth of French tarragon and a carpet of purple sage. This, indeed, is a cook's dream of a herb garden.

The seedheads of garlic add their spiralling arabesques to the herb garden in autumn. Highly esteemed all over the world and way back into the mists of time, garlic is indispensable in many kitchens and an essential ingredient in Mediterranean cooking. It is also rich in vitamin C, has strong antiseptic qualities and reduces blood cholesterol levels.

FORMAL HERB GARDENS

Most of us find the ordered symmetry of a formal herb garden pleasing. The artful arrangement of straight lines and curves satisfies both the eye and the brain, and even gardeners who prefer a more informal style usually admit an admiration for a well-groomed formal garden. For the formality of clipped hedges and neat paths with tidy planting can produce an atmosphere of peace and tranquillity in a garden – as if man and the unruly forces of nature have come to terms with each other to produce harmony.

From the damask roses and myrtle bushes of the ancient Persian paradise gardens, to the clipped box trees and rosemary hedges that surrounded beds of violets in the garden of Pliny's Laurentian villa, formal gardens have traditionally been the work of herb gardeners who take pride in growing their plants following a plan or pattern. Indeed, herbs such as rosemary, lavender and thyme which grow in clumps are ideally suited to a formal garden arrangement, offering not only a structured form but an opportunity for creating a delightful collection of herbal aromas. Such formal gardens are in sharp contrast to the freely romantic style of the unstructured medieval 'flowery mead' or meadow.

Court life has always favoured the formal garden as a private space where the sovereign and friends could spend time in gentle exercise or leisure. In Italy and France a palace garden invariably contained a pavilion or 'gloriette' large enough for dining or music-making. Good King René of France (1409–1480), a gifted gardener

Plays of light and shade can be used to add depth to a formal axis. Here at Cranborne Manor in Dorset a pale stone sundial is picked out against a dark yew backdrop, while mounds of grey-green santolina complete the tonal range.

OPPOSITE *Rosemary Verey's delightful herb garden at Barnsley House in Gloucestershire is cleverly divided into diamonds and triangles by clipped box borders. The central diamonds contain herbs such as sage, lovage and rosemary. Around the edges grow chives and pennyroyal.*

and patron of the arts, was said to have spent much of his later life writing and drawing in his elegant little garden house.

In 1447, in the Royal garden at Greenwich, an elevated and galleried arbor was built for the Queen so that she could admire the hedged garden below. And in the first year of the following century Henry VII fashioned a new garden at Richmond Palace to welcome Catherine of Aragon; it was 'under the King's windows, Queen's, and other estates, most fair and pleasant gardens, with royal knots alleyed and herbed'.

Within a few decades the style of garden known as the 'knot' had become highly popular. The classic knot garden is a level, rectangular bed planted in an intricate pattern, often based on a maze or a sinuous knotted coil of rope, that is delineated by means of a low, clipped hedge. The spaces between the hedges were either planted with herbs or filled with coloured gravels and sand. The whole effect was reminiscent of a faceted jewel or a tapestry cushion. Though fun to admire at ground level, the knot garden was best viewed from a nearby upper window where the overall pattern could be seen more clearly.

At Hampton Court, Henry VIII employed an army of gardeners to lay out elaborately designed gardens, planted with miniature box hedges and aromatic herbs that were clipped to shape. Although no longer miniature, his magnificent maze is still growing today.

The highly decorative designs of a Tudor knot garden resemble the embroidery patterns of the

time. These, in turn, were inspired by the architectural decoration known as strapwork.

In fashionable gardens of the seventeenth century, the Italian-inspired knot garden gave way to the 'parterre' style from France. The parterre garden was usually a symmetrical arrangement of knot gardens separated by paths of fine gravel or raked sand. In the *parterre de broderie* garden, the herbs planted within the low, clipped hedges were trimmed to an even height so that the effect was like that of a subtle, embossed embroidery.

By the time of the reign of William and Mary (1689–1702), an alternative form of parterre developed which is known as *Parterre Anglais.* Here the herbs and aromatic plants enclosed by the low, clipped hedges are allowed to grow and flower in a more relaxed style. Large houses had parterre gardens built on the south- or west-facing sides so that the ladies of the house could step straight into the decorative enclosed garden.

The next resurgence of interest in the formal herb garden began around the beginning of the present century. Gertrude Jekyll, renowned for her strong, simple garden design and planting schemes of subtle foliage and colour, designed a few herb gardens, all of them in a formal style. One of these designs, for Knebworth House in Hertfordshire, was the subject of an extraordinary and historic discovery in the early 1980s. The gardens at Knebworth were then undergoing restoration, and in the course of his work a young gardener found a plan dated 1907 for a herb garden. He was astonished to discover that it was the work of Gertrude Jekyll. Edwin Lutyens, the celebrated architect and her great associate, had married a daughter of the family (much to their disapproval) in 1897, but no one had ever suspected that Miss Jekyll had drawn up any plans for Knebworth, nor did any evidence exist to suggest that this design had ever been carried out. So it was that, over seventy years after it had been conceived, Miss Jekyll's scheme for the herb garden at Knebworth was finally brought to fruition. Her design, which was carried out to the letter, is based on five interlocking circles edged with concentric rings of brick. Lavender in the centre bed and rosemary in the satellite beds provide a strong architectural framework to the planting, with clipped rosemary linking the circles and a variety of other herbs, mostly perennials,

filling the gaps. This herb garden is a very fine and beautiful example of a formal layout that is carefully ordered and yet at the same time unconventional in design.

The considerable interest in herb gardening of the last 50 years has resulted in a revival of older styles of formal herb garden. Today in Britain there are many examples of both knot and parterre gardens to be found. Two particularly fine parterre gardens, each with immaculate box hedges, are to be seen at Hatfield House in Hertfordshire and at the Tradescant Garden at the Museum of Garden History in Lambeth, London.

In Kent, the lovely garden at Sissinghurst Castle, planted with culinary and medicinal herbs by Vita Sackville-West, has inspired countless herb gardeners. The last of the gardens at Sissinghurst to be planted, it was begun in 1938, then replanted and enlarged after the war, when it expanded from a dozen or so herbs for the kitchen to twenty beds arranged in a traditional cross-shaped design. The formal herb garden also works well in a public situation as illustrated by the delightful garden designed by John Codrington for Emmanuel College, Cambridge: a commission for which he was recommended, as it happens, by Vita Sackville-West. Based on an early seventeenth-century design, this large formal garden was also inspired by John Codrington's realistic appreciation of the average student's tendency to cut corners: 'Having been an undergraduate myself, I knew that no undergraduate, when late for a lecture, could ever go round a corner without cutting it off, so I drew straight lines from every door in the court to every other door.' Three triangular beds edged with box are subdivided into smaller compartments by a network of box hedges. Each of these small plots is filled with a single species of herb or with coloured chippings. The herbs, chosen chiefly for their ornamental foliage, include some rarities such as dwarf white lavender and the native medicinal herb elecampane, a tall, architectural and very good-tempered perennial which used to be made into an infusion for the treatment of consumption.

A monochrome geometrical knot outlined in box is the ultimate in elegant restraint.

SCENTED HERB GARDENS

A scented herb garden is the ultimate pleasure garden, planted and maintained for the delectation of the senses, yet, a garden of 'use and delight' according to William Lawson's *The Country Housewife's Garden* of 1618.

The loveliest scented herb gardens are sheltered spaces, usually enclosed so that the perfumes from the aromatic leaves and fragrant flowers are trapped in the warm, still air. For most people a scented garden is an enchanted place, a blissful sanctuary.

As far as we know, the earliest scented gardens were built in the courtyards of Persian houses over 2,000 years ago. These gardens were generally square or rectangular, and often they were divided into four by streams flowing from a central fountain. The name for these enclosed gardens was *pairidaeza*, the origin of our word 'paradise'. The Persians, who were superb gardeners, required three main qualities of their paradises: running water, shade and scent.

It was through the Byzantine church that such gardens found their way into western Europe, initially in the form of the cloister gardens soon to be found in every monastery. The idea of a walled, perfumed garden found ready echoes in the medieval Christian tradition, accustomed as it was to viewing the whole of creation in symbolic terms. Biblical references, from the Garden of Eden to the *Song of Songs*, had by now confirmed such gardens as images of Paradise itself.

In 1260 Albertus Magnus, a Dominican monk, specified the requirements of a perfect pleasure

What could be more delightful to all the senses, or more evocative of the long and fascinating history of herb gardens, than a walled garden filled with fragrant herbs and flowers? Havens for people and wildlife, they are of course useful as well. Bergamot and marigolds (above) are both valuable ingredients in traditional pot-pourris: marigolds chiefly for their colour, and bergamot flowers and leaves for their heady scent. Bergamot flowers share with hyssop (opposite) the virtue of retaining their perfume when dried. In this enclosed garden the combined fragrances are intoxicating.

garden: there should be a fountain and a lawn of 'every sweet-smelling herb such as rue, and sage and basil, and likewise all sorts of flowers, as the violet, columbine, lily, rose, iris and the like'. He also suggested that 'Behind the lawn there may be great diversity of medicinal and scented herbs, not only to delight the sense of smell by their perfume but to refresh the sight with their flowers'.

The rose had been introduced into western Europe by the crusaders. In fact, the original meaning of the word rosary is a round rose garden dedicated to the Virgin Mary. Although the earliest rosaries were built on holy ground, sixteenth-century paintings show that the style was adopted in private gardens where rose gardens and arbors were built by royalty and the rich.

Circular rose beds were commonly surrounded by plaited hurdles and the roses were trained over pergolas, arches and trellises to make an arbor. The rose became a sacred flower and the symbol of joy and love. Paintings and allegorical tales of the time portray young men transfixed by the beauty and scent of the flower.

The other sacred flower of the early Christian church was the beautiful and highly scented Madonna lily, *Lilium candidum*. In monastery gardens, roses and lilies were grown together with specially aromatic herbs such as lavender and rosemary. Garden historians believe that the medieval romance garden and the Renaissance love garden were primarily rose and herb gardens, as much esteemed for their aesthetic qualities as for their usefulness.

The heyday of the scented garden was undoubtedly during the reign of Elizabeth I when public taste enjoyed sweetly scented food, rooms and clothes. The mistress of an Elizabethan manor house cultivated fragrant flowers and aromatic plants in a secluded formal garden – usually hedged with rosebriars and fruit trees – not only for the pleasure of walking and sitting there, but also to provide the ingredients for her stillroom. Here, she prepared 'sweet waters' from rose petals and rosemary flowers and healing lotions from the stems of the Madonna lily and spikes of lavender. Aromatic herbs like hyssop and rue were grown for strewing over the floors of rooms to purify the air, and their dried flowers were stuffed into cushions and pillows to encourage unbroken sleep.

With the arrival, in the eighteenth century, of the landscape school of gardening, exemplified by Capability Brown and Humphry Repton, the enclosed scented garden disappeared from many English gardens. However, during the nineteenth century, the public appreciation of a more naturalistic approach to the garden and an awareness of the beauty of individual flowers was awakened by John Ruskin. He influenced the work of the Pre-Raphaelites whose paintings often depicted romantic scenes of love-struck people wearing or holding blooms of English flowers like the rose and the lily. The social reformer William Morris used English flowers such as the honeysuckle and the hop as a basis for his designs for fabric and wallpaper, many of which are still popular today. At that time large Victorian gardens became a series of outdoor rooms which included a kitchen garden, a flower garden, a rose garden and so on. In .many houses a splendid glass conservatory became a scented garden with climbing roses, gardenias and lilies luxuriating in the heat. It was customary for pots of scented-leaved geraniums to be carried into the house to sweeten the drawing room and to decorate the dining table.

At the same time, one of the century's greatest gardeners, William Robinson, preached in his horticultural journal, *The Garden*, the merits of individual plants. He was strongly opposed to the practice of carpet bedding – much in vogue at the time – where annual flowers are bedded out in regimented rows. Robinson favoured a natural approach to gardening as advocated in his book,

Many herbs with aromatic leaves do not release their fragrance until bruised or crushed. At Denmans in Sussex, paving stones are interspersed at random with drifts of chamomile, creeping thyme and other low-growing herbs.

OPPOSITE *The lily and the rose, often growing together, were the most prized of all flowers in medieval gardens. Charged with symbolism, both spiritual and erotic, they were treasured as much for their fragrance as for their beauty. Every part of the plants had its use, and the petals in particular would be strewn on floors to perfume the air or used to make pot-pourri or beautiful scent.*

The Wild Garden, published in 1870. In his own garden at Gravetye Manor in Sussex he paved the small, enclosed flower garden with old London flagstones and planted the beds with highly perfumed carnations and fragrant climbing roses – two of his favourite flowers. He planted carpets of sweetly scented violets as ground cover in beds of hardy plants. In 1895 Robinson wrote the foreword to *Scented Flowers and Fragrant Leaves* by Donald Macdonald.

When the Arts and Crafts Movement became established during the latter half of the century, its influence on architects and gardeners could be clearly seen. There was an emphasis on English craftsmanship in the widespread use of brick and untreated wood in a style that harked back to Tudor times. The distinguished work of Sir Edwin Lutyens and Gertrude Jekyll influenced several generations of gardeners, and many English gardens still retain the obvious Jekyll characteristics of strong, simple design and carefully detailed planting.

In the present century, the revival of herb gardening which was fostered by members of the herb movement has left a legacy of fine scented herb gardens. One of my favourites belongs to a friend in London who owns a tall, narrow house. The glass doors of her second-floor sitting room open onto a balcony and a circular staircase which leads down to the small square herb garden at ground level. Here, a round, brick terrace is surrounded by narrow beds of herbs and fragrant plants. The walls of the garden are clothed in summer jasmine and honeysuckle, and pots of lilies, scented roses and basil plants stand at the foot of the steps. On a late summer's evening, as you climb the staircase through a cloud of heavenly scent that drifts up from the garden, you can gaze down on the star-like flowers of the poet's jasmine and the gleaming satin petals of the Madonna lilies which face skywards, exuding their powerful perfume. This delightful garden truly recaptures the feel of the ancient scented herb garden: sheltered, enclosed and tranquil, the air suffused with scent. Yet it is not only ornamental, for underlying its fragrance and beauty is the practical nature of the herbs, with their medicinal and culinary uses. William Lawson would be pleased that over 350 years later there are still such gardens of 'use and delight'.

CREATING
A HERB GARDEN

The Knotte Garden Serveth for Pleasure:
The Potte Garden for Profitte.
HORMAN, 1519

Your dream herb garden may already exist in your mind's eye and it may only be a matter of time, money and effort to make it a reality. For those of you, though, who feel short of inspiration, my advice would be to start by visiting existing herb gardens, consult books on herb gardens and examine herb garden designs of the past. Not only will this help you to clarify your ideas about your future herb garden, but sometimes you will also discover an established design that is both attractive and appropriate for your situation.

Quite often your house itself can lead you towards the right garden design. If you live in an old house, then the period or style of its architecture may inspire you to take your herb garden style from the same time. For example, a red-brick Edwardian house, influenced by the Arts and Crafts Movement, would incline one towards a brick-paved herb garden with a bower or pergola made from dark-stained wood which would complement the house. Occasionally, however, a blend of period styles can work well, such as a simple interpretation of a *Parterre de Broderie* built in the courtyard of an ultra-modern house.

First, though, it's only sensible to consider the practicalities of a design. How much time do you wish to spend on the weeding and maintenance of your herb garden? Sometimes it is more convenient to construct an intricate herb garden in two stages, starting with the central part of a strong design and enlarging it by adding extra borders later, when you have more time. In my own garden, the design has changed slightly over the years because the herb beds spread a little every time I add more plants. Of course, some garden designs allow for slight changes in the dimensions or arrangement of the borders as the garden becomes established, while other designs are handsome because their formal style is fixed and remains unchanged with the passage of time.

Only a year after I had built my herb garden I changed my mind about the paths because I found that the lawn paths with their neatly trimmed edges took longer to maintain than the herb borders themselves. So I sliced off the layer of turf with a spade and laid gravel over matting (landscape fabric) that requires hardly any maintenance to keep it looking attractive.

The position and site of a herb garden play a vital role in how well the plants grow. In the early 1900s, Frances A Bardswell wrote in *The Herb Garden*, 'The one thing most needful for the Herb-garden is sunshine'. Since the majority of herbs prosper in full sun it is clearly desirable to design your garden to face or slope south in order

A simple trellis arch wreathed with roses cannot
fail to lend enchantment to the view. It also
provides the practical benefit of shade for
comfortable summer seating in your herb garden.

to catch the sun for as much of the day as possible. This, however, is a counsel of perfection and many herb gardens – mine included – grow perfectly well with only half a day's sun. Herbs are wonderfully accommodating plants and, depending on the latitude, they often withstand partial shade surprisingly well. Even if all you can offer is a light but sunless backyard, you can still grow herbs. Simply choose moisture-loving herbs such as sorrel, chives and angelica.

When drawing up your plan, use squared paper and work out the best scale – 1m (3ft) to 2.5cm (1in) usually works well. Make sure that you include all nearby walls, buildings and fences as they affect the quality of light and the feel of the garden. Work out where north is and show it on your plan so that you can take account of the direction of the sun when positioning the herbs.

One of the most appealing aspects of a herb garden is its private air of calm, offering a retreat from the cares of the world. This atmosphere of repose is sometimes easier to create in an enclosed garden, so it is wise to consider the boundaries of your herb garden. Should you grow a hedge or erect walls or fences? These will also shelter the plants and help to create a beneficial micro-climate for the more tender herbs. Existing walls and fences could possibly be extended – perhaps at a lower height – to help enclose the garden or, if necessary, their appearance might be improved by adding a pretty wooden trellis or an arched entrance that will frame a visitor's first glimpse of the garden.

How important are the paths in your design? In some gardens they play a minor role, in others they are designed to be as prominent as the beds of herbs. Do you favour paved, gravel or grassed walkways? Or would brick be the best choice? In a meadow-style herb garden, stepping stones of paving slabs or sections of tree trunks can work well. If it is at all possible make sure that your choice of paving blends with the material of any nearby buildings.

Defining the herb beds requires special consideration. Low, neat hedges of dwarf box look charming but need a lot of maintenance. I like chive and parsley edgings because they more or less look after themselves and I use so much of both herbs. Lavender, hyssop and rosemary make particularly delightful low hedges in a herb

garden, either left to grow freely or trimmed to shape. In a town garden, decorative tiles or even scallop shells can make an attractive frame to each border. It is still possible to find the dark grey scroll-edge Victorian garden tiles in demolition yards – otherwise reproduction ones can also be easily obtained.

Before you choose which herbs to grow, find out what kind of soil you have and whether it has good or poor drainage. Refer to the cultivation charts on pages 218–219 to check ideal growing conditions. Unless you have naturally well-drained ground it may be necessary to excavate the garden area, lay agricultural drainage pipes and replace the topsoil with a mixture of gritty sand and loam. In their natural habitat, Mediterranean herbs love dry, parched conditions, so, on heavy clay soils, I find raised beds or low stone walls with drainage holes provide an ideal environment for these herbs.

After you have considered all these points and are ready to transfer your herb garden design to the site, first of all pace it out to make sure that it fits the space. Use string and wooden pegs driven into the ground, or a hose-pipe, pebbles or bricks to mark out the design before you start to dig, so that, if need be, you can make alterations at this early stage. To mark out a circular bed, secure a string to a post in the centre of the bed, measure its radius along the string, and at this point tie a bottle filled with fine sand to the post. Then, keeping the string taut, drag the bottle along the ground to mark out the circle with a line of sand.

Every herb garden benefits from having a focal point such as a sundial, a garden statue or a magnificent urn or jardiniere. The imposing marble bowl resting on three lions in the centre of the herb garden at Sissinghurst is a particularly splendid example. Alternatively, if you have room, a deciduous tree like a mulberry, *Morus nigra*, or a fringe tree, *Chionanthus virginicus*, planted in the right place, can provide a beautiful pivot to the garden. Depending on the tree you choose, consider also planting a fragrant old-fashioned rambling rose to climb through its branches, such as the beautiful creamy-white 'Kiftsgate', or pure white 'Rambling Rector'. If you can, install or plant such a feature as soon as you start your construction work, then the herbs will grow naturally around it and add a timeless look to the garden.

ABOVE *Enclosing walls and hedges help to create a special atmosphere, making the herb garden feel like a world apart. More practically, they also provide shelter for tender species and surfaces for climbers to cling to. For hedging, rosemary, hyssop and lavender all make good alternatives to box.*

LEFT *However informal the planting is to be, every herb garden benefits from having a focal point of some sort. In the gorgeous grey garden at Lambrook Manor in Somerset, paths diverge and plants cluster around the base of a beautifully weathered bird bath, which makes a subtle centre piece.*

ABOVE *Paths merit more thought than they often receive, not only from the aesthetic point of view but also because the material you choose will have important implications for both cost and maintenance. Here the edges of a brick path are softened, if not completely hidden, by an emphatic planting of chives.*

PLANTING

Choosing which herbs to plant in your garden is a pleasurable task and, above all, a matter of personal choice. On the whole, a cook will prefer to grow culinary herbs, whereas somebody wanting to make pot-pourri will choose aromatic plants and so on.

Whatever your needs it is useful to bear in mind that the most successful plantings have a harmony of shade and shape. To me every garden, every border has a mood depending upon its design and its choice of plants. Gertrude Jekyll described planting as 'painting a landscape with living things' and it holds this kind of magic for me, too.

Foliage colour is one of the most effective ways of achieving the mood or 'landscape' you desire. For example, if you want a quiet, restful garden, select herbs with muted, grey-green and blue-green leaves. Why not recreate the lovely combination of white roses and silver-grey rosemary bushes favoured by the Duke of Bedford in his Royal garden in Paris. In complete contrast, a jolly, showy midsummer herb garden would contain yellow-green herbs like tansy, golden marjoram and feverfew as well as lots of bright yellow and orange marigolds and nasturtiums. For a serene and peaceful effect during early summer, borrow one of Miss Jekyll's happiest planting schemes by growing hostas and scented violets at the foot of heavily perfumed Madonna lilies, and provide a backdrop of dark green, glossy bay trees, clipped to make a hedge.

To achieve the most harmonious and natural look possible, it pays to consider the shape of

Colour is one of the most important factors in setting the mood in any garden. It may be a deciding factor in your choice of plants, and it will also affect the way you group them. The muted palette of silver, soft pink and mauve shown here will tend to create an atmosphere of soothing tranquillity.

each plant. The gardening writer Christopher Lloyd talks in terms of 'buns and cones', which I find helpful when planning new planting schemes. The garden can look dull unless you vary the shape and leaf colour of adjacent plants. The feathery grey spikes of the curry plant look well when placed next to red sage and clumps of clove pinks for example.

First of all, decide where to plant the trees and shrubs in your herb garden as these are going to stay in position for some time and may reach a considerable size. Though I might have planned the position on paper I double-check before planting a bay tree or juniper bush by fixing a stake in the ground to get some idea of how the full-grown herb will look. Unless you trim it to shape, a bay tree can grow very large – up to 6m (19½ft) high and as much around – and a tall variety of rosemary can reach from 1 to 2m (3¼ to 6½ft) if left to grow unchecked.

Next, plan the positions of the medium and small perennial herbs, bearing in mind that herbs like thyme, marjoram and hyssop do spread and are best planted not too close to the edge of a border unless you intend to trim them to shape. Allow 20–30cm (8–12in) between the plants. Once established, some herbs such as borage, fennel and chives seed themselves so readily that they need to be thinned in the spring.

Finally, once all danger of frost has passed, the annual herbs and edible flowers can be sown or planted in position.

Tender specimens, such as scented-leaved geraniums, are best planted in pots. Either transplant them to an antique urn or an attractive jardinière and position them where it is easy to brush your hands over their leaves as you pass, so they perfume the air. Alternatively, simply leave the plants in their pots and sink them into the ground up to their rims so that they can be returned quite easily to a frost-proof place at the end of the summer.

An established and successfully planted herb garden has a rich and varied appearance with little or no soil visible. Newly planted herbs soon spread out to cover most of the ground, however, and any remaining bare soil can be given a mulch of peat mixed with sand, wood bark or even gravel – this not only suppresses the weeds but gives the herb garden a neat and attractive look.

For those people who are fortunate enough to have large gardens, where space is not a problem, bold, impressionistic splashes of colour can have a quite spectacular and dazzling visual effect, as with these interlocking drifts of the common and golden form of marjoram covering a bank.

CREATING
A PAVED HERB GARDEN

A paved garden, having its origin in the brick and tiled courtyard gardens of early Islamic culture, has an aesthetically pleasing formality. The smooth surfaces of stone, tiles or brick that reflect both light and heat make an admirable setting for a wide variety of hardy perennial herbs.

The air of ordered calm that paving contributes to a garden, allied to the low maintenance that it requires, makes a paved garden eminently suitable for a town house. Some particularly fine examples are to be found in Paris, London and Madrid where they are distinguished by the high quality and originality of their design and imaginative choice of plants.

On the whole, a paved herb garden works best on a fairly small scale. It might be enclosed like a courtyard, or it could be surrounded with an informal hedge – perhaps of shrub roses or rosemary. However, a paved herb garden with a good strong design can also work well when placed in an open situation and set in an expanse of gravel or lawn.

One of the best positions for a paved herb garden is where it adjoins the house. Here the all-weather surface provides an ideal setting for your favourite herbs and also the perfect site for an outdoor room. To allow space for garden furniture and for sitting, drinking and eating it's

advisable to design the paved garden so that the herbs frame the space rather than obstruct it. The herb borders can be at ground level or slightly higher, in a raised bed set behind a low brick or stone wall. In a woodland garden raised beds tend to look more in keeping with the landscape when surrounded by tree off-cuts, peat blocks or weathered railway sleepers.

The paved bee-skep herb garden at the American Museum at Claverton Manor near Bath is well sited, close enough to the house to be used often. The small, square garden is built at the sunny, sheltered end of the main terrace that stretches along the back of the house. The central circular border holds an old-fashioned straw bee-skep, and flowering herbs such as melissa, bee-balm and lavender, that are always visited by bees, are planted in the box-hedged beds around it.

As an alternative to a rectangle or square herb terrace, a semi-circle forms a good strong garden design. Constructed with the straight side against the house – its doors and windows opening onto it – the pattern is properly exploited by making wedge-shaped beds of herbs resemble the spokes of a wheel radiating from the centre.

Traditional geometric patterns, like a chequerboard or wheel, work well in the garden when paved with bricks or stone sets. It is important,

Neat and stylish, a paved garden combines minimum maintenance with an air of ordered calm. Here, the simple design of the sundial and birdbath complements this style.

though, to use a paving material that is sympathetic to the design of the garden and the character of nearby buildings.

The variety of materials available is wide: stone flags and bricks in different colours and patterns are traditional choices, but slate, quarry tiles or even ceramic ones, wood, granite sets, cobbles and pebbles are all possible alternatives. A little judicious mixing can be successful too: patterns of cobbles or pebbles, for instance, can look attractive if let into bricks or granite sets. If you use them to make a path, however, lay them with care so that they are comfortable to walk on. And whatever you are using, try to make sure that the surface the path is to be laid on is as level as possible.

Costs also vary enormously, but as the area of most herb gardens is small and having the right colour and texture of the paving is so crucial, it may be tempting to splash out a little. Old or second-hand materials, if you are lucky enough to find them, have the double advantage of keeping costs down and looking beautifully weathered immediately. But any hard surfaces – even utilitarian concrete – can be mellowed and made more friendly-looking by careful planting. Tufts and cushions of creeping herbs such as thyme and pennyroyal will quickly soften edges and fill crevices, as well as releasing their heady, aromatic fragrance as you crush their leaves underfoot.

On the whole it is wisest, and also often most practical, to choose materials that will complement the house. Sometimes paving can exactly match the fabric of an adjacent building. Years ago I lived in a small red-brick cottage in the Thames Valley. The house took its name from the fine herringbone pattern of brickwork in its walls. From the wooden picket gate on the road, a smooth moss-encrusted brick path led up to the front door which was flanked by a large rosemary bush and a clump of silver-grey lavender. The path had been cleverly converted into a long narrow herb garden by planting pockets of herbs in the crevices between the bricks. Low, creeping herbs such as woolly thyme, Corsican thyme, chamomile and pennyroyal made small puffy cushions along its length. Taller herbs such as rue and lavender, santolina and marjoram were planted in narrow borders on each side of the path. The more tender herbs, tarragon and basil, grew in old

terracotta pots so that they could be overwintered under the wide porch.

The paved herb garden opposite has a strong practical appeal. The overall size is about 6 × 4m (19½ × 13ft) although, if space is at a premium, just half the design could be planted and would work equally well.

The framework of paths gives the garden a formal aspect that is softened by the clumps of herbs spreading over their edges. Stone paving slabs, measuring 46cm (18in) square, and frost-proof stock bricks are laid on a dryish mortar mix foundation, with the bricks grouped in blocks of three – two in one direction and the third laid lengthways across them. The pattern is reversed for the next block, and so on.

The garden is set in level lawn a fraction higher than the paving so that the grass can be mown straight over it, thereby saving time on edge trimming. The open position gives a light, airy feel to the design and one of its charms is that within a short time it looks well established and mature. The herbs, with their many different shapes and colours, create a beautiful display which is complemented by the textures and tones of the red brick and weathered stone paths.

Making clever use of limited space, this design manages to accommodate a good selection of common culinary herbs while at the same time keeping them accessible from the all-weather paved paths. A strongly symmetrical plan such as this can even be subdivided: for a more compact garden half the design could stand on its own, remembering to keep the central bay tree in order to provide a vertical accent.

PAVED HERB GARDEN

1 **SAGE**, *Salvia officinalis*
2 **SOUTHERNWOOD**, *Artemisia abrotanum*
3 **BISTORT**, *Persicaria bistorta*
4 **FOXGLOVE**, *Digitalis purpurea*
5 **CLOVE PINK**, *Dianthus caryophyllus*
6 **ROSA MUNDI**, *Rosa gallica* 'Versicolor'
7 **BAY**, *Laurus nobilis*
8 **POT MARJORAM**, *Origanum onites*
9 **PARSLEY**, *Petroselinum crispum*
10 **SILVER POSIE**, *Thymus repandia* 'Silver Posie'
11 **GARDEN ORACH**, *Atriplex hortensis*
12 **ALLIUM**, *Allium*
13 **PURPLE TOADFLAX**, *Linaria purpurea*
14 **LAVENDER**, *Lavandula angustifolia*
15 **MARJORAM**, *Origanum vulgare*
16 **MUSK MALLOW**, *Malva moschata*
17 **PURPLE SAGE**, *Salvia officinalis* 'Purpurascens'
18 **WALL GERMANDER**, *Teucrium chamaedrys*
19 **ROSA MUNDI**, *Rosa gallica* 'Versicolor'
20 **GERANIUM**, *Geranium macrorrhizum roseum*
21 **APPLE MINT**, *Mentha sauveolens*
22 **PEPPERMINT**, *Mentha X piperita*

CREATING A
CULINARY HERB GARDEN

To a gardening cook the deliberations about the style and location of a herb garden have more than just horticultural or aesthetic significance. On the whole, the best culinary herb garden is practical, inspiring and sited as near as possible to the kitchen. That said, clearly not every kitchen door opens onto the ideal spot for growing herbs. So, as with cooking itself, you may need to be ingenious and resourceful.

It is surprising, though, how often an unpromising corner of the garden can be transformed into a delightful herb garden provided that you can come up with the right design.

Even if your starting point is a sunless backyard, there is usually a solution to be found, given a modicum of imagination and flair. In this instance, why not paint the walls white and create a *trompe-l'oeil* effect by affixing large sheets of mirror glass to reflect all available light, then framing it with grey-painted trellis and shine carefully installed outdoor grow-lights onto the plants to promote vigorous, healthy growth.

If, however, you have more space at your disposal, your scope for designing the perfect cook's garden is limitless. The history of herb garden design illustrates the vast number of possible arrangements that work well for culinary herbs. Perhaps a medieval *herbarium* with a series of rectangular beds each assigned to a different herb is appealing, or a *parterre anglais*, planted with your favourite cooking herbs, each bed neatly corralled with box hedging. Or then again, an attractive Elizabethan herb garden might be your choice, with its rich medley of herbs and scented flowers.

The beautiful culinary herb garden opposite has been created in the sheltered, walled orchard of a house in Wiltshire.

One's first impression is of generous abundance: large verdant clumps of lemon balm jostle with mounds of chives and marjoram, a cloud of old-fashioned roses in full bloom is glimpsed through a colonnade of gauzy fennel, and rows of garden peas, French beans and onions fill in the gaps, in the style of a *jardin potager*.

The herbs are cultivated in large, triangular borders almost like a crop – and I imagine that there is enough of each one to satisfy even the most demanding cook. A further advantage of this attractive design is that you can quite easily develop a similar style in an existing kitchen garden either by gradually replacing vegetable plants with herbs or by colonizing unused space.

Once you've decided on the position and size of your herb garden, it is sensible to think next about its principal directions or axes, and, also,

A glorious cornucopia of herbs, vegetables and old-fashioned flowers fills this potager to the brim. The planting scheme is complex but the garden is both attractive and space-saving.

the focal point of the design. In the Wiltshire garden, the framework of diagonal grass paths intersects at an open square in the centre of the garden, to make a clearing large enough for a seat or a table. At the widest point of each border a young standard apple tree has been planted to maintain the continuity of the old orchard. A wigwam of beansticks makes an ideal support for a rambling golden hop or trailing nasturtiums. Like the trees, it provides another vertical feature to balance the high stone wall that stands at the back of the garden.

The unobstructed, well-drained paths are a boon to a cook in a hurry or during a downpour. Wide borders may need firm, level stepping stones set among the plants so that you can gather the herbs without trampling on the soil. Alternatively, you can extend the path into the border by making a series of bays or inlets so that you can reach the herbs easily. And why not place a wooden seat or a stone figure in one or more of the bays to add interest to the garden?

To some people a culinary herb garden may appear simply functional – just a way of producing fresh herbs for the kitchen. Yet every good cook knows how a beautiful garden inspires one's cooking and leads to fresh gastronomic ideas. Then, gathering home-grown herbs becomes one of the most pleasurable preludes to a fine meal.

For me, the most outstanding culinary herb garden of the past flourished during the sixteenth century; a present-day Elizabethan herb garden is not only a place of dazzling beauty but an unending source of inspiration. The Elizabethan fondness for flowers which was eloquently expressed in the paintings, fabrics and tapestries of the time sprang from their enthusiasm for the garden, where they grew flowers for pleasure and for medicinal, cosmetic and culinary purposes.

In my own herb garden I plant both annual and perennial edible flowers. Neat cushions of grey-leaved, pink-flowered dianthus grow next to the shaggy-headed bee-balm, blue cornflowers and heavy-scented stocks. Some of these flowers make a charming last-minute addition to a salad or a cool, sweet custard. Others I use as a garnish for a plate or a tray of food. Over the years I have compiled a list of flowers that are safe to eat. Some, such as violets, rose petals and marigolds have a delightful and unique taste, whereas the

flowers of herbs such as rosemary and lavender usually have a delicate flavour of the herb itself. Edible herb flowers are listed below:

EDIBLE HERB FLOWERS
Basil, bay, bergamot, borage, chamomile, chervil, chive, claytonia, dill, elderflower, fennel, hyssop, lavender, lemon balm, lemon verbena, lovage, marjoram, mint, pineapple sage, purslane, rocket, rosemary, sage, salad burnet, sorrel, sweet cicely, sweet woodruff, tarragon, tansy, thyme.

PLANTS WITH EDIBLE FLOWERS
Allysum, anchusa, begonia, carnation, chrysanthemum, clover, coleus, cornflower, cosmos, cottage pink, cowslip, dahlia, day-lily, dianthus, forget-me-knot, geranium, gladioli, hawthorn blossom, hibiscus, hollyhock, honeysuckle, hop, jasmine, lilac, lime, mallow, marigold, mesembryanthemum, monarda, nasturtium, heart's-ease pansy, rose, sedum, stock, tiger lily, violet, zonal pelargonium.

As any cook knows, the best culinary herb gardens are not merely functional but also inspirational. Of course they must be practical, for there is no point in growing a mouthwatering range of herbs if you then cannot reach them to gather a few sprigs, but they must also tempt you on to new gastronomic delights. In this garden generous and relaxed abundance is the keynote.

A SCENTED AND CULINARY HERB GARDEN

1 **COMFREY,** *Symphytum officinale*
2 **SUNFLOWER,** *Helianthus annuus*
3 **POPPY,** *Papaver*
4 **TANSY,** *Tanacetum vulgare*
5 **SCOTS LOVAGE,** *Ligusticum scoticum*
6 **SWEET CICELY,** *Myrrhis odorata*
7 **ANGELICA,** *Angelica archangelica*
8 **ROSEMARY,** *Rosmarinus officinalis*
9 **EVENING PRIMROSE,** *Oenothera biennis*
10 **ELECAMPANE,** *Inula helenium*
11 **WOAD,** *Isatis tinctoria*
12 **DILL,** *Anethum graveolens*
13 **VALERIAN,** *Valeriana officinalis*
14 **ALKANET,** *Anchusa officinalis*
15 **BERGAMOT,** *Monarda didyma*
16 **SAGE,** *Salvia officinalis*
17 **LAVENDER,** *Lavandula angustifolia*
18 **MARJORAM,** *Origanum vulgare*
19 **CLARY SAGE,** *Salvia sclarea*
20 **ROSEMARY,** *Rosmarinus officinalis*
 COTTON LAVENDER, *Santolina chamaecyparissus*
21 **CORNFLOWER,** *Centaurea cyanus*
22 **CARAWAY,** *Carum carvi*
23 **CORIANDER,** *Coriandrum sativum*
24 **WINTER SAVORY,** *Satureja montana*
25 **WHITE HYSSOP,** *Hyssopus officinalis* 'Albus'
26 **SUMMER SAVORY,** *Satureja hortensis*
27 **COMMON MINT,** *Mentha spicata*
28 **PARSLEY,** *Petroselinum crispum*
29 **GARDEN THYME,** *Thymus vulgaris*
30 **ENGLISH MACE,** *Achillea decolorans*
31 **ANISE HYSSOP,** *Agastache anethiodora*
32 **CHIVES,** *Allium schoenoprasum*
33 **BUCKLER-LEAFED SORREL,** *Rumex scutatus*
34 **SALAD BURNET,** *Sanguisorba minor*
35 **OREGANO,** *Origanum vulgare*
36 **HORSERADISH,** *Armoracia rusticana*
37 **TARRAGON,** *Artemisia dracunculus*
38 **BRONZE FENNEL,** *Foeniculum vulgare* 'Purpurascens'
39 **WELSH ONION,** *Allium fistulosum*

CREATING A SMALL FORMAL HERB GARDEN

Many gardeners with a sense of history are attracted to the idea of recreating a garden style from the past. The formal garden which most immediately evokes the past is the knot garden. This pattern of interweaving plants exerts an almost hypnotic charm, as you allow your eyes to follow the intricate paths of the plants, curving and looping like an unfurled ribbon.

A knot garden, though, is definitely not for the impatient: it takes time to establish and then requires the continual care of weeding and clipping to maintain its pristine beauty. The Connecticut knot garden overleaf measures 3.5m (12ft) square and its symmetrical pattern is composed of two squares, a circle and a continuous four-loop knot.

Blue-grey-leaved thrift with its rose-pink flowers forms the outer square, with the knot garden favourite, wall germander, planted in the inner square. The circle is planted with common rue and the knot ribbon is defined with the 'Blue Mound' variety of the same herb. Ground-hugging woolly thyme frames each corner of the garden while clumps of silver-leaved lamb's ears and glaucous-blue circle onion fill the spaces inside the smaller square.

To achieve the authentic tapestry-like effect, the planting must adhere to the pattern of the knot. In this case the line of rue 'Blue Mound' crosses over the squares of thrift and germander as it travels out from the centre, but passes under them as it returns. Accordingly, the garden achieves a rhythm and movement that is most engaging. Like its Tudor forebears, the garden has been designed to be viewed from above or from the first-floor window of the owner's house.

In summer the varied shades of green and blue herbs set against a background of white gravel define its pattern. In winter, in this all-weather garden, a layer of powdery snow reveals the pattern of the knot just as clearly.

From the knot garden an arbor of pleached Seckel pears leads to a second, slightly larger formal garden – this time based on a Renaissance style and ornamented with an antique sundial.

The symmetry of this rectangular garden is achieved by means of a pattern of raised beds separated by grey brick paths. The central circular border is carpeted with the felty leaves of lamb's ears and studded with mounds of *Artemisia schmidtiana* and creeping lemon thyme. Above it the sundial is placed on a weathered terracotta plinth. This vertical focal point is echoed by four white stone jardinières that flank both entrances to the garden. The silver theme is underscored by the *Helichrysum petiolare* with its trailing growth.

A pair of mop-head standard junipers flanks this delightful exercise in domestic-scale formality. The combination of square, stone plant pots creates a symmetrical order.

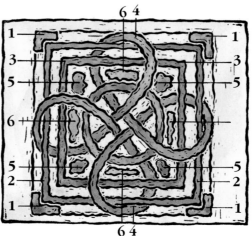

The swooping curves and labyrinthine interlocking lines of this Renaissance knot garden in miniature are almost mesmerizing in their charm. Subtle gradations of colour and texture add to the complexity, requiring meticulous care in planting and equally painstaking maintenance.

Dwarf hedges define the L-shaped beds of herbs, and dark green prisms and spheres of close-clipped box are a reminder of the topiary of the Renaissance garden. Wooden benches, each shaded by a trellis arbor, offer a welcome retreat during the heat of the day and emphasize the feeling of an outdoor room. At one side, two fine mop-head standard junipers highlight the domestic scale of this delightful herb garden.

Aspiring herb gardeners who are looking for ideas will be able to learn quite a lot from both the American gardens on this page. One aspect that is important yet is easily overlooked is the scale of both gardens – neither is very big and either would fit comfortably into the average size plot. Even a small city garden could accommodate the simple and compact knot design.

Generally, in a small formal herb garden the number of different herbs is deliberately restricted. This restraint extends to the range of surfaces that the garden utilizes – it is characteristic of a formal herb garden that less is more. Although it might appear easier to design a garden with less in it, it usually proves more of a challenge, because the most successful result depends upon every element working perfectly – both separately and together – and there is little room for mistakes. For this reason, careful deliberation is needed before you actually start to construct the garden.

First of all, it is necessary to decide on the landscape of the garden. Should it be predominantly soft and leafy with plenty of plants? Or would you prefer a more organized and ordered appearance, where the fixed elements of paths, paving, walls and steps are well emphasized? Perhaps the idea of making the plants themselves the formal element, by means of trimmed box hedging and clipped topiary, answers your needs.

Gardeners of the past have dealt with questions like these in a rich variety of ways. At Castle Drogo in Devon, the problem of how to make the gravel path that leads down from the herb terraces more interesting has been solved by breaking the straight edge of the path with a series of semicircles, arranged in pairs opposite each other, each a mirror image so that the border narrows on one side of the path as it widens on the other. It's the kind of clever, unobtrusive solution typical of the best garden design.

In Italy, I discovered a charming formal herb garden that had been built at the foot of a high stone wall. To overcome the dwarfing effect of the wall, a series of garden statues each set on a stone column were arranged alternatively with narrow, clipped juniper bushes along the main paths of the garden. These acted as a visual bridge between the height of the wall and the low carpet of herbs at ground level. The idea could easily be adapted, on a simpler scale, by using tall pots instead.

To many of us, there is an air of peace and balance in the formal herb garden that is most seductive. With its classical symmetry and its atmosphere of intimacy and seclusion, it can be scaled down to fit even the tiniest pocket handkerchief of a garden. In a world of increased pressure a small formal herb garden can become a heavenly oasis.

KNOT GARDEN

1 **WOOLLY THYME,** *Thymus pseudolanuginosus*
2 **THRIFT,** *Armeria maritima*
3 **GERMANDER,** *Teucrium chamaedrys*
4 **'BLUE MOUND' RUE,** *Ruta graveolens* 'Jackman's Blue'
5 **LAMB'S EAR,** *Stachys byzantina*
6 **CIRCLE ONION,** *Allium senescens* var. *glaucum*

SMALL FORMAL HERB GARDEN

1 **LAMB'S EAR,** *Stachys byzantina*
2 **SILVER MOUND,** *Artemisia schmidtiana*
3 **'SECKLE' PEAR TREES**
4 **GOLDEN SAGE,** *Salvia officinalis* 'Aurea' (in containers)
WOOLLY THYME, *Thymus pseudolanuginosus* (in containers)
5 **DWARF BOXWOOD,** *Buxus sempervirens* 'Suffruticosa'
6 **BOX,** *Buxus sempervirens*
7 **HIBISCUS,** *Hibiscus syriacus* (pots sunken into ground, taken indoors in winter)
8 **SOUTHERNWOOD,** *Artemisia abrotanum* var. *camphorata*
9 **LAVENDERS,** *Lavandula angustifolia* 'Munstead'; *L.a* 'Hidcote'; *L.* x *intermedia* 'Vera'
10 **JUNIPERS,** *Juniper virginicina*
11 **BURNET,** *Sanguisorba canadensis*
12 **CATNIP,** *Nepeta cataria*
13 **FENNEL,** *Foeniculum vulgare*

A plan inspired by the designs of the sixteenth century, cool and classical yet full of romantic period charm. This herb garden is surprisingly practical too, as the brick paths between the beds provide handy access to the herbs themselves.

CREATING
A SCENTED HERB GARDEN

A scented garden is the most romantic form of herb garden and one with a long and historic pedigree. In the medieval world fragrance was accorded a mystical spiritual quality akin to the power of music. The authority of the Bible, especially of course the intoxicating litany of perfumes which opens the *Song of Songs*, was quoted in support of the medieval belief that fragrance was a higher form of beauty. In the medieval and Renaissance world it must all too often have seemed an unattainable form of beauty, too: smells of all sorts would have assaulted the nose, but few of them would have been pleasant. Scented leaves and petals – used for strewing floors and for making garlands and pot-pourris, pillows and sachets, lotions and perfumes – were the only means available to most people for sweetening the air around them, and were treasured as such. Imagine, then, what a place of delight a scented garden would have been, with aromatic thyme and sweet woodruff underfoot, borders full of roses, pinks and lavender, a chamomile seat flanked by hyssop and rosemary, and perhaps a bower of jasmine and honeysuckle overhead. This is the legacy that we have inherited, which even now seems to endow the idea of a scented herb with a special and elusive magic.

And yet there is no secret to creating a garden like this, nor is it difficult. In fact people who have existing gardens often find it quite simple to convert to this style of garden since established borders, walls, arches and walks can be utilized by replacing non-scented plants with alternative fragrant varieties and well-chosen aromatic herbs.

In the delightful garden opposite, the designer has created a perfumed and pleasing environment composed of several smaller elements. This is an ambitious garden with over 50 herbs artfully arranged to form colour harmonies and precise architectural effects.

Although originally intended to fill a space of 18.25 × 15.25m (60 × 50ft), the asymmetric design could be adapted to a smaller space by laying out just part of the scheme. The design also provides an excellent blueprint for the gardener who wants to grow herbs in raised beds, a style of garden especially appreciated by the elderly, the wheelchair-bound and the blind.

A low, dwarf box hedge almost surrounds the focal point of the garden – a stone sundial. Four small gardens bounded by the box hedge each have a colour theme. The pink-flowered border, for instance, contains wall germander, soapwort, gravel root and cottage pinks. The three other borders contribute white, yellow and purple

A rustic bench invites you to linger among the heady fragrances of catmint and thyme. The location and style of the seat have been selected at an early stage of garden planning.

themes. Anyone unfamiliar with these versatile plants would be surprised that every single plant in this garden is a herb.

The all-pervading scents will attract dozens of bees and butterflies, and a cat will adore the 15.25m (50ft) border of catmint, which displays to advantage this glorious herb. The rustic bench placed among the riot of purple-blue blooms faces a cushioned bed of highly aromatic varieties of flowering thyme.

Culinary herbs are easy to gather from a charming U-shaped border that follows one of the boundaries, while beds of old-fashioned roses encircled with lavender and santolina form two islands of perfume at the side.

The gravel paths, laid over compacted hard-core, make a quick-draining surface. To provide an extra variation of height, some of the tender herbs, like pineapple sage and scented-leaved geraniums, might be grown in pots that stand directly on the gravel. Large, grand pots make an interesting feature and change of texture in a herb garden, and flowering herbs add splashes of colour. Of course, in some circumstances – where a garden is entirely gravelled or paved – a gardener may decide to grow all the herbs in pots (for more detailed advice on creating a container herb garden, see pages 60–63).

A scented herb garden is intended for lingering in – it should be so deliciously fragrant that you should find it impossible to drag yourself away from it. Pretty effects can be achieved by growing the plants at several different levels, from lavender in low beds, to basil in old terracotta pots and jasmine and honeysuckle creeping over trellises. I am particularly fond of the rose arbor herb garden that I designed in this way for a friend. It comprises a colour scheme of pale pinks, white and grey. The scheme is easily adaptable to a variety of circumstances. Although based on a series of round-topped wooden trellis arches, these could as easily be made from metal painted white or black. The arches are placed next to each other to form a circle, a square or an octagon, large enough, ideally, to accommodate some chairs and a table for outdoor dining. The enclosed space can be paved with stone or bricks, although gravel or a chamomile lawn would work well too. A collection of favourite fragrant climbing roses, summer jasmine and honeysuckles are

planted at the base of each arch so that they can clothe the framework and entwine overhead. At the foot of each climbing plant a circular border is planted with herbs that have aromatic leaves, such as rosemary, lavender, southernwood and lemon verbena. Madonna lilies, pale pink cottage pinks and grey-leaved white single daisies are grown in lead-grey troughs and pots so that they can be moved around and grouped to catch the sun or to flank a seat. The garden was not only a joy to plan and establish but it should continue to give pleasure for many years.

A scented herb garden outside the back door thus offers delight and refreshment to all the senses. And for dedicated cooks it also offers a wide variety of culinary herbs, with the bonus, according to John Worlidge, who wrote these words in 1677, of having the ability to aid digestion: 'Endeavour to make the principle Entrance into your garden out of the best Room in your House, your Walks being places of divertisement after a sedentary repast. The Aromatick Odours they yield, pleasant refreshments after a gross diet, and such innocent Exercises the best digestive to weak Stomacks. And let your principle Walk extend itself as far as you can . . . adorned with the choicest Plants for Beauty and Scent, and that there may be a succession of them through the year, not without Flower pots, which grace the best of Gardens.'

Nothing can equal the nostalgic, evocative romance of a perfumed garden, where the air hangs heavy with scents both lingering and fleeting, always changing with the rhythm of the seasons and the day. This is a garden where one should be able to dawdle and take time to enjoy the beautiful aromas of the herbs. The pleasurable experience is enhanced by the carefully planned paths and borders. One can make a scented herb garden from an existing garden simply by replacing plants with fragrant varieties or aromatic herbs.

A SCENTED HERB GARDEN

1 **CATMINT,** *Nepeta cataria*
2 **THYME,** *Thymus* species
3 **ALPINE STRAWBERRY,** *Fragaria vesca*
4 **MARJORAM,** *Origanum vulgare*
5 **COMMON ELDER,** *Sambucus nigra*
6 **RED SAGE,** *Salvia officinalis* 'Purpurascens'
7 **PINKS,** *Dianthus*
8 **GRAVELROOT,** *Eupatorium purpureum*
9 **WALL GERMANDER,** *Teucrium chamaedrys*
10 **SOAPWORT,** *Saponaria officinalis*
11 **FRENCH ROSE,** *Rosa gallica*
12 **SANTOLINA,** *Santolina chamaecyparissus*
13 **ROSA MUNDI,** *Rosa gallica* 'Versicolor'
14 **GRAPPENHALL LAVENDER,** *Lavandula X intermedia* 'Grappenhall'
15 **PURPLE HYSSOP,** *Hyssopus officinalis*
16 **BRONZE FENNEL,** *Foeniculum vulgare* 'Purpurascens'
17 **COMMON BOX,** *Buxus sempervirens*
18 **WINTER SAVORY,** *Satureja montana*
19 **RUE,** *Ruta graveolens*
20 **GOLDEN ELDER,** *Sambucus nigra* 'Aurea'
21 **APPLEMINT,** *Mentha suaveolens*

22 **SILVER POSIE THYME,** *Thymus repandia* 'Silver Posie'
23 **FENNEL,** *Foeniculum vulgare*
24 **SALAD BURNET,** *Sanguisorba minor*
25 **COMMON SORREL,** *Rumex acetosa*
26 **MINT,** *Mentha species*
27 **FRENCH TARRAGON,** *Artemisia dracunculus* 'Sativa'
28 **PARSLEY,** *Petroselinum crispum*
29 **SAGE,** *Salvia officinalis*
30 **CHIVES,** *Allium schoenoprasum*
31 **ROSEMARY,** *Rosmarinus officinalis*
32 **CURRY PLANT,** *Helichrysum italicum*
33 **EVENING PRIMROSE,** *Oenothera biennis*
34 **JERUSALEM SAGE,** *Phlomis fruticosa*
35 **SAGE,** *Salvia glutinosa*
36 **ELECAMPANE,** *Inula helenium*
37 **WOOLLY YARROW,** *Achillea tomentosum*
38 **MULLEIN,** *Verbascum thapsus*
39 **DYER'S CHAMOMILE,** *Anthemis tinctoria*
40 **TANSY,** *Tanacetum vulgare*
41 **GOLD VARIEGATED SAGE,** *Salvia officinalis* 'Icterina'
42 **WORMWOOD,** *Artemisia absinthium*
43 **BLUE LAVENDER,** *Lavandula angustifolia* 'Hidcote'
44 **SOUTHERNWOOD,** *Artemisia abrotanum*
45 **MULLEIN,** *Verbascum thapsus*
46 **ROCK HYSSOP,** *Hyssopus officinalis aristatus*
47 **WHITE LAVENDER,** *Lavandula angustifolia* 'Nana Alba'
48 **SWEET WOODRUFF,** *Galium odoratum*
49 **ANGLELICA,** *Angelica archangelica*
   SWEET CICELY, *Myrrhis odorata*
50 **SWEET ROCKET,** *Hesperis matronalis*
51 **SNEEZEWORT,** *Achillea ptarmica*
52 **SAGE,** *Salvia hispanica*
53 **PINK LAVENDER,** *Lavandula angustifolia* 'Hidcote Pink'
54 **ALECOST,** *Tanacetum balsamita*

CONTAINER HERB GARDENS

On the hillsides of Provence or Umbria, clumps of wild herbs growing in their natural habitat flourish in remarkably little soil. In my garden in the Ardèche I often transplant tussocks of wild thyme and mint and find them very difficult to dislodge from their home among the rocky outcrops. But after several strong tugs the herb eventually comes free and emerges with its dry, wiry roots denuded of soil. Once replanted in the damper, richer soil down near the house, the herbs often grow more lushly but rarely as aromatically. However, if planted in a clay pot and placed on a sun-baked terrace or windowsill, the wild thyme or mint regain their former vigour and scent – for pot-grown herbs invariably prosper.

A container herb garden not only looks delightful and is highly convenient, but also has the great charm of being created almost overnight. Once you've assembled the containers and your selection of herbs, planting up the most compatible partners is easy and enjoyable.

Just like larger herb gardens, container herb gardens are found in a variety of styles: a white-painted olive-oil can overflowing with flowering rosemary outside a Greek taverna, a clump of mint sprouting from an old china teapot on an English cottage windowsill or a series of neat wooden boxes of herbs in the garden of a Connecticut

Marrying herbs to the huge variety of containers available is a great source of instant pleasure and satisfaction.

Pots and troughs of culinary herbs on a kitchen windowsill (above) not only look charming, but are also handy for cooking. Mint and strawberries planted in a hanging basket (below) make a pretty and quite delicious combination.

containers. So, even if your budget does not allow for beautiful antique jardinières, there are inexpensive wooden tubs and reasonably priced terracotta urns widely available. Even cheap plastic pots can be improved by the addition of a thin coat of mortar or household filler tinted grey or green. Almost all porous pots can be aged by brushing them with rainwater, milk or yoghurt every few weeks until they develop a patina.

Among my favourite containers are clusters of ordinary clay flowerpots discovered in country markets and second-hand shops. And wooden fruit boxes stained with blue-grey wood dye and planted up with groups of herbs can make a useful and comprehensive herb garden.

Statuesque urns and jardinières, or a fine lead cistern or stone sink, can provide the necessary focal point in a garden. On a terrace of weathered stone, a softly romantic look can easily be achieved with an urn of blush pink dwarf roses, trailing scented-leaved geraniums, cottage pinks and grey-leaved santolina.

Some herb gardeners prefer the restrained formalism of topiary, such as clipped bay trees in tubs placed at the doorway of a town house. Other woody herbs such as rosemary and lavender can also be trained and clipped into mop-head shapes. On a windy site, it's a good idea to cover the growing medium with gravel or heavy pebbles to weigh down the container. Matching pots well planted and artfully positioned can achieve a dramatic and attractive effect. Containers of tall-growing herbs can form an attractive and informal screen in a garden.

The best growing medium for containers is a mixture of equal parts of gritty sand, loam and peat plus a dose of slow-release fertilizer, or use one of the proprietary blends of peat specially designed for pot-grown plants. Every container should have one or more drainage holes to prevent the plant getting waterlogged. I like to place a good layer of broken clay pots, or crocks, in the base of the container to help lower the centre of gravity and improve the drainage.

If a pot is large, place a length of perforated hose-pipe vertically in the middle of the pot so that you can water the plant through it. Surround the pipe with the growing medium and finally plant the herbs. A strawberry pot or tub, which looks charming planted up with different varieties

farmhouse all look charming because they are appropriate to their setting. It is important to consider carefully the style of your container herb garden, as well as the scale and proportion of each container, before you start.

Fortunately, interest in herb growing has encouraged potters, garden centres and nurseries to extend their range of interesting pots and

of thyme, is best planted as you fill it with the soil mixture. Make a layer of crocks in the base of the pot and wedge a length of perforated hose-pipe vertically in the centre, then cover the crocks with soil until level with the first opening in the side of the pot. Place the herb plant on the soil and gently push its leaves out through the hole, then spread out the roots and cover with soil, pressing it down gently to hold the plant in position. Now add more soil with a trowel until level with the next opening and plant another herb in the same way.

Hanging baskets are best lined with sphagnum moss to facilitate drainage and to cut down on weight. To fill a wire basket, place pieces of moist moss with their green tufty growth flat against the wire. Then half fill with the growing medium, place the plants in position and bed them in well with extra medium. If the soil in a newly planted container looks too bare, try covering it with bark chippings or gravel, or even sow some mustard and cress which will germinate quickly and provide a green edible sward which can be cropped as the main herbs grow and spread.

Water the herbs as they require it, bearing in mind that leafy fleshy herbs such as basil prefer a damp soil while those from the Mediterranean such as rosemary like slightly arid conditions. Each time you water the pots, give them a good drenching. Hanging baskets tend to lose much more moisture than other containers. During the summer give fast-growing herbs an occasional feed of liquid organic fertilizer. Woody herbs, like hyssop, rosemary and lavender, should be pruned after flowering to ensure strong healthy growth for the following year. Trim herbs regularly to keep them in good shape and, if necessary, winter the tender perennial herbs such as tarragon and chives under cover in a light frost-proof place.

Containers are a good and inexpensive solution to problems such as a lack of space or sun. A salad bowl of oakleaf lettuce, mint, parsley, chives and other shade-tolerant herbs, for instance, will thrive in a sunless corner of your garden.

GUIDE TO PROPAGATION

When it comes to propagation, herbs are no different from other members of the plant kingdom in that they can be raised from seed or produced vegetatively by means of cuttings, layering or root division.

Whatever one's age, the thrill of growing plants from seed never diminishes. All of the annual herbs such as basil and rocket, and some of the biennial herbs such as angelica and smallage are best raised from seed in the spring.

Sow seed thinly by shaking it from a folded paper cone. In the case of very small seed, mix in a little fine sand. Sprinkle the seed on top of a pot or pan of slightly damp sowing compost. Sprinkle a thin layer of sifted compost over the seed and very gently tamp down with a piece of wood. Either place the pot in a propagating case or cover it with a layer of newspaper and a sheet of glass. Move the pot to a warm windowsill or to a staged plant stand in a greenhouse – a minimum night temperature of 18°C (65°F) is required – until germination takes place. At that point remove the covering and, if necessary, water sparingly.

When the seedlings have produced two true leaves prick them out by lifting a few at a time with a spatula, taking care not to dislodge the soil from their roots. Repot by planting 1–3 seedlings in a pot of compost and grow on until large enough to transplant to the herb garden.

Alternatively sow 2–4 seeds of the herb in small peat pots and leave to germinate in the same way. At the seedling stage remove the weaker ones and leave the stronger seedling to grow on until large enough to transplant with its ball of compost.

Some herbs such as French tarragon cannot be raised from seed. These are increased by cuttings taken from midsummer onwards. Select 7.5–10cm (3–4in) long tip cuttings from the plant, trim away the leaves from the lower half of the stem and dip the base into hormone rooting powder. Using a pencil or narrow dibber make a hole at the edge of a pot of cuttings compost, pop in the cutting and gently firm the compost around it. Place in a mist propagator or cover the pot with a roomy plastic bag with a few airholes punched in it, and leave in a light, warm place for 2–4 weeks until the cuttings have formed roots. Remove the bag and grow on for 2–4 weeks until the root system is strong enough to allow you to transplant the cutting to another pot. It can then be overwintered under glass. After hardening off in the following spring, plant in the herb garden in late spring or early summer. All the woody-stemmed herbs such as rosemary, bay, juniper and lavender can be grown from tip cuttings.

French tarragon can also be increased by root division. This is best carried out when the plant is dormant in late autumn or early spring. Gently dig up the herb and carefully separate some of the long straggly roots, select some with growing tips and cut off cleanly from the parent plant. Replant each root to the same depth in potting compost in pots or in sifted soil in the herb garden. In an exposed garden, cover the new plants with a glass or plastic cloche to give them protection from the wind. Most of the herbaceous herbs such as marjoram, oregano and thyme can be increased by root division.

Perhaps the easiest method of all for increasing your number of herb plants is to use layering. Any straggly herb, particularly the prostrate varieties of thyme, hyssop and summer jasmine, work well with this method. Choose a trailing and healthy-looking stem of the herb and gently stretch it out away from the parent plant. Place a small heap of sifted cuttings compost about halfway along the stem or sink a pot of the compost into the ground. Cover the stem with 2.5–5cm (1–2in) of compost and, if necessary, pin it down with a piece of bent wire. Leave for 6–8 weeks, or longer in cold weather, until fine roots have formed, then cut the new plant from the parent and transfer to permanent quarters. Layering can be done at any time during the growing season.

Happily some herbs propagate themselves with little help from the gardener. Among others, borage, angelica, fennel and clary sage, if allowed to form seedheads, will shed their seed on the ground around the parent plant. This seed germinates easily in warm, damp weather enabling the gardener simply to transplant the seedling herbs to their proper place in the herb garden when large enough to handle.

The prudent gardener saves seed of his favourite herbs in order to produce plants for his own garden or to give as gifts or to sell. The best time to collect herb seeds is just before the plant itself disperses them, usually in late summer. In this way, the seeds will be mature and well dried, by the air and the sun, and they should store well until needed for sowing. Cut off the seedhead and place it upside down in a paper bag. Tie up the open end and hang the bag in a warm, dry place for two weeks or longer. The seeds are ready to remove from the bag when they are dry enough to rattle when shaken. Sort out the seeds and discard the rest of the plant. Transfer the seeds to an airtight container, label and date it and store in a cool, dry, dark place until required for sowing.

Herb gardeners seem to be fecund creatures – forever producing seedlings and cuttings from their favoured plants. It is useful, if you have room, to set some space aside for a nursery bed in which to raise herb plants. This is also a good place to

cosset that slip of pink-flowered rosemary or a cutting of yellow-leaved bay – given by a friend or snaffled from another garden, as keen gardeners are wont to do.

The nursery bed is the best place to grow stock plants from which you can take cuttings. A new formal herb garden, like a knot or a parterre, will require a large number of young hedging herbs when it is planted up. If you plan well ahead it is easy to produce all the plants yourself, which is not only considerably cheaper but also highly satisfying. Tip cuttings can be taken from all the herbs suitable for low hedging such as box, curry plant, hyssop, lavender, rue, santolina and wall germander.

Occasionally, the nursery bed has to become a hospital bed, where ailing plants are nursed back to health. When a herb fails to flourish, it may well be because it was planted in the wrong place – a Mediterranean herb, like rosemary, does not enjoy growing in a cold, damp situation and would prefer to bask in the sunshine with its roots in a light, well-drained soil, along with other heat-loving herbs such as catmint, lavender, santolina, nasturtium, rue and many others. Do not make the mistake either of thinking that you will be giving these plants a treat by enriching the soil: the majority of herbs with Mediterranean origins actually prefer poor soil, and over-manuring can result in abundant growth at the expense of scent and flavour.

Other herbs relish rich, moist conditions and are wretched in a sun-baked site: green, crisp-leaved sorrel, for example, or fragrant sweet violets, or pungent horseradish. In between there lies the whole spectrum of herbs, from those like sweet woodruff which like rich deep soil to others like valerian which will seed themselves in the tiniest crevice in a wall. The surest approach is to try and match the conditions in which any herb grows in the wild.

Since much of your success as a herb gardener depends on knowing what conditions each herb prefers, a checklist is helpful when making a planting plan for a new herb garden. Almost all herbs will grow well in full sun, though many are tolerant of a wide range of conditions and therefore appear in more than one category. See the cultivation chart on pages 218–219 for a complete guide to planting herbs.

HERB DIRECTORY

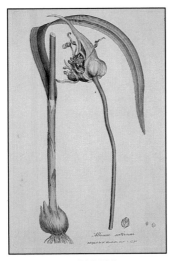

Allium sativum, **GARLIC**

Allium sativum
Liliaceae
GARLIC

CULTIVATION A hardy perennial, garlic has aromatic, narrow, green leaves and white flowers in its second summer of growth. It reaches 30–45cm (12–18in) and prefers well-drained, moderately fertile soil and full sun. Propagate it by planting the cloves of garlic in early spring or late autumn. Grow it as a companion plant in fruit and vegetable gardens to reduce aphid activity. Harvest it in late summer when the top growth has shrivelled, digging up the heads of garlic. Dry the heads outside for several days, then tie them in bundles or plaits and store in a cool, dry, dark place until needed. A useful garden, border and container herb.

USES Culinary, horticultural, medicinal
In a wide range of cuisines from all over the world, garlic is regarded as an essential flavouring. Its pervasive

but delicious flavour is a natural partner to many meat, fish, vegetable, egg and cheese dishes. The herb is also cooked on its own to produce a mellow, less pungent-tasting form.

The medicinal claims for garlic are considerable. The herb contains a sulphide of the radical Allyl, which is antiseptic and therefore combats bacterial infections such as common colds, dysentery and typhoid. Garlic has also been recommended as a treatment for hypertension, rheumatism and baldness.

Allium schoenoprasum
Liliaceae
CHIVES

CULTIVATION This hardy perennial has aromatic, hollow, grass-like leaves and purple or white flowers from late spring. It grows to a height of 15–75cm (6–29in) and prefers fertile, well-drained soil and sun or light shade. Propagate it by sowing seeds or planting bulblets in spring or by dividing the plant in autumn, planting them 15–23cm (6–9in) apart. Harvest the leaves and flowers whenever they are available. It is an attractive garden, border, edging, container and conservatory herb. The essential oils in chives have anti-fungal and insecticide properties, so they can be used as companion plants for vegetables and fruit vulnerable to aphids.

USES Culinary, household, medicinal
All members of the Allium *family provide essential ingredients for good cooking. The slim, cylindrical leaves of chives give a delicate onion flavour to a wide variety of dishes, such as sauces and soups, and the needle-like*

Aloysia triphylla, **LEMON VERBENA**

blooms of the puffball-shaped flowers are both beautiful to look at and delicious to eat when scattered over a green salad. Other Alliums *that deserve a place in the herb garden are Chinese chives,* Allium tuberosum; *the everlasting Welsh onion,* Allium fistulosum; *and the architectural Egyptian tree onion,* Allium cepa, *'Proliferum'.*

Aloysia triphylla
Verbenaceae
LEMON VERBENA

CULTIVATION A half-hardy perennial, it has aromatic, narrow, lance-shaped leaves and spikes of small pale-pink flowers from midsummer. It grows to a height of 45cm–1m (18–36in) and prefers light, poor soil and full sun in a sheltered position. Propagate it by sowing seeds or taking stem cuttings in spring, planting them 60cm (2ft) apart. Harvest the leaves whenever available and the flowers in full bloom in midsummer. Grow lemon verbena as a border, container or conservatory herb.

USES Culinary, cosmetic, household, medicinal
Use fresh leaves to make a delightful tisane, scent sugar, oil or vinegar or to float on the surface of a jug of chilled rum punch. Dried, the leaves can be used in pot-pourri mixtures. The essential oil from lemon verbena is prized by the perfume industry and aromatherapists.

Amoracia rusticana, **HORSERADISH**

Amoracia rusticana
Cruciferae
HORSERADISH

CULTIVATION The horseradish is a hardy perennial with long, elliptical, dark-green leaves and small, star-shaped white flowers in midsummer. It grows to a height of 45–60cm (18–24in) and the roots generally grow from 15 to 30cm (6 to 12in) long. The horseradish prefers fertile, moist soil and light shade and to be planted 30cm (1ft) from its neighbour. Propagate it by sowing seeds or dividing the plant or taking cuttings in spring. Harvest the small, tender leaves in spring, and the roots all year round, whenever the ground is workable. Dig up the whole root and remove the top growth and peel before using. In cold areas with severe winters, store freshly-dug roots in a box of damp sand until needed. Grow it as a garden or border herb and, because horseradish can be invasive, try growing it in vertical drainage pipes, sunk into the ground.

USES Culinary, cosmetic, medicinal
Young, tender leaves taste like the root and can be added to a salad. Horseradish sauce is a mixture of grated root, lemon juice and cream.

Anethum graveolens
Umbelliferae
DILL

CULTIVATION A hardy annual, dill has aromatic, feathery, dull-green leaves with clusters of sulphur-yellow flowers from midsummer. Reaching 45cm–1m (18–36in), it prefers fertile, well-drained soil and full sun in a sheltered position. Propagate it by sowing seeds in spring and again in midsummer, thinning the seedlings to 15cm (6in) apart. Harvest the leaves and flowers whenever they are available.

Grow dill as a garden, border, container and conservatory herb.

USES Culinary, cosmetic, household, medicinal
Both the leaves and flowers have a valuable culinary role as a flavouring for fish, egg and potato dishes. The flower heads are an essential seasoning in the vinegar for dill pickles or gherkin cucumbers. Dill vinegar, dill butter and dill cream are all tasty served with dishes of summer vegetables. A tisane of dill leaves or seed is an effective digestive.

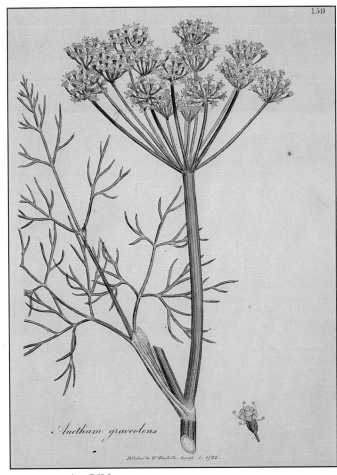

Anethum graveolens, **DILL**

Angelica archangelica
Umbelliferae
ANGELICA

CULTIVATION A biennial, hardy herbaceous herb, it has aromatic, bright green, divided, glossy leaves with mop-headed sulphur-yellow flowers from midsummer. It reaches 1–2m (3–6ft) and prefers rich, damp soil and light shade. Propagate it by sowing seeds in late summer and early autumn, when the freshly harvested seed germinates more

Angelica archangelica, **ANGELICA**

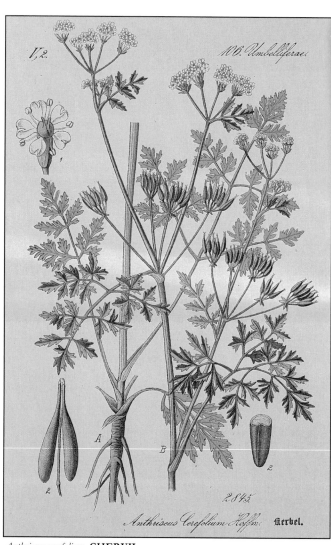

Anthriscus cerefolium, **CHERVIL**

successfully, and transplant seedlings to 75 cm (2ft) apart. Harvest the young stems from late spring, the leaves at any time and the flowers from midsummer. To extend the life of the plant to three to four years, remove the flower stems and leave one flower head to provide seed. Angelica is a versatile garden, border and specimen herb.

USES Culinary, cosmetic, household, medicinal

This tall, attractive herb is grown principally for its fleshy, hollow stems that, crystallized, make the delicious green sweetmeat that cannot be equalled as a flavouring for cakes and desserts. The aromatic leaves with their distinctive flavour are also valuable in the kitchen. When used in the cooking of sharp-tasting fruits you do not need to use so much sugar.

Anthriscus cerefolium
Umbelliferae
CHERVIL

CULTIVATION Chervil is a hardy annual with aromatic, lacy, light-green leaves and delicate white clusters of flowers from late spring. It grows to a height of 20–30cm (8–12in) and prefers loamy, well-drained soil and light shade. Propagate it by sowing

seeds (it will often self-seed) from spring until late summer for a continuous crop of its lacy leaves, and thin or plant seedlings 15cm (6in) apart. Harvest the leaves and flowers whenever they are available. Pick the herb just before adding it to a dish and cut down the tall stems to stimulate the plant to produce more fresh, tender leaves. Chervil can be grown as a garden, border, container and conservatory herb.

USES Culinary, cosmetic
Chervil leaves have a subtle aniseed flavour. Simply divide them into sprigs, or pluches, for a delicious addition to salads of young leaves or as a garnish to dishes of vegetables, fish and poultry. Chop the leaves to give a delicate flavour to soups and sauces. The herb is one of the constituents of the French mixture fines herbes *which is widely used to flavour omelettes and egg dishes, as well as chicken and salads.*

Apium graveolens
Umbelliferae
SMALLAGE, WILD CELERY

CULTIVATION A hardy herbaceous biennial, smallage has aromatic, bright-green, fan-shaped leaves and greenish-yellow flowers from late summer in its second year of growth. Growing to 30cm–1m (1–3ft), it prefers fertile, well-drained soil and full sun. Propagate it by sowing seeds in late spring, thinning the seedlings to 30cm (1ft) apart. Harvest the leaves from spring to autumn and the flowers as and when they appear. Grow it outdoors only as a garden and border herb.

USES Culinary, medicinal
Smallage is a useful herb as you can use it to replace the flavour of celery in a wide range of stocks, soups and savoury dishes. The herb goes well with fish, cheese and poultry and the finely ground seed can be used instead of salt. Serve it with hard-boiled quails' eggs, for example, or as a salt-replacement in a low-salt diet.

Chop the leaves finely to make a good garnish for vegetable soup. A tisane of smallage has a sedative effect and a tea made of the dried seeds may be prescribed by herbalists as a treatment for rheumatism. Do not use during pregnancy.

Artemisia abrotanum
Compositae
SOUTHERNWOOD

CULTIVATION A hardy semi-evergreen perennial, southernwood has aromatic, grey-green, feathery or deeply indented, fern-like leaves. It grows to a height of 60cm–1m (2–3ft) and prefers light, well-drained soil and full sun. Grow it at a slight distance from culinary and medicinal herbs and give it a summer trim. A good companion plant in a hot, dry border where its foliage can soften the edge. It can usefully be grown in the vegetable garden and orchard, too, as the herb has insecticidal properties, in particular as a deterrent to cabbage butterflies. Propagate it by sowing seeds in spring or taking hardwood cuttings in late summer, planting them 60–90cm (2–3ft) apart. Harvest the leaves at any time of year. A lovely border and hedging herb.

USES Culinary, household
The cottage garden names for southernwood are 'Old Man' and 'Lad's Love'. This ancient and attractive herb can be used to make a tisane. The leaves can be placed in a wardrobe as a moth repellent. Also, place a sprig near you when you are driving on a long journey as the herb is reputed to allay tiredness. Do not use during pregnancy.

Artemisia dracunculus
Compositae
TARRAGON

CULTIVATION An almost hardy deciduous perennial, tarragon has mid-green, narrow, aromatic leaves and small, white, ball-shaped flowers in late summer. Reaching 30–60cm (1–2ft), it prefers fertile, well-drained soil and a sheltered site in full sun. Propagate it by dividing the plant in spring or taking cuttings in late summer. Harvest the leaves at any time. A useful and attractive garden, border, container and conservatory herb.

USES Culinary, household
For culinary purposes, only French tarragon is worth consideration. The flavour of this magnificent herb is one of the finest in gastronomy. French cooking has celebrated the herb's natural alliance with poultry and eggs for centuries. This affinity is illustrated by the dish of poulet à l'estragon, *which remains a classic of* cuisine bourgeoise *all over France. Tarragon is an essential herb in the cook's garden: use sprigs to flavour stocks and sauces, butter, white wine vinegar and olive oil and, along with chervil and parsley, as an essential component of* fines herbes. *A tisane of tarragon is recommended as both a digestive and tonic.*

Borago officinalis
Boraginaceae
BORAGE

CULTIVATION A hardy annual herb with hairy, dull-green, oval leaves, it has bright blue (and sometimes pink), star-shaped flowers with prominent black

Borago officinalis **BORAGE**

stamens from early summer. It grows to a height of 45–75cm (18–30in) and prefers light, well-drained soil and sun or light shade. Propagate it by sowing seeds in spring and autumn (the herb seeds itself easily in light soils) and thin or transplant the seedlings to 30cm (12in) apart. Harvest leaves and flowers at any time. A good garden, border, woodland and container herb.

USES Culinary, cosmetic, household, medicinal
Borage flowers strewn over vegetable and fruit salads and used as a garnish for sweet dishes not only look delightful, but are edible, too. Crystallized flowers will store for several weeks in an airtight container.

Calendula officinalis
Compositae
MARIGOLD

CULTIVATION This hardy annual has hairy, mid-green, tongue-shaped leaves and yellow, cream or orange, daisy-like flowers

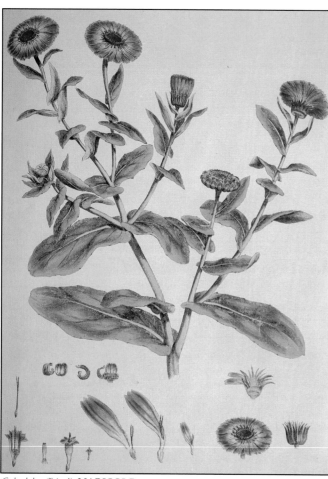

Calendula officinalis **MARIGOLD**

Carum carvi, **CARAWAY**

Carum carvi
Umbelliferae
CARAWAY

CULTIVATION A biennial, it can be grown as an annual and is hardy. It has aromatic, feathery, light-green leaves with flat heads of tiny white flowers from midsummer. Reaching 25–45cm (10–18in), it likes rich, moist soil and full sun. Propagate it by sowing seeds in early spring or late summer, thinning seedlings to 15cm (6in) apart. Harvest the leaves and flowers when available, but, for drying, pick the flower heads before the seeds explode from their husks in late summer. Caraway is a good garden and border herb.

USES Culinary, cosmetic, medicinal
The feathery leaves of this herb resemble a cross between yarrow and chervil and their flavour is a more delicate version of the caraway seed. Add sprigs of leaves to a salad of young leaves and misticanza, or chop them finely to make a tasty addition to vegetable soups or herb butters for

beef and game. Caraway seeds are used widely in the cooking of northern and eastern Europe, especially Scandinavia and Hungary. The thick roots can be cooked.

Chamaemelum nobile
Compositae
CHAMOMILE

CULTIVATION Chamomile is a hardy evergreen perennial with aromatic, feathery, light-green leaves and white, daisy-like flowers from midsummer. Reaching a height of 20–30cm (8–12in), it prefers light, well-drained soil. Propagate it by sowing seeds in spring, taking cuttings during summer or dividing the plant in autumn, planting them 15–30cm (6–12in) apart. Harvest the leaves at any

Chamaemelum nobile, **CHAMOMILE**

from late spring. Reaching a height of 30–50cm (12–20in), it prefers moist, medium-rich soil and full sun. Propagate it by sowing seeds in spring or autumn, thinning to 15cm (6in) apart. Harvest the leaves and flowers at any time, but pick flowers you want to dry from midsummer. A garden, border, container or conservatory herb.

USES Culinary, cosmetic, household, medicinal
The shape of all daisy-type flowers reminds us of the sun, though none

more clearly than the cheerful orange-yellow marigold with its radiant petals and its golden eye. The golden marigold petals look charming strewn over a green salad and the young leaves lend a welcome peppery flavour to a plain lettuce salad. The dried flowers or petals look lovely in pot-pourri for they add a welcome note of colour; and their essential oil is used either alone or added to creams as a very effective skin treatment and in aromatherapy. As well as brightening a room like few other flowers can, a vase of fresh marigolds deters flies due to certain insecticidal properties.

time and the flowers from midsummer. Grow it as a garden, edging and carpeting herb. The non-flowering variety makes a fine chamomile lawn.
Recommended varieties Apple-scented chamomile, *C.n. 'Flore Pleno'*; non-flowering chamomile, *C.n. 'Treneague'*.

USES Culinary, cosmetic, household, medicinal
The flowers, used fresh or dried, of the apple-scented variety and German chamomile are recommended for making chamomile tea, which has a relaxing effect. You can also dry chamomile leaves and use them in pot-pourri.

Claytonia perfoliata
Portulacaceae
CLAYTONIA, WINTER PURSLANE, MINER'S LETTUCE

CULTIVATION A hardy annual with fresh, green, heart-shaped leaves and tiny white flowers borne on thin stalks above the leaf from late spring. It grows to a height of 15cm (6in) and prefers moist, fertile soil and light shade. Sow seeds in early spring and under glass in early autumn, thinning the seedlings to 10cm (4in) apart. Harvest whenever it is in leaf. A useful garden, border, edging, container and conservatory herb.

USES Culinary
Claytonia is an excellent salad herb with its bright green, generous leaves and high vitamin C and iron content. It can be a useful ingredient in the medley of salad leaves known as misticanza (page 99). The leaves are cooked like spinach.

Coriandrum sativum
Umbelliferae
CORIANDER

CULTIVATION This half-hardy annual has aromatic, toothed, bright green lower leaves and feathery upper leaves with clusters of small, pinkish-white flowers from early summer. Reaching a height of 30–45cm (12–18in), it prefers light, fertile soil and full sun. Sow seeds in early spring or under glass during autumn and thin the seedlings to 15cm (6in) apart. Water well, especially during dry weather, to promote production of the lower leaves. Harvest the leaves and flowers whenever they are available, trimming off the top growth to promote new, flavoursome leaves, or, if you primarily want the seeds, let the plant flower and cut off the seed heads when they are just turning brown in late summer. Grow it as a garden, border, container and conservatory herb.

Coriandrum sativum, **CORIANDER**

USES Culinary, horticultural, household, medicinal
Coriander is grown for both its fresh leaves and the dried seed. The fan-shaped leaves have a distinctive and unusual flavour and the aromatic seeds taste of dried orange peel. The fleshier young leaves are very good added whole to salads and vegetable dishes and are an essential ingredient in much Indian and Thai cuisine. Crushed and ground coriander seed is used to flavour cakes and biscuits and lightly spiced savoury dishes.

Eruca vesicaria sativa
Cruciferae
ROCKET

CULTIVATION Rocket is a half-hardy annual with mid-green, tongue-shaped leaves and creamy-white, four-petalled flowers. It grows up to 60cm (2ft) tall and prefers moist, fertile soil and sun or light shade. Sow seeds every few weeks from early spring, thinning seedlings to 15cm (6in) apart. Harvest the leaves at any time and the flowers from midsummer. A garden, border, container and conservatory herb.

USES Culinary, medicinal
Both the leaves and flowers are excellent in green salads and the herb is one of the constituents of the Provençal winter salad known as 'mesclun'. Rocket leaves can also be cooked like spinach.

Foeniculum vulgare
Umbelliferae
FENNEL

CULTIVATION A hardy herbaceous perennial, fennel has

aromatic, feathery, mid-green or copper-bronze leaves and flat heads of sulphur yellow flowers from midsummer. It grows to a height of 1.5–2m (5–6½ft) and prefers well-drained, poor to medium-rich soil and full sun. Propagate it by sowing seeds in spring or summer or by dividing the plant in autumn, planting them 45cm (18in) apart. Harvest the leaves at any time, the flowers from midsummer and the seeds from late summer. A garden and border herb.

USES Culinary, cosmetic, medicinal
Fennel is an indispensable herb in the kitchen as its aniseed flavour has a natural affinity with fish and summer vegetables. Small sprigs of tender fennel leaves are best strewn over a green salad just before serving. Fennel seed makes a good addition to home-made bread and drained cheeses. Both the leaves and the seed can also be used to make a digestive tea that helps prevent constipation, and seeds can be chewed to stave off hunger and relieve indigestion.

Foeniculum vulgare, **FENNEL**

Fragaria vesca
Rosaceae
WILD STRAWBERRY

CULTIVATION The wild strawberry is a hardy, evergreen perennial with mid-green, toothed, three-lobed leaves and small, white and yellow-centred flowers from early spring, producing sweet-tasting, scented, red fruits from early summer. Reaching a height of 15cm (6in), it prefers well-drained, peaty soil and a sheltered position in light shade. Propagate it by sowing seeds or dividing the plant in spring or late summer, planting them 30cm (1ft) apart. A gorgeous garden, border, edging, container and conservatory herb.

USES Culinary, cosmetic, household, medicinal
A small number of wild strawberries, freshly picked, are so perfect they need no adornment, but if you must, then add no more than a sprinkling of rose-scented sugar and a little pouring cream. Both the flowers and leaves may be added to a green salad or used as a garnish and a tisane made from the leaves is prescribed as a remedy for blood and kidney disorders. The dried leaves make a delightful addition to pot-pourris.

Galium odoratum
Rubiaceae
SWEET WOODRUFF

CULTIVATION A hardy perennial, sweet woodruff has shiny, light green leaves, growing in a 'ruff' at intervals along the stems, and clusters of pure white flowers from late spring. Reaching 30cm (12in), it prefers moist, fertile loam and light shade. Propagate it by sowing seeds in late summer or by dividing the plant during the autumn. Harvest the leaves and flowers from late spring. Grow it as a garden, border and woodland herb.

USES Culinary, household, medicinal
Sweet woodruff is a delightful plant. Dried leaves of woodruff contain coumarin and this gives the herb a scent reminiscent of new-mown hay, making the dried leaves perfect for deliciously scented pillows and sachets.

Helichrysum italicum
Compositae
CURRY PLANT

CULTIVATION The curry plant is a half-hardy evergreen. It has aromatic, needle-like, silver-grey leaves and clusters of small, round, yellow flowers from midsummer. Reaching 45cm (18in), it prefers well-drained soil and full sun. Propagate it from cuttings taken in early spring or late summer, planting them 45cm (18in) apart. Harvest the leaves at any time and the flowers from midsummer while they are still bright yellow. A rewarding garden, border, container and edging herb.

USES Culinary, decorative, horticultural, household
On a warm, still day, the spicy scented foliage of the curry plant perfumes the air around it in the herb garden. The leaves can be added to soups and stews to give a delicate flavour of curry and, when separated into their individual blooms, the small yellow flowers make a pretty garnish to Indian dishes.

Hyssopus officinalis, **HYSSOP**

Hyssopus officinalis
Labiatae
HYSSOP

CULTIVATION This hardy evergreen perennial has aromatic, narrow, dark-green leaves and blue, pink or white flowers from midsummer. It grows to a height of 30–60cm (1–2ft) and prefers light, well-drained soil and full sun. Propagate it by sowing seeds or dividing the plant into sprigs or taking stem cuttings in spring and autumn. Hyssop planted in a kitchen garden lures cabbage-white butterflies from brassicas and other leaf crops. Harvest the leaves all year round and the flowers during summer and early autumn. Grow this lovely herb in the garden, border or container or as an edging.

USES Culinary, cosmetic, medicinal
The highly aromatic leaves of hyssop have a spicy taste that hints at mint and thyme. In Gascony, cooks add a sprig of hyssop to rich meat dishes and tomato preserves.

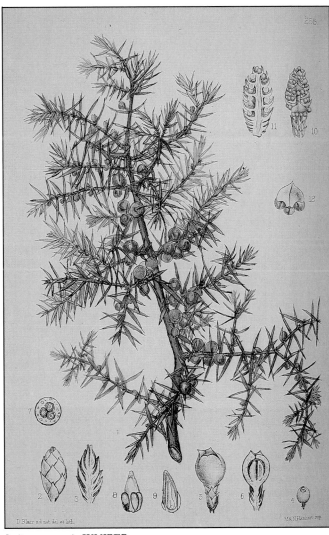

Juniperus communis, **JUNIPER**

Juniperus communis
Cupressaceae
JUNIPER

CULTIVATION Juniper is a hardy, evergreen shrub with grey-green, needle-like leaves and small, creamy-yellow flowers that appear from midsummer. Growing to a height of 1–3m (3–9ft), it prefers poor, well-drained, alkaline soil and full sun. Propagate it by sowing seeds or taking cuttings in spring. Harvest the aromatic, navy-blue berries in their third summer when they are ripe and covered in a grey bloom. Use some berries freshly picked and dry the rest in a warm room for one to two weeks, then store them in a screw-top jar. The juniper is lovely as a garden, border, hedge or container herb. There are dwarf, prostrate, creeping and columnar varieties available, so choose one appropriate to the site. *Plant both a male and a female, so berries will appear on the female plants.*

USES Culinary, household
Juniper berries have a distinctive and unique flavour which they impart to gin. The berries can also be used to season game and rich meats beautifully and, added to a wine marinade, give a delicious flavour to slowly cooked meat dishes. Pâtés and terrines made from pork or goose are improved by the addition of a few crushed juniper berries. Do not eat juniper during pregnancy.

Laurus nobilis
Lauraceae
BAY, SWEET BAY, LAUREL

CULTIVATION A semi-hardy evergreen tree with aromatic, glossy, mid-green, lance-shaped leaves and small, creamy-white flowers from midsummer. It reaches a height of up to 8m (26ft) and prefers a sheltered position, rich, well-drained soil and sun or light shade. Propagate it by taking 10cm (4in) stem cuttings in late summer. Plant them in sandy soil in a frost-free corner of the garden or under glass. Harvest the leaves at any time when using them straight away, but, for drying, pick them from midsummer. Bay is an elegant garden, border, hedging, specimen, container and conservatory herb.
Recommended varieties
Common green bay, *L.n.*; golden bay, *L.n.* 'Aurea'; willow leaf bay, *L.n. angustifolia.*

USES Culinary, cosmetic, household, medicinal

Bay leaves are immensely valuable in the kitchen. When young they are mid-green, then they gradually thicken and darken with age until they resemble glossy leather, the fragrance of the fresh leaf being balsamic, a delicate balance of lemon and nutmeg, becoming spicier and less subtle as it dries. Apart from the bay leaf's outstanding culinary uses, the herb is a most handsome plant of Mediterranean origin and can live for over 50 years. For a fine specimen tree, one should trim the leaves to shape in late spring.

Lavandula angustifolia
Labiatae
LAVENDER

CULTIVATION A hardy evergreen shrub, lavender has aromatic, slim, grey-green leaves and mauve, blue, white or pink flowers. It grows to a height of 30–75cm (12–30in) and prefers poor, well-drained soil and full sun. Propagate it by taking stem cuttings in spring or summer or by dividing the plant in the autumn, planting them 30cm (1ft) apart. Harvest the flowers as they open and the leaves all year round. Lavender is a versatile garden, border, hedge and container herb.

Recommended varieties Blue-flowered, *L.a.* 'Munstead'; white-flowered, *L.a.* 'Nana Alba'; purple-flowered, *L.a.* 'Hidcote'; French lavender, *L. stoechas*; silver-leaved purple-blue, *L.* 'Sawyer's'; Dutch lavender, *L.* x *intermedia* 'Vera'.

USES Culinary, cosmetic, household, medicinal

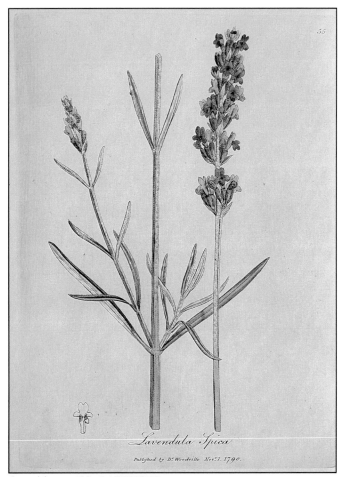

Lavandula angustifolia, **LAVENDER**

This Mediterranean herb is an essential one in both the house and the garden for its delightful fragrance and charming appearance. In the kitchen, both the leaves and the flowers can be used to flavour sweet dishes and creams and, medicinally, a tisane of lavender is a calming antidote to anxiety and depression. The oil of lavender is widely used in cosmetics as it is a good skin cleanser.

The dried flowers of lavender are an important component of many pot-pourri mixtures and herbal wreaths and their scent will discourage moths and insects.

Levisticum officinalis
Umbelliferae
LOVAGE

CULTIVATION Lovage is a hardy herbaceous perennial with aromatic, toothed, glossy, dark-green leaves and lime-green umbels of flowers from late summer. It reaches 60cm–2m (2–6ft) and prefers moist, fertile soil and full sun or light shade. Propagate it by sowing seeds in spring or summer or by dividing the plant in spring or autumn, planting them 60cm (2ft) apart.

Levisticum officinalis, **LOVAGE**

Harvest the leaves at any time and the seed in late summer. Perfect both as a garden and a border herb.

USES Culinary, medicinal

The flavour of lovage leaves is reminiscent of celery and angelica and the herb has the unusual characteristic of giving a yeasty, almost meat-like flavour to other ingredients that can make vegetarian dishes more appealing to meat eaters. The seed is excellent added to wholemeal bread dough and a lovage leaf butter is an appetizing garnish for vegetable soups, potatoes, beetroot and other root vegetables. Lovage tea is known for its diuretic properties. Lovage should not be used during pregnancy.

Malva moschata
Malvaceae
MUSK MALLOW

CULTIVATION The musk mallow is a semi-evergreen perennial with slightly aromatic, feathery, bright green leaves and white or rose-coloured flowers from midsummer. Reaching 60cm–1m

(2–3ft), it prefers well-drained, poor soil and full sun. Propagate it by sowing seeds or taking stem cuttings in the spring, planting them 60cm (2ft) apart. Harvest the leaves and flowers at any time. A very pretty garden and border herb.

USES Culinary, cosmetic
The petals of the edible flowers of musk mallow can be used to decorate summer desserts and sorbets, while whole flowers look pretty embedded in ice plates and bowls. The Malvaceae family has over 1,000 members and they are valued for the gum-like substance made by crushing the seeds that is a remedy for inflammation.

Melissa officinalis
Labiatae
LEMON BALM

CULTIVATION Lemon balm is a hardy herbaceous perennial with aromatic, oval, puckered, dull-green or variegated leaves and tiny white flowers from midsummer. It grows to 60cm–1m (2–3ft) and prefers poor, moist soil and full sun or light shade. Propagate it by sowing seeds or taking stem cuttings in spring, or dividing the plant in the autumn, planting them 50cm (20in) apart. Harvest the leaves from spring to autumn and the flowers during the summer. Lemon balm can be grown as a garden or border herb.

USES Culinary, cosmetic, household, medicinal
The leaves of this vigorous and easy-to-grow herb make a refreshing tisane known as Melissa tea. The tea can be served hot with honey or cold with ice cubes. Alternatively, a sprig of lemon balm may also be added to a pot of Earl Grey or Ceylon tea. Use it, too, to give custards and ice-cream a delicate lemon flavour by steeping the herb in hot cream or milk, then using the flavoured liquid in the recipe. Small, tender leaves are delicious added to a green salad, or, chopped, in chilled summer soups and hot vegetable dishes. Lemon balm vinegar is easily made by slipping two or three sprigs of the herb into a bottle of white wine vinegar and leaving the bottle in a sunny place for two weeks before using. Medicinally, a handful of fresh leaves held against the skin are a soothing treatment for insect bites and sores.

Mentha species
Labiatae
MINT

CULTIVATION A hardy herbaceous perennial, mint has highly aromatic, oval or spear-shaped leaves and white, pink or pale mauve flowers. It grows to a height of 1cm–1m (½in–3ft) and prefers rich, damp soil and sun or light shade. Because the plant spreads easily, sending out runners underground, plant mint in a bed on its own or in a container sunk into the ground. Plant mint 30cm (1ft) apart. Harvest the leaves from early spring until the first frost and the flowers from midsummer. An attractive and useful garden, border and container herb.
Recommended varieties Apple mint, *M. suaveolens*, or Bowles mint, *M.* x *villosa alopecuroides*; Corsican mint, *M. requienii*; eau-de-cologne mint and lemon mint, *M.* x *piperita citrata*; ginger mint, *M.* x *gentilis*; Japanese mint, *M.*

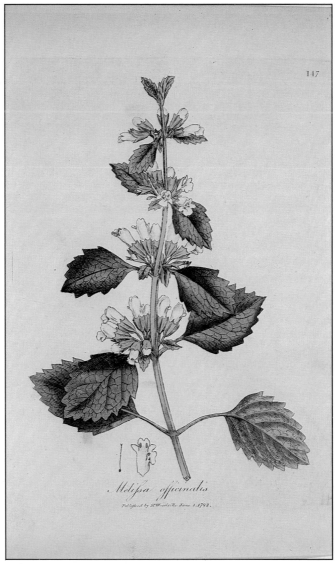

Melissa officinalis, **LEMON BALM**

Mentha, **MINT**

arvensis; pennyroyal, *M. pulegium*; spearmint and Moroccan mint, *M. spicata*; peppermint, *M. x piperita*; water mint, *M. aquatica*.

USES Culinary, cosmetic, household, medicinal
Defining and classifying all 2,000 members of the 'Labiatae' family – whose 40 species of mint form just one branch – is a formidable task, and an ever-growing one, since the mint hybridizes easily. However, the most common culinary mints number just a dozen or so.

The distinctive essential oil in the plant is menthol and its refreshing flavour has made mint popular in cuisines all over the world – from the cooling yoghurt drink from India known as 'lassi' to the well-known mint sauce that British cooks serve with roast lamb. Both fresh and dried mint are especially popular in Mediterranean cooking. A tisane made from the leaves, served hot or chilled, is delightful and candied mint leaves make a charming decoration for summer desserts and chilled drinks. See the recipe for Southern Mint Julep on page 162.

Monarda didyma, **BERGAMOT**

Monarda didyma
Labiatae
BERGAMOT, BEE BALM

CULTIVATION A perennial, hardy, herbaceous herb with aromatic, oval, pointed, mid-green leaves and shaggy heads of tubular scarlet flowers in late summer. Reaching a height of 50cm–1m (18–36in), it prefers fertile, well-drained soil and full sun or light shade. Propagate it by taking root cuttings in spring or autumn, or stem cuttings in summer, planting them 45cm (18in) apart. Harvest the leaves

and flowers at any time, but pick flowers you want to dry from late summer. Grow it as a border herb and in fruit and vegetable gardens as it attracts bees.
Recommended varieties
Purple-flowered bergamot, *M.* 'Blue Stocking'; pink-flowered bergamot, *M.* 'Croftway Pink'.

USES Culinary, cosmetic, household, medicinal
Both the leaves and flowers of the scarlet-flowered bergamot are valuable in the kitchen. The flavour of the aromatic leaf is a blend of mint and lemon. The flowers – fresh or dried – give a distinctive flavour to green or blackleaf teas. Indeed, the tisane made from the fresh or dried leaves is known as Oswego Tea after the North American Indians who drank it. The separated tubular blooms look and taste delightful when strewn over a green or fruit salad. The flowers are lovely in pot-pourri mixtures.

Myrrhis odorata, **SWEET CICELY**

Myrrhis odorata
Umbelliferae
SWEET CICELY, MYRRH

CULTIVATION Sweet cicely is a hardy herbaceous perennial with light to mid-green, aromatic, lacy leaves and flat umbels of white flowers from late spring, with attractive, slim, curved seeds following. It prefers fertile soil and light shade and grows to a

height of 1m (3ft). Propagate it by sowing seeds in autumn or by dividing the plant in late spring, planting them 60cm (2ft) apart. Harvest the leaves at any time, the flowers from late spring and the seeds from midsummer. Grow it in a garden or border; especially good for orchards or bee gardens as it flowers early.

USES Culinary, household, medicinal

This herb's botanical name comes from the Greek word for perfume, and, to my mind, no herb garden seems complete without this lovely herb that springs into leaf very early in the year. The leaves, flowers and seeds all have a delicate aniseed flavour and each play valuable roles in the kitchen. The small young leaves are excellent added to a green salad or misticanza, the flowers are an attractive addition to fruit compôte or summer tart and the seeds give a delightful flavour to fruit syrup or apple pie. Like angelica, the leaves of sweet cicely 'sweeten' sharp-tasting fruit like rhubarb and gooseberries.

Myrtus communis
Myrtaceae
MYRTLE

CULTIVATION A half-hardy evergreen perennial, the myrtle has small, shiny, lance-shaped leaves and creamy-white flowers from midsummer. Reaching 2–3m (6–10ft), it prefers a sheltered site with moderately rich, well-drained soil and full sun. Plant 1m (3ft) apart. Harvest the leaves all year round, the scented flowers when in bloom, the blue-black berries in early autumn and dry the leaves and flowers from midsummer. A handsome garden, hedge, conservatory and container herb.
Recommended variety *M.c. tarentina.*

USES Culinary, cosmetic, household, medicinal
The plant is native to southern Europe and sprigs are used to flavour pork and lamb in Tuscan and Cretan cooking. The fresh berries are added to some Mediterranean dishes and the dried berries used as a seasoning for meat in Turkey. Short branches of myrtle placed over hot charcoal just before barbecuing meat or fish gives a delicious juniper-like flavour to the food. Myrtle flowers are edible, too. A tisane of myrtle leaves is prescribed as a remedy for chest infections. Both the flowers and the leaves are lovely dried in pot-pourri.

Nepeta cataria
Labiatae
CATMINT, CATNIP

CULTIVATION Catmint is a perennial, hardy herbaceous herb. It has aromatic, downy, grey-green leaves with spikes of small, soft blue or white flowers from early summer. It grows to a height of 45cm–1m (18–36in) and prefers well-drained, poorish soil and sun. Propagate it by taking softwood cuttings in spring or by dividing the plant in late summer, planting them 30cm (12in) apart. Harvest the leaves and flowers whenever they are available, picking leaves you intend drying from midsummer.

Nepeta cataria, **CATMINT**

A lovely garden, border, edging and container herb, it deters insects and beetles so grow it as a companion plant in kitchen, fruit and herb gardens. For edging, the low-growing catmint, N. mussinii is recommended.

USES Culinary, cosmetic, household, medicinal
Both the toothed, triangular leaves and the scented blue flowers are highly aromatic. The fresh leaves, which are rich in vitamin C, make a fresh, healthy tisane, and can be used to flavour meat pâtés and terrines. The young shoots may be added to a green salad. Catmint contains several volatile oils that have medicinal and horticultural value.

Ocimum basilicum
Labiatae
BASIL

CULTIVATION Basil is a tender annual, bearing aromatic, oval, pointed, light-green leaves and clusters of small white flowers from late summer. It grows to a height of 20–45cm (8–18in) and prefers rich, damp soil and full sun in a sheltered position or under glass. Propagate it by sowing seeds in spring, thinning or transplanting the seedlings to 20cm (8in) apart. Harvest the leaves and flowers at any time, removing the flowers as they appear so the plants grow more leaves. It is a lovely garden, border, edging, container and conservatory herb.
Recommended varieties Greek basil, *O.b. minimum*; French basil, *O.b. communis*; Opal basil, *O.b. purpurascens*; Lemon basil, *O.b. citriodorum*; Genoese basil *O.b.* 'Genovese'; Aniseed basil.

USES Culinary, cosmetic, household, medicinal
No herb evokes so strongly the cooking of Italy and the South of France as the clove-like fragrance of basil. The leaves are fragile and highly aromatic, so add them whole to salads and vegetable dishes, but chopped or pounded to sauces, especially those based on olive oil such as pesto. The small-leaved Greek basil is the best for sauces, while the fleshy-leaved Italian basil is recommended for salads and pesto. The purple-leaved Opal basil is beautiful for garnishes and for adding to salads, but has a less pronounced flavour than the other varieties.

Origanum species
Labiatae
MARJORAM

CULTIVATION Marjoram is a hardy herbaceous perennial with aromatic, woolly, small, oval leaves and white or pink flowers from midsummer. Reaching 15–30cm (6–12in), it prefers poor soil and full sun. Propagate

Origanum majorana,
SWEET MARJORAM

marjoram by sowing seeds in spring or by dividing the plant in spring or autumn or by taking stem cuttings during the summer, planting them 30cm (1ft) apart. Harvest the leaves and flowers at any time to use fresh, but dry the leaves in midsummer just as the plant comes into flower. A useful garden, edging, container and conservatory herb.

Recommended varieties Sweet, or knotted, marjoram, *O. majorana*; pot or French marjoram, *O. onites*, also the rarely flowering *O. onites* 'Crinkle Leaf'; Oregano, *O. vulgare*; golden marjoram, *O. onites Aureum*; winter marjoram, *O. vulgare hirtum*; Dittany of Crete, *O. dictamnus.*

USES Culinary, cosmetic, medicinal
The herb is used for tisanes, and in tomato, egg, fish and cheese dishes. Marjoram leaves contain thymol, which is a powerful antiseptic and the delicious flavour of the herb is akin to thyme but spicier. Marjoram is one of the characteristic herbs of the eastern Mediterranean and, on the hillsides of Italy and Greece, wild marjoram, which is known as oregano, flowers freely, forming sheets of pale pink.

Pelargonium species
Geraniaceae
GERANIUM

CULTIVATION A tender evergreen perennial with highly-scented, green or variegated decorative leaves, usually toothed or deeply cut, and white or pale pink flowers from midsummer. It grows to a height of 30cm–1m (1–3ft) and prefers

gritty potting compost in full sun or light shade. Propagate it by sowing seeds or taking tip cuttings in spring or late summer. Harvest the leaves and edible flowers all year round. An excellent garden, border, container or window-box herb that can be also be grown indoors quite easily.

Recommended varieties Rose-scented, *P. graveolens*; rose-peppermint, *P. tomentosum*; rose-lemon, *P. radens*; pineapple, *P. x fragrans*; orange, *P.* 'Prince of Orange'.

USES Culinary, cosmetic, household, medicinal
The geranium's highly aromatic leaves easily transfer their flavour to sugar, custards, cakes and other sweet dishes and both the leaves and flowers make an attractive and edible garnish to summer desserts and delightful tisanes. The dried leaves can be added to pot-pourris and the essential oils in the herb are used in the perfume industry and aromatherapy.

Petroselinum crispum
Umbelliferae
PARSLEY

CULTIVATION A hardy biennial with aromatic, bright green leaves that are either curly or flat and trifoliate with flat heads of yellow-green flowers. Reaching 25–45cm (10–18in), it prefers moist, fertile soil in sun or light shade. Sow seeds outdoors in late spring or, under glass, at any time of year, remembering not to cover the seeds with soil and to thin the plants to 15cm (6in) apart. Harvest the leaves at any time, the flowers from midsummer. An attractive and

useful garden, border, edging, container and conservatory herb.
Recommended varieties Curled parsley; turnip-rooted Hamburg parsley, *P.c.* 'Tuberosum'; Flat-leaf Italian or French parsley, *P.c.* 'Neapolitan'.

USES Culinary, cosmetic, household, medicinal
Every part of the parsley plant is useful in the kitchen – the leaves, stalks and roots all have a part to play in cooking, and have done since the time of Pliny. The delicious flavour gives a well-rounded taste to soups and sauces and works wonderfully well with all fish and vegetable dishes. The leaves of flat-leaf parsley also make a simple and appealing garnish. A French persillade is composed of finely chopped parsley and garlic; an Italian gremolata is finely chopped parsley combined with grated zest of lemon, used as the final garnish to meat dishes like osso buco. *Parsley is also the essential herb in a classic* maître d'hôtel *butter, which is the ideal finishing touch to a dish such as grilled steak or fish.*

Petroselinum crispum, **PARSLEY**

Pimpinella anisum
Umbelliferae
ANISE/ANISEED

CULTIVATION Aniseed is a half-hardy annual with aromatic, toothed, bright-green lower leaves, lacy upper leaves and clusters of small white blooms from midsummer. Reaching a height of 40cm (15in), it prefers rich, well-drained soil and full sun. Sow seeds in mid-spring, thinning the seedlings to 12cm (4in) apart. Harvest the leaves and flowers whenever they are available and the seed from late summer. Grow it as a garden, border, container and conservatory herb.

USES Culinary, cosmetic, household, medicinal
The aromatic leaves have a more subtle flavour than the seeds, indeed whole leaves make an excellent addition to a green salad. Green, freshly-gathered seeds are often more popular than the dried seed. Aniseed is chiefly used in the cooking of the Middle East and India and in some European breads and biscuits. The seeds are used in aperitifs like pastis and anisette.

Portulaca oleracea
Portulacaceae
PURSLANE

CULTIVATION Purslane is a half-hardy annual with fleshy, tongue-shaped, light green leaves and small, daisy-like yellow flowers. It grows to a height of 15cm (6in) and prefers moist, fertile soil and sun. Sow seeds outdoors in late spring or under glass at any time of year, thinning the seedlings to 15cm (6in) apart.

Pimpinella aniscum, **ANISE**

Portulaca oleracea, **PURSLANE**

Harvest the leaves at any time, the flowers from midsummer. A useful garden, border, container and conservatory herb.

Recommended varieties Common, or green, purslane, Yellow-leaved purslane, *P. sativa*.

USES Culinary, medicinal
For centuries, this herb has been widely grown in southern Europe and the Middle East, it is a native of southern France, where the herb grows wild, and its leaves, which are rich in vitamin C, are valuable in salads, while the yellow blooms can be used to garnish a green salad. In Provence the herb is cooked, either alone or mixed with spinach, as a green vegetable. In the past, in the Midi, the reddish stalks and fleshy leaves were pickled in vinegar for winter eating. A tisane of purslane, made with fresh or dried leaves, has diuretic properties.

Rosa species
Rosaceae
ROSE

CULTIVATION The rose is a hardy deciduous perennial with oval leaves on prickly stems and fragrant or unscented blooms that produce green, yellow or red hips. Reaching up to 2m (6ft), or taller for climbing species, it prefers well-drained, moderately fertile soil and sun or light shade. Propagate it by taking cuttings in late summer and plant them 1–2m (3–6ft) apart. Harvest the flowers from early summer and the hips from late summer until the first frosts. A beautiful garden, border, hedging, container and conservatory herb.

Recommended varieties Pink and red, scented varieties, like 'Madame Isaac Pereire', 'Guinee', 'Alec's Red', and Damask roses.

USES Culinary, cosmetic, household, medicinal
Use rose petals to make preserves and rose-scented vinegar and sugar. Rose-hips are very rich in vitamin C and can be used to make syrups and jams.

Rosmarinus officinalis
Labiatae
ROSEMARY

CULTIVATION Rosemary is a hardy evergreen with aromatic, needle-shaped, grey-green leaves and scented, blue, white, pink or mauve flowers that appear from early spring and at any time during mild weather. Reaching 30cm–2m (1–6ft), it prefers slightly limy, well-drained soil and a sheltered position in full sun. Propagate it by sowing seeds in spring or by taking tip cuttings during summer and early autumn. Plant them 45cm–1m (18–36in) apart. Harvest the leaves and flowers at any time. An attractive and extremely versatile garden, border, hedging and container herb.

Recommended varieties Lilac-blue-flowered wild rosemary; blue-flowered *R.o.* 'Suffolk Blue'; pink-flowered *R.o.* 'Majorcan Pink'; white-flowered *R.o. albus*; pale blue-flowered *R.o.* 'Miss Jessopp's Upright'; blue-flowered prostrate *R.o. prostratus*; semi-prostrate half-hardy blue-flowered *R.o.* 'Severn Sea'.

USES Culinary, household, medicinal
Rosemary grows wild around the shores of the Mediterranean and is used to give a distinctive flavour to the cooking of Provence and Southern Italy. Sprigs of rosemary added to pork, lamb and fish dishes bring out their flavour and a faggot of rosemary branches burnt over charcoal when barbecuing smells and tastes good. The highly aromatic leaves give a delightful flavour to honey, sugar and syrups. A tisane of rosemary tea is an effective digestive and the essential oil from the herb is antiseptic.

Rosmarinus officinalis, **ROSEMARY**

Rumex acetosa
Polygonaceae
SORREL

CULTIVATION Sorrel is a hardy perennial with bright green, spear-shaped leaves and rust-coloured, small, disc-shaped flowers from midsummer. Reaching 30–90cm (1–3ft), it prefers fertile, moist soil and light shade. Propagate it by sowing seeds in spring or by dividing the plant during the autumn. Thin seedlings to 25cm (10in) apart. Harvest the leaves whenever they are available. A useful garden, border, edging and container herb.
Recommended varieties *R.a.* 'Large de Belleville' and 'Oseille de Belleville'.

USES Culinary, household, medicinal
The delicious, lemony flavour of young sorrel leaves is one of the luxuries of springtime. This citrus-like sharpness makes sorrel an admirable partner to rich food or oily fish such as salmon, mackerel or trout. Sorrel sauce also goes well with eggs and rich meats.

The herb is also cooked with spinach to develop the flavour of the vegetable. It is rich in vitamins A, B1 and C.

Ruta graveolens
Rutaceae
RUE

CULTIVATION A hardy, evergreen perennial, rue has small, aromatic, blue-green leaves and yellowy-green, daisy-like flowers from midsummer. It grows to a height of 30–60cm (1–2ft) and prefers poorish, dry soil and a sheltered site in full sun. Propagate it by sowing seeds in spring or by dividing the plant or taking stem cuttings in late summer. Harvest the leaves all year round and the flowers from midsummer. A pretty garden, border, edging and container herb.
Recommended varieties *R.g.* 'Jackman's Blue'; *R.g.* 'Variegata'.

USES Culinary, household, medicinal

Salvia horminum
Labiatae
CLARY

CULTIVATION Clary is a hardy annual with green-veined bracts, coloured in shades of pink, purple, blue and white from midsummer. It reaches 30–45cm (12–18in) and prefers moderately rich soil and full sun. Sow seeds sparingly in spring and thin the plants to 10cm (4in) apart. Harvest the leaves whenever they are available. It is a pretty garden, border, container and conservatory herb.

USES Culinary, household
The attractive bracts of clary are delightful strewn over a leaf salad and small sprigs plucked from the top of each stem make an excellent edible garnish. Leaves and sprays of clary also dry well for use in pot-pourris and dried herb wreaths.

Salvia officinalis
Labiatae
SAGE

CULTIVATION A hardy evergreen perennial, sage has aromatic, velvety leaves that are grey, green, purple or variegated according to the variety and blue, pink or mauve, scented flowers from midsummer. Reaching 30–75cm (12–30in), it prefers light, well-drained soil and full sun. Propagate it by sowing seeds in spring or by taking tip cuttings from spring

Salvia sclarea, **CLARY SAGE**

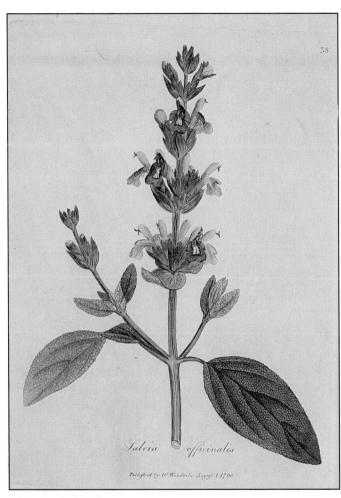

Salvia officinalis, **SAGE**

USES Culinary, cosmetic, household, medicinal
The happy marriage of sage with rich meats is well exploited by Italian cooks who use the herb widely in savoury dishes. Sage vinegar and sage butter make good accompaniments to pork and veal sausages. Sage tea is recommended as a nerve and blood tonic and as a digestive.

Sambucus nigra
Caprifoliaceae
ELDER

CULTIVATION Elder is a deciduous perennial shrub or tree with aromatic, oval, toothed, mid-green leaves and flat umbels of tiny, creamy-white flowers from early summer. It grows to a height and spread of 3–5m (10–16ft). Propagate it by sowing ripe berries or taking hardwood cuttings during spring or late summer. Prune elder to shape during the winter. Harvest the flower heads as soon as they appear from early summer onwards and the berries from late summer. Grow elder as a garden and specimen herb.

USES Culinary, cosmetic, household, medicinal
Elderflower, with its lovely muscatel flavour, can magically transform the taste of light summer desserts, sorbets and ice-creams and a syrup made with the blossom can be stored for use in winter. The shiny, purple-black berries, which are rich in vitamin C, make splendid pies and summer puddings. Elderflower can also be put to medicinal use as cool elderflower water is recommended for bathing sun-burnt skin and the eyes. A glass of elderflower champagne is a delicious non-alcoholic drink.

Sambucus nigra, **ELDER**

Sanguisorba minor
Rosaceae
SALAD BURNET

CULTIVATION Salad burnet is a hardy herbaceous perennial with leaves that are formed from pairs of mid-green, toothed leaflets and it has pinky-green, ball-shaped flowers. It grows to a height of 10–40cm (4–16in) and prefers poorish, alkaline soil and sun or light shade. Propagate it by sowing seeds in spring or autumn. Harvest the leaves at any time – doing this regularly promotes the growth of new leaves – and the flowers from midsummer. A very useful garden, border and edging herb.

USES Culinary, cosmetic, medicinal
The herb grows wild in Provence and its decorative, toothed leaves have a slight taste of cucumber. Add salad burnet leaves to green salads and use as a garnish with some borage flowers for summer dishes and chilled wine cups. A tisane of salad burnet is a remedy for gout and if some leaves are added to cool water, the result is a soothing lotion for sunburn.

until autumn. Harvest the leaves all year round – although they are at their best during the spring – and the flowers from early summer. Grow sage as a garden, border, container, edging and hedging herb.
Recommended varieties
Spanish narrow-leaf sage, *S. lavandulifolia*; prostrate sage, *S. prostrata*; gold variegated sage, *S.o.* 'Icterina'; broad-leafed sage, *S.o.* broad-leaved variety ; purple or red sage, *S.o.* 'Purpurascens'; green- pink- or white-leaved sage, *S.o.* 'Tricolor' with a mild flavour.
S. rutilans PINEAPPLE SAGE
A half-hardy annual with smooth, red-tipped, mid-green, pineapple-scented leaves and narrow, scarlet, trumpet-shaped flowers. Both leaves and flowers are excellent for flavouring and garnishing sweet dishes.
S. sclarea CLARY SAGE
A hardy biennial member of the sage family with large-toothed, hairy leaves and aromatic, columnar lilac and white flowers.

Santolina chamaecyparissus
Compositae
SANTOLINA

CULTIVATION Santolina, a hardy evergreen perennial, has aromatic, narrow, feathery, silver-grey leaves and bright yellow, button-shaped flowers. Reaching 23–45cm (9–18in), it prefers poor, sandy soil and full sun. Its grey foliage and neat habit make it ideal for edging, though clip it to shape during the summer. Propagate it by taking tip cuttings from spring until late summer, planting them 30cm (12in) apart. Harvest the leaves all year round and the flowers from midsummer. Grow santolina as a garden, border, edging and container herb.
Recommended varieties *S.c.* 'Lemon Queen'; *S. virens*.

USES Household, medicinal
This attractive herb is also known as cotton lavender.

Sanguisorba minor, **SALAD BURNET**

Satureja montana
Labiatae
WINTER SAVORY

CULTIVATION Winter savory is a hardy evergreen perennial with aromatic, narrow, dull-green leaves and pale mauve flowers in late summer. Reaching 30cm (1ft), it prefers well-drained, alkaline soil and full sun. Propagate it by sowing seeds or dividing the plant in late summer, planting them 30cm (1ft) apart. Harvest the leaves at any time and the flowers when they bloom. Winter savory is an attractive and useful garden, border and edging herb.
Recommended varieties
Creeping winter savory, *S. repanda*.

USES Culinary, cosmetic, medicinal
The flavour of winter savory resembles a peppery thyme, making the herb useful in dishes of rich meats and game. A more valuable variety, however, is the annual summer savory, S. hortensis, *whose paler green leaves and pale pink flowers have a more delicate flavour. Summer savory is a famous partner for broad beans and, indeed, the herb does go well with them and grows well alongside the vegetable, too. Finely chopped leaves of either savory make an excellent flavouring for butter.*

Stachys officinalis
Labiatae
BETONY

CULTIVATION A hardy perennial herbaceous herb, it has aromatic, felty, dull green leaves with spikes of pink or purple flowers from late summer. It reaches 45– 60cm (18–24in) and prefers fertile soil and light shade. Propagate it by sowing seeds in early spring or by dividing clumps in spring or autumn, planting them 30cm (1ft) apart. Harvest the leaves at any time and the flowers from late summer. It is a good garden, border and woodland herb, but it can become invasive.

USES Culinary, medicinal
Betony's aromatic oval leaves are highly valued for making medicinal teas and tisanes as the herb has sedative and antispasmodic properties, particularly valuable in the treatment of migraines and nervous exhaustion.

Symphytum officinale
Boraginaceae
COMFREY

CULTIVATION A hardy, herbaceous perennial with long, lance-shaped, dull-green leaves, comfrey has mauve-blue, bell-shaped flowers from midsummer. It grows to a height of 1m (3ft) and prefers well-drained, fertile soil. Start with a small plant and, for more plants, divide it during early spring or late summer, planting them 50cm (20in) apart. A useful garden or border herb.

USES Culinary, horticultural, household, medicinal
Comfrey is a vigorous and attractive plant with many valuable medicinal and horticultural qualities. The leaves are rich in vitamins A, C and B12 and in the minerals calcium, phosphorus and potassium. They also have a higher protein content than any other vegetable. Recent research has indicated that comfrey should only be consumed under medical supervision.

Symphytum officinale, **COMFREY**

Tanacetum parthenium, **FEVERFEW**

USES Culinary, cosmetic, household, medicinal
Due to the bitter flavour, the herb has limited culinary use, but both the leaves and the flowers can be used to make a mildly sedative tisane. Herbalists, however, have been making use of feverfew as a treatment for headaches for centuries. More recently, scientists have supported their assertions, establishing that feverfew taken each day is an effective treatment for migraine. Do not use during pregnancy.

Tanacetum vulgare
Compositae
TANSY

CULTIVATION The tansy is a hardy herbaceous perennial with aromatic, indented and toothed, bright green leaves and buttercup-yellow, button-shaped flowers from midsummer. It grows to a height of 1–1.25m (3–4ft) and prefers light, well-drained soil and sun or light shade. Propagate it by sowing seeds in spring or by dividing

the plant in autumn. Harvest the leaves when they are available from spring until early winter and the flowers from midsummer. A pretty garden, border and container herb.

USES Culinary, cosmetic, household, medicinal
The bitter-tasting tansy leaf should be used with discretion in cooking. The herb has given its name to the springtime dishes of fruit with custard, usually made with rhubarb or gooseberries, that date from Elizabethan cooking. Although John Evelyn recommends cooking the leaves with butter and serving them with orange juice and sugar, I regard tansy more as a decorative herb for growing in the herb garden and orchard as its insecticidal properties are very useful there. Both the leaves and flowers can be picked in midsummer for drying for pot-pourris and filling anti-moth sachets. Although a lotion made with tansy is recommended for bathing bruises, sensitive skins may react to the herb's toxicity. Do not use during pregnancy.

Teucrium chamaedrys
Labiatae
WALL GERMANDER

CULTIVATION A hardy evergreen perennial with aromatic, mid-green leaves, similar in shape to an oak leaf, and mauve-pink flowers from midsummer. It grows to a height of 10–20cm (4–8in) and prefers well-drained soil and full sun. Propagate it by sowing seeds or taking cuttings in late spring or by dividing the plant in early autumn, planting them 30cm (1ft) apart. Harvest the leaves at any time but principally during midsummer,

A benefit for gardeners is that, if steeped in water for 3–4 weeks, the leaves can be used to make an organic fertilizer, specially suited to potatoes and tomatoes. Wilted leaves make an excellent soil mulch for garden beds.

Tanacetum parthenium
Compositae
FEVERFEW

CULTIVATION Feverfew is a hardy perennial with aromatic, lacy-edged, lime or yellow-green leaves and single or double, daisy-like, white flowers from early summer. Reaching 45–60cm (18–24in), it prefers well-drained, medium soil and full sun. Propagate it by sowing seeds in spring or divide the plant in autumn and one can take stem cuttings from the plant in summer. Harvest the leaves whenever they are available and the flowers from midsummer. A lovely garden, border, container and conservatory herb.

and the flowers when they are available. An attractive garden, edging and container herb.

USES Cosmetic, household, medicinal
A tisane made from wall germander is good for gout and rheumatism.

Thymus species
Labiatae
THYME

CULTIVATION Thyme is an evergreen perennial with small, aromatic, green or yellow, lance-shaped leaves and pink, purple or white flowers. Growing to a height of 2–30cm (½–12in), it prefers well-drained, alkaline soil and full sun. Propagate it by planting seeds in spring or by layering or taking stem cuttings in summer or by dividing the plant during autumn, planting them 15–30cm (6–12in) apart. Harvest the leaves at any time and the flowers from early summer. An excellent garden, border, edging, container and conservatory herb.
Recommended varieties
Garden thyme, *T. vulgaris*;
Lemon thyme, *T. x citriodorus*;
Silver-leaf thyme.

USES Culinary, cosmetic, household, medicinal
Thyme is a native of the Mediterranean where the clumps of pink-flowered wild thyme growing on the rocky hillsides of Provence and Calabria scent the air and is used to give flavour to the cooking of the region. A sprig of thyme is part of the classic bouquet garni, *and British cooking, too, has made much use of the herb since the Middle Ages. The herb's ability to aid digestion*

Thymus, **THYME**

makes thyme a natural ally of rich meats like goose and game, roast beef and pork. Thyme is a herb that dries supremely well and is one of the eight herbs in the blend known as herbes de Provence. *Dried thyme is added to pot-pourris and makes one of the most beneficial of all tisanes as it stimulates the circulation and even speeds recovery from a hangover.*

Tilia cordata
Tiliaceae
LIME

CULTIVATION A deciduous tree, the lime has heart-shaped, mid-green, glossy leaves and scented, creamy-yellow flowers with yellow-green flattened false petals like bracts from midsummer. It grows up to 10m (33ft) high and prefers moist, moderately fertile soil and full sun or light shade. Propagate it by sowing seeds or taking stem cuttings in spring, planting them 10m (33ft) apart. Harvest the flowers as soon as they bloom in midsummer, dry them in a dark, airy place and store in a screw-top jar.

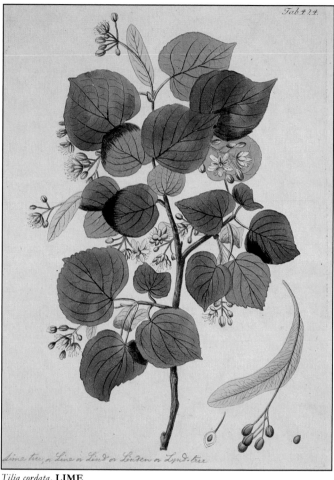

Tilia cordata, **LIME**

USES Culinary, cosmetic, medicinal
The fragrant lime tree deserves a place in any large garden. The mature tree has a handsome shape and, in midsummer, the scent from the clusters of flowers travels some distance. Lime flowers attract bees, and lime-flower honey is particularly sweet and delectable.

The fresh or dried flowers can be used to make a soothing tea or tisane, sometimes known as linden tea, that is often served as a digestive or a calming tonic and an infusion of lime flowers makes an excellent skin toner.

Trigonella foenum-graecum
Leguminosae
FENUGREEK

CULTIVATION A tender annual, it has small, oval, bright-green leaves appearing in threes and creamy-yellow flowers from midsummer. It grows to a height of 30–60cm (12–24in) and prefers fertile, well-drained soil. Propagate it by sowing seeds in spring and midsummer, thinning the seedlings to 15cm (6in) apart. Harvest the leaves and flowers whenever they are available and the seeds from late summer. A pretty garden, border, container and conservatory herb.

USES Culinary, household, medicinal
Fenugreek is mainly grown as a salad herb and for its aromatic seeds. The leaves can also be cooked as a green vegetable. Dried fenugreek leaves contain coumarin and this sweet-smelling, hay-like scent makes the herb a good ingredient for pot-pourri mixtures. The slab-sided, light brown seeds, ground, resemble curry powder and so the powder is useful in Indian and oriental dishes. Tisanes can also be made from the seed and herbalists prescribe this as a tonic for stimulating digestion. Fenugreek seed also yields a yellow dye, suitable for dyeing cotton and wool.

Tropaeolum majus
Tropaeolaceae
NASTURTIUM

CULTIVATION A hardy annual with peppery-flavoured round leaves and trumpet-shaped, orange, yellow and red flowers. It grows to a height of 15–30cm (6–12in) and prefers poor, well-drained soil and full sun. Sow seeds in spring, 15–20cm (6–8in) apart. Good companion plants in kitchen gardens as their roots discourage soil pests and the flowers attract aphid-eating hover flies. Harvest the leaves and flowers when they are large enough to eat. Nasturtium is a delightful garden, border and container plant.
Recommended varieties
Dwarf, climbing and trailing types are ideal for most gardens, and the Atlantic hyrids have pretty, variegated leaves.

USES Culinary, cosmetic, household, medicinal
The nasturtium is a decorative plant native to Peru. Both the leaves and flowers have a high vitamin C content and the small leaves give a welcome piquancy to a green salad, while a handful of freshly-picked flowers strewn over the surface give a jewel-like brilliance to the dish. In the south of France, both the leaves and flowers are stuffed as you would vine leaves. Wine vinegar flavoured with nasturtium flowers develops a delicious peppery flavour and orange colour.

Tropaeolum majus, **NASTURTIUM**

Valeriana officinalis
Valerianaceae
VALERIAN

CULTIVATION This hardy herbaceous perennial has spear-shaped, bright green leaves and pink, white or rose-coloured flowers from midsummer. Growing to a height of 60cm–1.5m (2–5ft), it prefers poor, well-drained soil and full sun. It attracts earthworms, so use it in mixed borders and vegetable gardens. Propagate it by sowing seeds in spring or by dividing the plant in autumn, planting them 60cm (2ft) apart. Harvest the leaves and flowers from spring to autumn whenever they are available. A useful garden, border, container and conservatory herb.

USES Culinary, household, medicinal
Small young leaves of the herb can be added to a green salad and the flowers can be dried for use in herb wreaths. A tisane of valerian root acts as a sedative. When you are tidying the garden during the autumn, collect valerian leaves for adding to the compost heap.

Viola odorata
Violaceae
SWEET VIOLET

CULTIVATION This hardy deciduous perennial has small, green or purple, heart-shaped leaves and perfumed, velvety flowers of purple or white appearing during spring. It grows 10 to 15cm (4 to 6in) high and prefers fertile, moist soil and light shade. Propagate it from its runners or by dividing the plant during early autumn or late spring. Harvest the leaves and flowers whenever they are available. A pretty, traditional garden, border or edging herb.

USES Culinary, household, medicinal
The sweet violet's flowers appear during mild weather early in spring, usually half-hidden by the leaves. The French toss the sweet-tasting blooms over a salad of young leaves. Violet leaves taste good in a green salad and can be made into a tisane.

Part 2

A TASTE OF HERBS

*Good living is an act of intelligence, by which we
choose things which have an agreeable taste
rather than those which do not.*
BRILLAT-SAVARIN, 'THE PHYSIOLOGY OF TASTE', 1826

To my mind it has always seemed simply intelligent to eat, and, if possible, to cultivate those plants which prosper in our own climate and to develop ways of preparing them which enhance their intrinsic good flavour. In all probability, no plant rewards the cook as agreeably as a fine herb.

The fortunes of these historic plants that have changed little in the course of time, have remained constant despite the ebb and flow of fashion in food, medicine and gardening. Few plants have survived so faithfully, for the hybridizer has rarely introduced new varieties. Indeed, left to their own devices some herbs such as mint hybridize themselves.

Some ways of cooking with herbs have also survived from ancient times. Consider the fondness for garlic which characterized the food of ancient Rome, and its present-day place in Californian cuisine. Or reflect on the role played by herbs such as sweet bay, tarragon and parsley in French cooking today – both bourgeois and haute cuisine. It is as vital as ever. This allegiance to particular plants has happened because the taste of herbs is too good to miss. And once adopted is never abandoned.

The versatility of herbs has never been in doubt. It seems extraordinary that a small sprig of fresh rosemary can embody so many valuable properties. In cooking, rosemary transfers its flavour to a dish and subtly transforms and elevates its taste. As, for instance, when a roast leg of lamb, imbued with the pervasive and haunting flavour of the herb, becomes a more complete dish requiring no embellishment. The rosemary, in effect, rounds out and amplifies the flavour of the meat and makes it taste more satisfying and pleasing to the discriminating palate. Yet when the same herb perfumes an ice-cream or a plate of warm, buttery biscuits a discreetly altered, more delicate scent is produced because the essential oils in the herb have reacted with different ingredients in the food.

The practised cook soon learns that herbs are an ingredient to be trusted – fresh herbs are pure, unspoilt and essential. No sensible cook would want to ignore herbs or banish them from his cooking. For the capacity of these generous and beguiling plants to transform our food, engage our senses and delight our palate appears infinite.

*Asparagus with Lemon and Tarragon Mousseline
Sauce – a delicious springtime taste of herbs.
See the recipe for this dish on page 138.*

SOUPS AND FIRST COURSES

*There's no doubt that first impressions matter, gastronomically speaking, however
one might wish to deny it. The table is laid, the plate is placed before you
and, full of expectation, you respond to the appearance and aroma of the dish.
The first course is an introduction or overture to any meal and as such it should
impart an obvious, appetizing appeal that says 'eat-me'.
Fortunately, most good food prepared with fresh seasonal ingredients to an
appropriate recipe does look attractive: it should not require any additional tweaking
on the plate. Learning how to trap the elusive scent of a herb in one's cooking takes time.
There are some useful guidelines though. It is usually helpful to know the native
habitat of culinary herbs. For example, rosemary is a Mediterranean herb
that grows wild on the hillsides of Provence. The herb is widely used
in the cooking of the region, most notably in the slowly cooked daubes of pork and beef.
From this starting point it is interesting to discover how well a sprig of rosemary
enhances other casseroled dishes, such as a chicken or beef stew.
So why not add the herb to a beef stock and use it in a soup?
Some of my recipes for cooking with herbs – for instance, the Tomato Tarts
(see page 101) – start with a nod to these well-established culinary alliances.
Others, like the Courgette and Sorrel Soup (see page 100), were inspired by my garden,
where the two principal ingredients grow alongside each other and reach a peak
of perfection at the same time. I hope that you will find all of them
not only delicious but also a starting point for your own culinary adventures.*

PREVIOUS PAGE *left to right* SCALLOPS WITH ROASTED PEPPERS AND MINT IN A FILO BASKET, *page 95;*
PUMPKIN AND ROSEMARY SOUP WITH SUN-DRIED TOMATO CROÛTES, *page 95;*
CHILLED AVOCADO AND BASIL SOUP WITH ASPARAGUS CRACKERS, *page 96.*

SCALLOPS WITH ROASTED PEPPERS AND MINT IN A FILO BASKET

This dish has become one of my favourite starts to a summer meal. Use fresh plump scallops for the best flavour, or replace the scallops with small slices of monkfish. The filo pastry baskets can be made well ahead of time and frozen until needed.

SERVES 4
6 shelled scallops with their corals
juice of 1 lemon
1 red sweet pepper
4–8 sheets of filo pastry
30g (1oz) butter, melted
salt
6 pink peppercorns, crushed
2 tablespoons extra virgin olive oil
a sliver of garlic, chopped
2 teaspoons chopped mint
4 sprigs of mint, to garnish

Use kitchen paper to pat the scallops dry and, if necessary, remove the fine black thread from each one. Detach the corals and then cut each scallop into three slices. Put the scallops and corals on a plate and sprinkle with a little lemon juice. Set aside in a cool place.

Roast the red pepper on a heatproof plate under a grill set on high, turning the pepper over until the skin is blistered and even blackened in places. Remove from the heat, cover with an upturned bowl and leave for 15 minutes (this makes the pepper easier to peel). Skin the pepper, cut it in half and remove the core and seeds, then cut the flesh into narrow strips. Set aside.

Spread a sheet of filo pastry on the work surface and brush it with butter. Cut the pastry in half and place one piece in a buttered bun tin, gently pressing the pastry into shape. Allow the surplus pastry to spread out from the tin like a handkerchief. Place the second piece of pastry on top of the first but slightly twisted round so that the pastry corners do not overlap. Slightly crinkle the edges of the pastry to make a basket shape. Make the other pastry cases in the same way.

Bake in a moderately hot oven (200°C, 400°F, gas mark 6) for 5–8 minutes until the pastry is golden and crisp. Cool in the tin for 2 minutes, then transfer to four individual plates and keep warm.

Season the scallops with salt and pink peppercorns. Heat the olive oil with the garlic in a frying pan and cook the slices of scallop briefly on each side. Add the corals and the mint and cook for 1 minute, then use a slotted spoon to transfer the fish to a hot plate. Add the roasted peppers to the pan and heat.

Spoon the peppers and the scallops into the pastry baskets. Add some lemon juice to the the pan and when bubbling, pour over the scallops. Garnish each basket with mint.

GARDEN HERB SORBET

The inspiration for this lovely sorbet came from Alan Ford, the talented chef at Hintlesham Hall, a magnificent Elizabethan country house in Suffolk with a beautiful herb garden.

SERVES 6–8
150ml (¼ pint) medium dry white wine
700ml (1¼ pints) water
225g (8oz) sugar
½ cinnamon stick
6 cloves
a large handful of 3 freshly picked garden herbs e.g. mint, parsley and basil
2 teaspoons finely chopped garden herbs
sprigs of mint, parsley or basil, to decorate

Measure the wine and water into a saucepan, add the sugar and stir over low heat until dissolved. Add the cinnamon and cloves and bring to the boil. Simmer steadily for 4 minutes. Remove from the heat and add the handful of herbs. Leave to infuse for 1 hour.

Strain the syrup into a bowl and stir in the finely chopped herbs. Freeze in a sorbetière or in a freezer until firm. Half an hour before serving, beat the sorbet until it is fairly smooth and then refreeze.

To serve, scoop the sorbet into stemmed glasses and decorate with sprigs of herb.

PUMPKIN AND ROSEMARY SOUP WITH SUN-DRIED TOMATO CROUTES

It is a charming idea to serve this soup in the pumpkin shell itself – it makes a natural tureen and even has its own lid.

SERVES 6
60g (2oz) butter
2 shallots, finely chopped
900g (2lb) pumpkin flesh, diced
a sprig of fresh rosemary
5cm (2in) stick of cinnamon
1 litre (1¾ pints) chicken stock
150ml (¼ pint) double cream
salt and freshly milled pepper
SUN-DRIED TOMATO CROUTES
2 sun-dried tomatoes
4 tablespoons hot water
1 slim clove garlic, chopped
120g (4oz) butter
a squeeze of lemon juice
1 French loaf, sliced

Melt the butter in a saucepan and stir in the shallots. Cook over medium heat for 5–8 minutes until soft, but do not allow the shallots to brown. Stir in the pumpkin until coated in butter. Add the sprig of rosemary and the cinnamon, cover the pan and cook over medium heat for 15 minutes.

Add the stock and cook, covered, for 20–30 minutes until the pumpkin is soft.

Meanwhile, prepare the croûtes. Soften the sun-dried tomatoes in the hot water. Drain and use scissors to snip the tomatoes into a food processor. Add the garlic and butter and process until the tomato is finely chopped and the butter is an attractive coral colour. Mix in the lemon juice to adjust the flavour.

Discard the sprig of rosemary and the cinnamon from the pumpkin mixture and purée the contents of the pan in a food processor. Return the soup to the pan. Add the cream, reheat and season. Keep hot until ready to serve.

Add a swirl of cream to the soup just before serving. Toast the slices of bread, spread with the tomato and garlic butter and serve.

Few ingredients contribute so much aromatic flavour to cooking in such abundance as fresh herbs. Just a sprig of tarragon, two leaves of sage or a single bay leaf added to a dish at the opportune moment can give food an astonishing depth of flavour and an exciting, lively taste that puts air-freighted exotic ingredients firmly in their place.

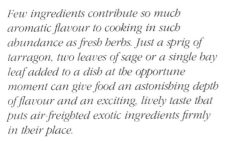

CHILLED AVOCADO AND BASIL SOUP WITH ASPARAGUS CRACKERS

This delicious soup is best made ahead and chilled. The asparagus crackers taste at their best hot from the oven, when the filo pastry is still crisp and golden and the asparagus in basil butter is tender and juicy.

SERVES 6–7
3 large, ripe avocado pears
1 teaspoon basil leaves snipped into pieces
a sliver of garlic, crushed
a few drops of elderflower vinegar (see page 161) or balsamic vinegar
juice of ½ lemon
300ml (½ pint) Greek-style natural yoghurt
about 450ml (¾ pint) asparagus or vegetable stock
salt
leaves of basil, to garnish
ASPARAGUS CRACKERS
24 asparagus tips, each 7.5–10cm (3–4in) long
120g (4oz) butter, softened
1 teaspoon finely chopped basil or a combination of chives and thyme
a squeeze of lemon juice
8 sheets of filo pastry, each measuring 18 × 38cm (7 × 15in)

Halve the avocado pears, discard the stones and scrape the flesh into a food processor. Add the basil, garlic, vinegar, lemon juice and yoghurt and whizz together until smooth. Thin to the desired consistency with the stock, then season with salt. Pour into a jug and chill.

Trim the end of each spear of asparagus, then cook them in boiling salted water for 5–8 minutes until tender. Refresh in cold water and drain well.

Blend the butter with the basil and lemon juice, and leave in a warm place until soft.

Stack the sheets of filo pastry and divide into three by making two even cuts in the shorter direction to produce 24 pieces, each measuring 18 × 13cm (7 × 5in). Take one piece of pastry and brush the centre with basil butter; also brush basil butter over a spear of asparagus. Place the asparagus in the centre of the piece of pastry and wrap up like a Christmas cracker. Tie each end together using several 15cm (6in) lengths of blanched chive stalks. Place on a buttered baking sheet and brush the pastry with basil butter. Make the rest of the asparagus crackers.

Bake in a moderately hot oven (200°C, 400°F, gas mark 6) for 8–12 minutes until the pastry is crisp and golden.

Pour the chilled soup into a tureen or ladle into individual soup bowls. Garnish each bowl with a basil leaf and place 3–4 asparagus crackers beside each bowl.

BABY VEGETABLES WITH HERB BUTTER EN PAPILLOTE

Cooking food in a paper bag, or en papillote, *is not only fun – it also makes good sense, because all the intense delicious flavour of these baby vegetables bathed in herb butter is contained in the parcel until the moment when you tear into the paper and the aroma bursts forth.*

SERVES 4

450g (1lb) mixed baby vegetables such as
baby leeks, baby sweetcorn, broccoli and
cauliflower florets, carrots, courgettes,
mangetout peas and baby turnips
2–3 faggots of garden herbs
salt
120g (4oz) butter, softened
2–3 tablespoons chopped mixed garden
herbs
a squeeze of lemon juice

Prepare the vegetables by washing and trimming as necessary. Place the faggots of herbs in a steaming basket and arrange the vegetables on top. Steam the vegetables until almost cooked, then remove from the basket and season lightly, if desired, with salt.

Cream the butter with the chopped herbs and add lemon juice to taste. Place a sheet of baking parchment on the work surface, fold it in half and then open again. Spread some herb butter in the centre of the sheet and arrange one-quarter of the vegetables on one side of the fold line. Spoon herb butter on top of the vegetables. Fold over the paper and secure the edges by folding neatly – or fasten the paper with old-fashioned wooden clothes' pegs. Make 3 more paper parcels in the same way.

Bake the vegetable parcels on a baking tray in a moderately hot oven (200°C, 400°F, gas mark 6) for 10 minutes until the vegetables are tender. Carefully transfer the parcels to 4 individual hot plates and serve straight away.

Baby vegetables cooked en papillote *(in paper) provide sealed parcels that, when opened on the dining table, reveal a delicious and colourful herb-scented dish.*

MISTICANZA
WITH WOOD-EAR MUSHROOMS

Misticanza *is the musical name for the Italian mixture of wild leaves and herbs collected from the fields and meadows of Castelli-Romani. According to Anna Del Conte's superb* Gastronomy of Italy, *Roman gastronomes state that* misticanza *should contain 21 different kinds of wild salad. She writes, 'Even if this is a little excessive, a good* misticanza *must contain rocket, chicory, sorrel, mint, radichella – a kind of dandelion – valerianella, lamb's lettuce, purslane and other local edible weeds.' For a late summer or early autumn dish, I have combined a lightly dressed* misticanza *with warm wood-ear mushrooms (oyster mushrooms are also highly delicious served this way) cooked in hazelnut oil.*

FOR EACH SERVING
a large handful of *misticanza* leaves
a dressing made with extra virgin oil,
tarragon vinegar, salt and freshly milled
pepper
about 1 handful of wood-ear mushrooms
sunflower oil
hazelnut oil
lemon juice
a few toasted hazelnuts, sliced

If necessary, wash and dry the leaves of *misticanza* by shaking them in a salad basket.

Make the dressing in a bowl and, just before serving, gently toss the leaves in it until very lightly coated, then arrange on a plate.

Cut the wood-ear mushrooms from their stalk and dice the stalk. Gently cook the mushrooms in sunflower oil until soft, adding a little hazelnut oil towards the end of the cooking time. Season with lemon juice and salt, if desired.

Spoon the wood-ear mushrooms over the *misticanza.* Add the hazelnuts to the hot pan, add a squeeze of lemon juice and stir to incorporate all the cooking juices. Spoon the hazelnuts and cooking juices over the mushrooms and serve straight away while the mushrooms are still warm.

MALAYSIAN SPICED FISH
IN NEW LEAVES

I devised this dish a year or so ago for a New Year's Day brunch – hence the pun. The oriental combination of hot fish balls wrapped in cool herbs and leaves of lettuce is always appetizing but not too filling.

SERVES 4
225g (8oz) fresh haddock, skinned and
boned
120g (4oz) prawns, cooked and peeled
60g (2oz) shelled almonds, blanched and
chopped
30g (1oz) cooked ham, diced
a sliver of garlic, chopped
a walnut-size piece of fresh root ginger,
peeled and grated
1 tablespoon safflower oil
1 teaspoon cornflour
¼ teaspoon salt
1 teaspoon soy sauce
oil for shallow frying
SAUCE
1 teaspoon light sesame oil
1 teaspoon light soy sauce
1 teaspoon white wine vinegar
½ teaspoon clear honey
¼ fresh green or red chilli, chopped
a sliver of garlic
2 tablespoons hot water
TO SERVE
1 small iceberg lettuce
leaves of mint
leaves of coriander

First make the sauce by combining all the ingredients together in a small bowl, mix gently then set aside.

Cut the haddock and prawns into small pieces. Place in a food processor with the almonds, ham, garlic and ginger and whizz until finely chopped. Add the oil, cornflour, salt and soy sauce and process until the mixture sticks together.

Take a teaspoon of the mixture and form it into a ball. Repeat with the rest of the mixture. Shallow-fry the balls, in batches, for 3–4 minutes until golden. Then transfer them to a

Not only are markets fascinating places to visit, they provide a truly local ambiance and an indispensable guide to the indigenous fresh produce which is vital for creating rich and interesting flavours in cooking. Herbs, particularly in France and Italy, are readily available from local markets. They look visually alluring and taste marvellous when added to soups and vegetable dishes.

pre-heated plate covered with kitchen paper and keep warm.

Divide the sauce among 4 bowls and place on individual plates. Surround the bowl of sauce with a few leaves of lettuce, mint and coriander, and divide the hot fish balls among the plates.

The way to eat this dish is to tear off a piece of lettuce leaf and place a fish ball and a mint or coriander leaf on it. Roll up the lettuce leaf like a small green parcel. Dip one end into the sauce and eat.

FRESH HERB PASTA WITH PESTO

This lovely green-flecked egg pasta is mixed with chopped fresh herbs. You can use a mixture of several compatible herbs like parsley, chervil and thyme, or use just one such as rosemary, tarragon or sage to give the pasta a distinctive flavour. Unless I'm very short of time, I make pasta by hand because I enjoy handling the soft dough. If you use a pasta machine, roll out the pasta on its thinnest setting. Pesto is, of course, the definitive sauce for pasta, but a well-blended herb butter is almost as delicious.

SERVES 2–4
140g (5oz) plain unbleached flour
¼ teaspoon salt
2–3 tablespoons chopped fresh herbs:
parsley, chervil, tarragon, rosemary,
thyme, sage
1 tablespoon olive oil
1 egg, beaten
1–2 teaspoons water as necessary
extra virgin olive oil
freshly ground black pepper
pesto sauce (see page 118)

Sift the flour and salt into a bowl. Stir in the herbs and olive oil and mix to a dough with the egg, adding sufficient water as necessary. Knead the dough together into a ball when it should start to feel elastic. Alternatively, mix all the ingredients in a food processor, then gather the dough together to form a ball.

Turn the dough on to a floured board and knead for 10 minutes. Cover dough with the upturned bowl and rest it for 45 minutes.

Cut the dough in half and roll out each piece until it is as thin as possible. Drape the dough over the back of a chair, rope or broomhandle and leave to dry for 20–30 minutes.

Fold the pasta into a loose roll and cut into strips according to your preference. Tagliatelle is cut to a width of 6mm (¼in), fettuccine is cut 3mm (⅛in). Unroll the folds of pasta so that they do not stick together and leave covered by a cloth until ready to cook.

Cook the herb pasta in plenty of boiling salted water. It will need only 2–3 minutes: it is cooked when it rises to the top of the pan. Drain well and return to the pan with some extra virgin olive oil and freshly ground black pepper. Toss well.

Serve in dishes with the pesto sauce spooned over the pasta.

COURGETTE AND SORREL SOUP WITH ALMOND AND CHIVE SABLES

As soon as I'd devised this soup I wondered why I'd not thought of it before. For during the summer months, both courgettes and sorrel grow in super-abundance and their flavours are truly complementary.

SERVES 5–6
60g (2oz) butter
1–2 spring onions, chopped
500g (1lb) young courgettes, trimmed and sliced
a sliver of garlic
a bay leaf
120g (4oz) sorrel leaves, washed, drained and roughly shredded
300ml (½ pint) well-flavoured chicken or vegetable stock
150ml (¼ pint) double cream
milk
salt
GARNISH
4–6 tablespoons double cream
1 teaspoon long shreds of lemon zest
ALMOND AND MARJORAM SABLES
60g (2oz) butter, softened
1 teaspoon finely chopped chives
120g (4oz) plain flour
30g (1oz) ground almonds
Parmesan cheese, grated
1 egg yolk
1–3 tablespoons cold water
30g (1oz) split blanched almonds

First make the almond and chive sablés: in a mixing bowl, cream the butter with the chives. Sift the flour and ground almonds into a bowl and stir in the Parmesan cheese. Rub in the chive butter and mix to a soft dough with the egg yolk and water.

Take a teaspoonful of dough and gently roll it into a ball on a floured surface. Slightly flatten the ball into an oval shape on a buttered baking sheet and press a split almond into the top. Make the remaining sablés in the same way (there should be 24–30). Bake in a moderate oven (180°C, 350°F, gas mark 4) for

15–20 minutes until the biscuits are golden and crisp. Cool on the baking sheet for 2 minutes, then transfer to a wire rack. Serve the sablés cold or warm.

Melt the butter in a saucepan and stir in the spring onions, courgettes and garlic until coated with butter. Add the bay leaf, cover the pan and cook over moderate heat for 10–15 minutes until the courgettes are tender. Remove the bay leaf, and stir in the roughly shredded sorrel with the stock. Cook for 4–5 minutes until the sorrel has wilted then purée the contents of the pan in a food processor. Add the cream and pour through a sieve back into the pan. Reheat gently, and thin with milk to the desired consistency. Season with salt.

Pour the soup into bowls and garnish with some double cream and shreds of lemon zest. Serve accompanied by the sablés.

TOMATO TARTS
WITH HERB BUTTER

The contrast of textures in these thin crisp pastry tarts covered with slices of hot tomato and herbs is very good indeed.

SERVES 6
250g (9oz) prepared puff pastry
90g (3oz) butter, softened
2 tablespoons finely chopped mixed herbs
– basil, parsley, thyme, chives
a little finely grated lemon zest
a squeeze of lemon juice
3 large marmande or beefsteak tomatoes
salt and freshly milled black pepper

Divide the pastry into 6 pieces and roll out each piece on a floured board to make a 15cm (6in) round.

Cream the butter with the herbs, lemon zest and juice until well combined. Spread the herb butter over each round of pastry and place on a sheet of baking parchment on a baking sheet. Slice the tomatoes very thinly and place 3 slices, slightly overlapping, on each pastry round. Season with salt and pepper.

Bake in a moderately hot oven (200°C, 400°F, gas mark 6) for 15–20 minutes until the pastry is crisp and golden. Serve straight away.

FISH AND SHELLFISH

The delicate nature of most fish and shellfish is invariably flattered by the presence
of an appropriate herb. Fish cooks quickly and is ready to eat
as soon as the flesh is opaque and the bone separates easily.
Consequently fragile and delicate herbs such as sorrel, mint and dill
often make the best partners for fish since they require
only brief cooking to release their flavour.
Once you become used to cooking fish with herbs you will find them indispensable.
A bouquet garni added to the court bouillon *(poaching liquid)*
not only adds a uniquely delicious flavour to the fish, but the strained liquor can
then be reduced to make a fumet, *or base, for a sauce with the simple addition*
of a knob of butter or a spoonful of cream.
Many of the classic sauces that accompany fish depend on just a few sprigs
of a fresh herb and a dash of wine for their character; the results have a subtle flavour and
vibrancy that is unequalled. Herb butters such as lime and chives, or tomato and basil,
added as a garnish to a fish dish just before serving produce a delicious
lift in flavour. The butter bathes the fish in a thin layer of glistening moisture
and the finely chopped herbs soak into the flakes of flesh, giving it a fine tang
that is far removed from the sickroom image of plainly cooked fish.
When cooking fish with herbs it is instructive and inspirational to study other
cuisines where fish comprises a large part of the daily diet.
The marinated fish cookery of Scandinavia and the Pacific, for example,
both of which make good use of herbs,
includes the superb dishes of gravad lax *and* ceviche, *which highlight*
some of the less familiar herbs such as dill, fennel and coriander.

PREVIOUS PAGE *left to right* BOILED LOBSTER WITH HERB MAYONNAISE, *page 105;*
SEAFOOD SALAD WITH CITRUS AND FENNEL DRESSING, *page 105.*

BOILED LOBSTER WITH HERB MAYONNAISE

A freshly-cooked lobster tastes superb served hot or cold, with a richly-flavoured herb mayonnaise. The flavour of the mayonnaise improves if it is made a few hours ahead – in fact, herb mayonnaise is a useful sauce to keep in the refrigerator for 2–3 days.

SERVES 2
2 egg yolks
1 coffeespoon Dijon mustard
75–100ml (3–4fl oz) mild-flavoured olive or sunflower oil, at room temperature
75–100ml (3–4fl oz) grapeseed oil
2–3 tablespoons very finely chopped mixed summer herbs: tarragon, parsley, chervil, chives, basil, marjoram
lemon juice to taste
150ml (¼ pint) crème fraîche or soured cream (optional)
1 live lobster, weighing about 1kg (2¼lb)
sea water or salt
bouquet garni of fresh herbs (see page 165)

Make sure that the bowl and the ingredients for the mayonnaise are at room temperature. Blend the egg yolks with the mustard and very gradually, drop by drop, add the oils, beating in each addition thoroughly. If the mayonnaise gets too thick, beat in a little warm water to thin it. Finally, mix in the herbs and enough lemon juice to adjust the flavour. Spoon into a dish or a lidded jar and chill for 4–8 hours. Just before serving, stir in crème fraîche if desired.

Put the lobster into a deep pot, cover to a depth of 15cm (6in) with seawater or salted water and add the bouquet garni. Bring to the boil and cook for 7 minutes per 450g (1lb) of lobster. For eating cold, remove the lobster and plunge it into ice-cold water to stop the cooking; for serving hot, leave the lobster in the cooking water until ready to serve.

To serve the lobster, place it on its back and cut it lengthways into 2 halves. Discard the feathery fronds in the centre and remove the intestinal tract. Crack the claws and remove the shell to expose the meat. Spoon some herb mayonnaise into the cavity in the shell.

SEAFOOD SALAD WITH CITRUS AND FENNEL DRESSING

Vary the seafood in this salad according to season and availability. During the summer months, squid, prawns and clams are probably easier to come by. Autumn and winter bring good supplies of excellent mussels, langoustines and shrimps.

SERVES 6–8
170g (6oz) poached baby squid, cut into rings
170g (6oz) each of cooked prawns, mussels, langoustines, gambas or Mediterranean prawns, clams, cockles etc., peeled or on the shell as you wish, to make a total weight of 450–675g (1–1½lb)
DRESSING
3–4 sprigs of fennel
1 clove garlic, halved
½ teaspoon finely grated orange zest
juice of 1 orange
juice of 2 limes or 1 small lemon
75–100ml (3–4fl oz) olive oil
2 tablespoons crème fraîche
salt and freshly milled green peppercorns
GARNISH
sprigs of fennel and heads of fennel flower if available
endive frisée

Once you have prepared the seafood ingredients according to your requirements, place all the seafood together in a large bowl.

Make the dressing by warming the fennel, garlic, orange zest and orange juice in a small pan. Bring almost to the boil, then remove from the heat and allow the flavours to infuse for 15 minutes.

Strain the liquid into a bowl and add the juice of the limes or lemon. Gradually whisk in the oil, then stir in the crème fraîche and season to taste with salt and the freshly milled green peppercorns. Pour the dressing over the seafood and leave to marinate in a cold place for 1–3 hours.

To serve, heap the seafood on to a large platter and garnish with sprigs of fennel and fennel flower and some endive frisée.

SALMON BAKED WITH A HERB CRUST

A mixture of fine white breadcrumbs and freshly chopped herbs makes an excellent coating for a delicate fish, retaining all the flavour and succulence of the fish during the cooking. Halibut is another fish with a delicate consistency which makes a very good alternative to salmon in this recipe.

SERVES 4
4 × 180g (6oz) salmon steaks
juice of 1 lemon
salt and freshly milled pepper
120g (4oz) fresh white bread with the crusts removed
¼ teacup of mixed chopped fresh herbs: parsley, chervil, chives, basil, tarragon, mint
½ teaspoon finely grated lemon zest
60g (2oz) butter, melted
1–2 tablespoons medium dry white wine

Pat the fish dry with kitchen paper, then sprinkle half the lemon juice over both sides of each salmon steak and season lightly with salt and pepper. Place the fish in a well-buttered ovenproof dish.

Break the bread into the bowl of a food processor, add the herbs and process until the bread has formed crumbs and the mixture is pale green. Add the lemon zest, some salt and pepper, and two-thirds of the butter with the remaining lemon juice. Process again until the mixture lightly binds together – if necessary carefully add a little cold water which should encourage the binding process.

Spoon the herb mixture over the salmon, pressing it down lightly to form an even layer. Pour over the remaining butter and spoon the wine into the dish around the salmon steaks. Cover the fish with a butter paper, or buttered greaseproof. Bake in a moderately hot oven (190°C, 375°F, gas mark 5) for 20–25 minutes or until the salmon is opaque and cooked. Serve straight away. There can be no better accompaniment to this dish than new potatoes tossed in mint butter (see page 153) and steamed mangetout peas.

*Although tuna is preferable for the grilled
fish recipe (bottom left), mackerel could also
be used if tuna were unavailable. Fish is
always delicious when served with a slightly
spicy sauce. Here, coriander provides an
excellent accompaniment and a good
contrast to the hot green chillis*

GRILLED TUNA FISH WITH COCONUT, LEMON GRASS AND CORIANDER SAUCE

*Tuna fish, mahi-mahi and mackerel have a
delicious dense, almost meat-like texture
which makes them excellent for grilling over
charcoal. Their flavour goes particularly well
with this delectable Thai-inspired sauce.*

SERVES 4
4 tuna steaks
2 lemons
2 tablespoons plain or lovage flavoured
sunflower oil
300ml (½ pint) coconut milk, fresh, tinned
or powdered
1 stalk of lemon grass, bruised and cut
into short pieces
1 fresh green chilli, halved and seeded
a walnut-size piece of fresh root ginger,
peeled and sliced
2 spring onions or 1 clove garlic, chopped
½ teaspoon Thai or Indonesian *nam pla*
(fish sauce)
a hand-sized bunch of fresh coriander
1 teaspoon arrowroot blended with 1
tablespoon cold water
finely grated zest and juice of 1 lime

First you must marinate the fish. Use kitchen
paper to dry the fish, then cut the lemons in
half, remove the flesh and squeeze it to extract
the juice. Reserve the lemon shells for serving
the dish later. Mix the lemon juice with the oil
and a little salt and pour over both sides of the
fish. Set aside in a cool place to marinate for up
to 2 hours until ready to cook.

Make the sauce by combining the coconut
milk with the lemon grass, chilli, ginger, spring
onions, fish sauce and the stalks (plus roots if
any) of the coriander in a saucepan. Bring to
the boil and simmer for 10–15 minutes until
reduced by one-third. Strain the sauce and
return to the pan, then add the arrowroot and
cook over moderate heat, stirring, until slightly
thickened. Remove from the heat and add the
lime zest and juice, season with salt, and add
the coarsely chopped coriander leaves. Keep
the sauce warm.

Grill the fish on both sides, preferably over
charcoal but otherwise place the fish under a
grill set on high, basting with any remaining
marinade while cooking. Serve the fish with
some of the sauce spooned into the empty
lemon shells and hand the rest separately.
Plain boiled rice goes well with this dish as it
leaves you to savour all the subtle flavours of
the fish and its sauce.

SMOKED SALMON TROUT MOUSSE WITH FENNEL

*This creamy-pink well-flavoured mousse is
nicest served as a first course with a small
salad of young leaves and hot Melba toast.*

SERVES 4–6
120g (4oz) smoked salmon trout, sliced
3–4 sprigs of fennel leaves, chopped
120g (4oz) unsalted butter, softened
120g (4oz) clotted cream
½ teaspoon finely grated orange zest
2 tablespoons orange juice
a good pinch of ground allspice
2–3 teaspoons elderflower vinegar (see
page 161) or Pernod
extra sprigs and flowers (if available) of
fennel to garnish

Flake the salmon trout into the bowl of a food
processor, add the chopped fennel and butter
and process until well mixed. Add the cream,
orange zest and juice, allspice and vinegar or
Pernod and process until well mixed but not
too smooth.

Spoon the mousse into a dish and smooth
level. Cover and chill for 1–2 hours. Garnish
with the sprigs of fennel before serving.

BAY TREE BROCHETTES OF COD WITH YELLOW PEPPERS AND BLACK OLIVES

Instead of cod, any very fresh white fish such as John Dory or monkfish may be used to make this attractive summer dish.

SERVES 4

700–900g (1½–2lb) skinned fillet of cod
1 lemon
1–2 tablespoons clear English or Greek
honey
2 tablespoons olive oil
1 tablespoon finely chopped mint leaves
salt and freshly milled black pepper
2 yellow sweet peppers
24–30 stoned black olives
8–12 fresh bay leaves
a little extra olive oil
8 skewers made from stems of fresh bay
or wooden skewers
boiled white rice cooked with olive oil,
bay leaves and garlic, to serve

Remove any errant bones from the fish, then cut the fillet into 30–40 even-sized pieces.

Wash and dry the lemon, then use a lemon zester to remove long shreds of zest. Place in a wide, shallow bowl and add the strained juice of the lemon, the honey, olive oil and mint. Stir, then check the taste and season lightly if you wish. Add the fish and turn over gently in the marinade until evenly coated. Set aside in a cool place to marinate for 30–60 minutes.

Remove the core and seeds from the peppers and cut into pieces about the same size as the fish. Put in a shallow bowl with the olives and bay leaves and dribble over a little olive oil.

Thread the fish, peppers, olives and bay leaves on to the skewers and place on a lightly oiled grill pan or ovenproof dish. Spoon any surplus marinade over the fish and cook under a high grill, turning the brochettes once, for 5–8 minutes or until the fish is pearly white but still very moist.

Spoon some of the hot rice on to 4 plates and place 2 brochettes beside it on each plate. Spoon the cooking juices over the rice.

SALMON AND DILL FISHCAKES
WITH SORREL SAUCE

These very good fish cakes can be made up to a day ahead if kept covered on a floured plate in a cold place.

SERVES 4
450g (1lb) tail piece of salmon
4 tablespoons medium-dry white wine
450g (1lb) old potatoes, peeled and freshly
boiled
30g (1oz) butter, softened
1 teaspoon finely chopped dill
1 teaspoon finely chopped chives
$\frac{1}{4}$–$\frac{1}{2}$ teaspoon peeled and finely grated fresh
root ginger
$\frac{1}{4}$ teaspoon finely grated lemon zest
salt
seasoned flour
sunflower oil for shallow frying
SORREL SAUCE
120g (4oz) sorrel leaves
30g (1oz) butter
150ml ($\frac{1}{4}$ pint) double cream
1 clove garlic
salt

Place the salmon in an ovenproof dish, pour over the wine and cover with a butter wrapper or buttered greaseproof paper. Bake in a moderate oven (180°C, 350°F, gas mark 4) for 20–30 minutes or until the flesh is opaque and just coming free of the bone.

Set aside to cool, then remove the skin and bones and flake the flesh into a bowl. Add the cooking juices.

Put the potatoes through a 'mouli-légumes', or mash them well, and add to the fish. Add the butter, dill, chives, ginger, lemon zest and salt to taste. Mix gently so that the fish flakes are still discernible. Shape into flat cakes 8–10cm (3–4in) across and 2.5cm (1in) thick. Coat in seasoned flour and store until ready to cook.

To make the sorrel sauce, wash the sorrel leaves in cold water and remove the stalks. Place in a pan over moderate heat with half the butter and stir until the leaves have collapsed into a soft mass. Cook until all the surplus water has evaporated.

Purée the sorrel in a food processor or blender and return to the pan with the cream. Peel the clove of garlic and impale it on a fork. Stir the sauce with the fork over low heat for 2–3 minutes until it has absorbed sufficient garlic flavour, then discard the garlic. Season with salt and add the remaining butter. Keep the sauce warm.

Shallow fry the fish cakes in sunflower oil for 3–4 minutes on each side until golden brown. Serve straight away on hot plates with some sorrel sauce spooned over.

There is no need whatsoever for fresh fish to taste bland. Simple cooking methods like poaching and grilling come into their own and an addition of herbs to the cooking process ensures a lively, appetizing flavour. Often the only extra flourish that is needed can be provided by the addition of fresh lemon juice, a pat of tarragon butter or a spoonful of cream infused with the flowers of chervil or thyme.

CRAB AND BROCCOLI GRATIN WITH CORIANDER LEAVES

The uniquely delicious taste of crabmeat is always enhanced by the flavour of fresh herbs. Although dill, fennel, parsley and tarragon all go well with crabmeat, I find that the oriental flavour of coriander leaves lightens and freshens the taste of this superb shellfish.

SERVES 4
225g (8oz) dressed crab
225g (8oz) broccoli or calabrese
salt
2 bay leaves
45g (1½oz) butter
30g (1oz) plain flour
400ml (14fl oz) single cream or creamy milk
1 teaspoon chopped chives
2 tablespoons chopped coriander leaves
60g (2oz) Gruyère cheese, finely grated
60g (2oz) dryish white breadcrumbs

If possible, separate the white crabmeat from the brown. Break the broccoli or calabrese into bite-size florets; cook in boiling salted water with a bay leaf until tender. Drain well.

Grease four small gratin dishes and divide the brown meat between them. Arrange the broccoli and half the white crab meat on top.

Melt the butter in a saucepan and stir in the flour for 1–2 minutes but do not allow it to change colour. Gradually stir in the cream, add the remaining bay leaf and cook, stirring, for 5–7 minutes until thickened. Discard the bay leaf, and stir in the chives, coriander, half the cheese and the remaining white meat. Check the flavour and add salt if necessary. Divide the sauce between the dishes, spooning it over the broccoli and crabmeat. Mix the remaining cheese with the breadcrumbs and sprinkle over the top of each dish.

Bake in a moderately hot oven (200°C, 400°F, gas mark 6) for 10–15 minutes or until the sauce is bubbling and the topping is golden and crisp.

MEAT, POULTRY AND GAME

Keen cooks quite soon discover that fresh herbs act like a seasoning for meat.
They bring out its true taste and provide an aromatic foil for its rich flavour.
Yet at each stage in the cooking process herbs contribute a subtly different effect.
A joint of beef or a saddle of hare, for instance,
slowly marinaded in a blend of thyme and juniper berries mixed with wine,
yoghurt or fruit juice can produce a sumptuous dish of complex yet harmonious flavours
that quite transforms the separate ingredients.
On the other hand, a purée of garlic crushed with finely chopped rosemary and olive oil
spread over lamb cutlets and chilled for 1–3 hours before grilling or roasting
contributes a fresh, vivid taste to the meat. Similarly, a
chicken or guinea fowl roasted under a crust of herbs mixed
with breadcrumbs develops a delicate herb-infused succulence.
Some herbs best enhance the flavour of meat when added after the cooking, as in an
escalope of veal served with a lemon thyme sauce. If prepared ahead
and stored in the fridge or freezer, such sauces and butters can embellish
the fastest of foods to give an almost instant and flavourful distinction.

PREVIOUS PAGE *left to right* ROAST DUCK WITH A SAUCE OF MORELLO CHERRIES AND HYSSOP, *page* 113;
BAKED SWEET POTATOES WITH CHIVE AND GINGER BUTTER, *page* 139.

ROAST DUCK WITH A SAUCE OF MORELLO CHERRIES AND HYSSOP

A simple roast duck served with a vibrant sauce always makes a good meal. Because my morello tree produces plenty of fruit, I devised this sauce based on them. Nevertheless, sweet red cherries can replace the morellos provided that you sharpen the flavour of the sauce with a little lemon juice.

SERVES 4–6

1.8–2.25kg (4–5lb) oven-ready duckling

1 onion, quartered

salt

5 tablespoons Côtes du Rhône wine

450g (1lb) ripe morello cherries, stoned

juice of 1 orange

45–60g (1½–2oz) light muscovado sugar

4 sprigs of hyssop

1 teaspoon arrowroot

1 tablespoon eau-de-vie de cerises or cold water

a pinch of ground allspice

30g (1oz) butter

cherries and/or sprigs of hyssop, to garnish (optional)

Remove the giblets from the duck and place the onion inside the body cavity. Pat the duck skin dry with kitchen paper and rub in some salt. Place the duck on a rack in a roasting tin and put the giblets in the bottom of the tin.

Roast the duck in a moderately hot oven (190°C, 375°F, gas mark 5) for 1–1¼ hours or until cooked. During the cooking, pour off the surplus fat occasionally and reserve it for other cooking, particularly potato dishes. When the duck is cooked, transfer it to a serving dish and keep warm in a low oven until ready to serve.

Pour off all surplus fat from the roasting tin and add the wine. Cook over high heat for 4 minutes, stirring to incorporate the cooking juices and sediments from the duck. Strain the liquid into a cup and keep warm.

Put the cherries in a saucepan with the orange juice, sugar and 2 sprigs of hyssop. Cook gently until the juice is released from the fruit, then remove from the heat and discard the hyssop. Blend the arrowroot with the eau-de-vie or water and add to the cherries together with the wine stock and the allspice. Cook, stirring, over a moderate heat for 3–5 minutes until the sauce has cleared and thickened. Add the leaves from the remaining sprigs of hyssop and check the flavour of the sauce, adding salt and/or sugar to taste. Remove from the heat and add the butter. When it has melted, spoon some sauce over the duck and serve the rest from a sauce boat.

PORK TENDERLOIN WITH HAM AND LOVAGE

This is delicious served with a crisp green salad for lunch or a picnic. I find one teaspoon of chopped tarragon in place of lovage can be used equally well.

SERVES 4–6

1 pork tenderloin or fillet

60g (2oz) butter, softened

3–4 lovage leaves, finely chopped

1 tablespoon fine white breadcrumbs

120g (4oz) lean cooked ham, thinly sliced

2 tablespoons finely chopped parsley, chives and thyme

Cut the pork in half lengthways and then across to make four pieces. Use a meat mallet to beat each piece of meat until slightly larger and thinner.

Cream the butter with the lovage and the breadcrumbs and spread over three pieces of the meat. Arrange the sliced ham, cut to fit, on top. Layer the pieces on top of each other with the plain piece on top, pressing them gently together. Tie with string in 3 places, season lightly all over and then roll the meat in the chopped mixed herbs and wrap in lightly oiled foil.

Roast in a moderately hot oven (190°C, 375°F, gas mark 5) for 35–40 minutes or until the meat is cooked.

Remove from the oven and allow to cool. Then unwrap and chill well before cutting the meat into slices. You will find that this dish slices easily when chilled.

FILLET OF BEEF WITH JUNIPER BERRIES AND CRIQUE ARDECHOISE

The fruity wine-like taste of juniper berries make them a perfect flavouring for many game and beef dishes. The crique ardèchoise *is a straw potato pancake made with finely chopped garlic and parsley.*

SERVES 4

4 beef fillet steaks

6 juniper berries

6 black peppercorns

90g (3oz) butter

150ml (¼ pint) red Côtes du Rhône wine

90ml (3fl oz) beef or vegetable stock

CRIQUE

450g (1lb) maincrop potatoes

1–2 cloves garlic, very finely chopped

1 tablespoon finely chopped parsley

salt

sunflower oil for shallow frying

4 sprigs of flat leaf parsley

Place the steaks on a plate. Crush the juniper berries and peppercorns with a pestle in a mortar until fairly fine. Rub the mixture into all the surfaces of the meat, then set aside in a cold place for 1–2 hours.

To make the *crique*, peel the potatoes and grate into a bowl. Stir in the garlic, parsley and salt. Divide the mixture into 4 rounds and shallow fry in the oil, allowing about 5 minutes on each side. The cooked *crique* should be golden brown and crisp on the outside.

Meanwhile, melt half the butter in a shallow pan and fry the steaks on both sides to your satisfaction. Transfer the meat to a hot dish and keep warm. Add the wine and stock to the pan, stirring and scraping with a wooden spoon to incorporate all the pan juices, and bring to the boil. Simmer fast until reduced by half, then strain into a small pan and keep warm. Just before serving beat the remaining butter into the sauce.

Cut each fillet steak into three or four slices and arrange on a hot plate. Spoon over some of the sauce and place the *crique* beside it. Garnish with a sprig of parsley and serve.

The combination of garlic and herbs is a classic association that has its roots in French cooking.

RABBIT PIE
WITH PARSLEY CREAM

A traditional English rabbit pie has long been associated with harvest time when meals were carried out into the fields so that farmworkers could eat in the shade of a tree. This pie is good at any time of the year, but late summer, around harvest time, seems particularly appropriate.

SERVES 4–6
1 medium-size rabbit, jointed
salt and freshly milled pepper
60g (2oz) butter
2 spring onions or 1 slim clove garlic, chopped
5 tablespoons medium dry white wine such as a riesling or a chardonnay
6 tablespoons water
2 sprigs of thyme
2 teaspoons cornflour
300ml (½ pint) crème fraîche or double cream
2–3 tablespoons finely chopped parsley
225g (8oz) puff or shortcrust pastry
egg yolk, to glaze

Wash the rabbit and dry with kitchen paper. Season the joints of meat with salt and pepper.

Melt the butter in a frying pan and lightly brown the rabbit joints all over. Stir in the spring onions or garlic for 1 minute, then add the wine and 5 tablespoons of the water. Transfer the contents of the pan to a pie dish and add the sprigs of thyme. Cover with a sheet of foil, sealing the edges well. Cook in a moderately hot oven (190°C, 375°F, gas mark 5) for 30 minutes. Remove the dish from the oven. Raise the oven temperature to 200°C, 400°F, gas mark 6. Remove the sprigs of thyme from the pie dish and discard. Blend the cornflour with the remaining water in a bowl and mix in the crème fraîche, the parsley and cooking juices from the pie dish. Pour this over the rabbit and, if desired, place a pie funnel in the middle of the dish.

On a floured board, roll out the pastry to fit the dish, lay it over the dish and trim the edges. Make a steam vent over the pie funnel, or make 2–3 vents in the pastry. Use any trimmings to make the pastry leaves and berries and arrange on the pie crust. Brush the pastry with egg yolk before heating in the oven.

Bake the pie for 25–30 minutes until the pastry is golden brown and crisp. Serve hot.

SIMPLE ROAST CHICKEN
STUFFED WITH HERBS

It is a truism that the simpler the cooking style, the more important the ingredients. Chicken roasted with just butter and herbs requires a high quality roasting bird, preferably maize-fed and free-range or a poulet de Bresse *to bring out the best in the method.*

SERVES 4–6
1 × 1.5–2kg (3–4lb) roasting chicken, without giblets
a bundle of fresh mixed herbs: parsley, chives, tarragon, fennel, thyme, marjoram or whatever is available
60g (2oz) butter, softened
60–90ml (2–3fl oz) medium dry white wine
60–90ml (2–3fl oz) water or fresh vegetable stock
1 teaspoon finely chopped fresh herbs

Place the chicken in a roasting tin. Stuff the bundle of herbs into the cavity of the chicken and spread the butter over the breast. Roast in a moderately hot oven (190°C, 375°F, gas mark 5) for 1–1½ hours or until the juices run clear when the bird is pierced below the joint on the leg. During cooking, baste the breast with the fat in the tin now and again.

Transfer the chicken to a hot serving dish and set aside in a warm place for at least 15 minutes so that the meat will be easier to carve. Meanwhile, make the gravy: pour off the surplus fat from the roasting tin and add the wine and water or stock. Boil fast on top of the stove for 3–4 minutes, scraping the pan with a wooden spoon to incorporate the cooking juices and sediment. Remove from the heat. Just before serving, add the chopped herbs to the gravy and bring almost to the boil.

BUTTERFLIED LAMB
A LA MAROC

This is one of the classic lamb dishes of the Mahgreb, the territory that stretches from Tunisia to Morocco. The flavours of the blend of spices and herbs seep into the meat while it marinates for 3–5 hours.

SERVES 6–8
1 leg of lamb, boned
1 teaspoon black peppercorns
1½ teaspoons cumin seeds
1½ teaspoons coriander seeds
1 tablespoon sweet paprika
3 cloves garlic, finely chopped or crushed
1–2 tablespoons olive oil
1–2 tablespoons water
2 handfuls of coriander leaves, chopped

Spread out the boned leg of lamb on a flat platter or wooden board and, if necessary, make incisions in the meat to ensure that it is almost the same thickness all over.

Grind together the peppercorns, cumin and coriander seeds in a pestle and mortar, or use an electric coffee mill but do not make the mixture too fine. Mix with the paprika, garlic, olive oil, water and coriander leaves to make a spreadable paste.

Rub and spread the paste over both surfaces of the leg of lamb, making sure that it penetrates all the crevices. Set aside in a cold place to marinate for 3–5 hours.

Cook the lamb either over charcoal or under a grill set on high, allowing about 15 minutes for each side, or until the meat is cooked to your satisfaction. The lamb is most delicious when still pink in the centre.

Remove from the heat and place on a wooden platter. Cut into thick slices for serving with a fresh green salad.

To dry small quantities of herbs place the leaves in a paper bag before drying, in the same way as you would with a bunch of herbs. An electric food dryer is also an efficient way of drying several different herbs at the same time.

GASCON LAMB WITH
GARLIC AND ROSEMARY

Right across the south of France lamb is studded with garlic and sometimes thyme, rosemary, herbes de Provence or fillets of anchovy. The joint is then roasted until the meat – indeed, the whole kitchen – is perfumed with this heady mixture.

SERVES 8–10
1 × 2kg (4–5lb) leg of lamb
1 small head of garlic, each clove cut into slices
3–4 sprigs of rosemary
salt and freshly milled pepper
goose fat or softened butter

Place the lamb on a wooden carving board and make sure that all the tough outer skin and any surplus fat has been removed. With a sharp-pointed knife, make a cut into the skin of the meat. Push a sliver of garlic and 2–3 rosemary leaves into the incision. Repeat all over the lamb, then place it in a roasting tin. Season with salt and pepper and smear with goose fat or butter.

Roast the meat in a moderately hot oven (200°C, 400°F, gas mark 6) for about 1½ hours or until the meat is cooked to your liking. Transfer the lamb to a carving dish or board and leave to rest in a warm place for at least 20 minutes before carving.

QUAIL COOKED IN VINE LEAVES WITH PESTO

The small delicious quail is now more commonly farmed than reared in the wild. The bird has been wrapped and roasted in vine leaves for centuries in France; however, a thin layer of pesto or a herb butter (see page 153) spread over the meat and under the vine leaf does wonders for the flavour.

SERVES 2–4
8–12 vine leaves, fresh and blanched or
brined and rinsed
4 oven ready quail
1 tablespoon olive oil
PESTO
100g (3½oz) basil leaves
8 tablespoons olive oil
30g (1oz) pine kernels
2 medium size cloves garlic, chopped
¼ teaspoon salt (optional)
60g (2oz) Parmesan cheese, freshly grated

Make the pesto by measuring the basil, olive oil, pine kernels, garlic and salt into a blender or food processor and whizzing until you have an even paste. Alternatively, pound the ingredients together with a pestle in a mortar. Gradually work in the freshly grated Parmesan cheese. Spoon the sauce into a dish (any left over from this recipe is best saved for serving with hot pasta).

Place 2–3 vine leaves, slightly over-lapping, in a lightly oiled gratin dish. Spread pesto all over the body of one quail, place on the vine leaves and wrap them round to enclose the bird. Repeat with the other quail. Brush the parcels with olive oil.

Roast the quail in a moderate oven (180°C, 350°F, gas mark 4) for 35–45 minutes or until cooked. Serve with boiled new potatoes.

For cooking over a wood fire or barbeque, wrap the vine-clad quail in foil and cook, turning them now and again, for 45–60 minutes depending upon the heat of the fire.

An Italian delicatessen is invariably a good source for buying fresh Parmesan cheese.

VEAL AND SAGE ROLLS

Saltimbocca, *the Italian name of this simple but very good dish, means 'leaps into the mouth'. Use slim young leaves of sage for the best flavour.*

SERVES 6

700–900g (1½–2lb) veal or turkey escalopes
salt and freshly milled pepper
200g (7oz) prosciutto or Parma ham
about 24 young sage leaves
3–4 tablespoons seasoned flour
60g (2oz) butter
2 tablespoons olive oil
150ml (¼ pint) dry white Italian wine,
Chianti or Marsala
cubes of white day-old bread for croûtons
extra olive oil or butter for frying

If necessary, beat the escalopes between two layers of plastic film until large enough to cut into a total of 24 pieces. Season the meat lightly with salt and pepper and cover each piece with prosciutto, cut slightly smaller. Place a sage leaf in the centre, roll up the meat and secure each roll with a wooden cocktail stick. Set the rolls aside in a cold place until ready to cook.

Toss the veal or turkey rolls in seasoned flour. Heat the butter and oil in a frying pan until foaming, then shallow-fry the veal rolls for 5–7 minutes (less for turkey) until golden-brown all over.

Add the wine to the pan, cover and cook for 5–8 minutes until the rolls are cooked right through. Meanwhile, fry the bread cubes in butter or olive oil to make the croûtons.

Transfer the meat to a hot serving dish and remove the cocktail sticks. Cook the pan juices over high heat until syrupy, then spoon over the meat and serve with the croûtons.

The classic Italian combination of veal and sage is a delicious one. There are several different varieties of sage, each with its own distinctive colour, flavour and texture. All varieties are particularly delicious when used to flavour savoury dishes and sage butter is a good accompaniment to pork and veal sausages.

PASTA, RICE, EGGS AND CHEESE

*Many centuries ago the Italians discovered the delicious combination of herbs
with pasta and rice dishes. Both these staple foods
have a fundamentally bland taste which herbs enliven in a dramatic way.
Some of the most delicious results are achieved by adding fresh herbs,
like finely chopped sage or thyme, to the raw pasta dough itself – a perfect example
of how herbs can elevate the taste of a simple dish to Lucullun heights.
Even plain pasta cooked in boiling salted water with a large bouquet garni of
fresh herbs gains in flavour. But my favourite method
is to return freshly cooked pasta to the pan with some very finely chopped garlic,
a large lump of butter, some olive oil and a handful of fresh chopped herbs. Stir over
moderate heat until all the pasta is flecked with the buttery herbs
and serve straight away with a good seasoning of milled black pepper and
plenty of freshly grated Parmesan cheese.
Freshly boiled rice can be given the same treatment with equally good results.
The Thai-inspired method of adding lots of chopped coriander leaves, some crushed
garlic and a couple of beaten eggs while you stir the mixture over low heat makes a
lovely supper dish or a separate course.
Certain herbs, notably those with an aniseed flavour such as chervil, dill, fennel
and tarragon have an affinity with egg and cheese dishes.
The digestive properties of the herbs appear to lighten the effect of
the rich ingredients. Cheese dishes are always enhanced by the presence of garlic
or chives and nobody could deny that an omelette* fines herbes
*with its rich flavour of parsley, chervil, chives and
tarragon is far more satisfying than a plain version that is sadly herbless.*

PREVIOUS PAGE *left to right* TEA EGGS IN A GREEN NEST, *page 123;*
WILD RICE SALAD WITH OEUFS EN GELÉE À L'ESTRAGON, *page 123;*
TAGLIATELLE WITH TOMATO AND BASIL SALSA, *page 124.*

WILD RICE SALAD WITH OEUFS EN GELEE A L'ESTRAGON

The eggs can be prepared some hours ahead. This dish makes a very good light luncheon or a first course to a summer meal.

SERVES 4
OEUFS EN GELEE
4 eggs
2 tablespoons fino sherry
3 sprigs of tarragon
600ml (1 pint) liquid well-flavoured aspic
½ small red sweet pepper, skinned and diced
2 miniature gherkins, halved
4 slices of cooked ham
SALAD
115g (4oz) wild rice
325ml (12fl oz) cold water
1 clove garlic
2 bay leaves
2 slices of lemon
½ teaspoon salt
DRESSING
1 tablespoon hazelnut oil
1 tablespoon mild olive oil
1–2 teaspoons lemon juice
½ teaspoon finely grated lemon zest
a handful of oak-leaf lettuce, to garnish

Poach the eggs until the whites are set and the yolks are still liquid, then drain and cover with cold water. Gently warm the sherry with 2 sprigs of tarragon, then set aside for 10 minutes to infuse. Strain the sherry into the liquid aspic and pour a 5mm (¼in) layer into the bottom of each of 4 oval or round 150ml (¼ pint) metal or china moulds. Chill until set.

Arrange some tarragon leaves, diced red pepper and half a gherkin cut into a fan shape on the layer of set aspic. Spoon a little liquid aspic on top and chill until set. Trim each poached egg to a neat shape and dry well on kitchen paper, then place an egg in each mould and spoon over aspic jelly to cover. Chill until almost set, then place a slice of ham trimmed to fit on top of the aspic and spoon over the remaining jelly. Chill until set.

Measure the wild rice and water into a pan, add the garlic, bay leaves, slices of lemon and salt and bring to the boil. Cover the pan and cook over low heat for 50–60 minutes until the rice is tender. Pour off any surplus liquid and discard the garlic, bay leaves and slices of lemon from the pan of rice.

Mix the oils and lemon juice and zest into the rice and season with salt. Set the wild rice aside, covered, until cool.

To serve, dip each mould briefly into hot water and unmould on to an individual plate. Spoon some of the rice salad beside each oeuf en gelée and garnish with oak-leaf lettuce.

POTTED CHESHIRE CHEESE WITH WALNUTS AND SAGE

Potted cheese is a traditional British dish made by blending finely grated cheese with softened butter, fresh herbs and wine. Cheshire cheese is usually potted with sherry and Wensleydale cheese with port, but other wines like a dry Madeira or even a Malmsey go equally well.

SERVES 4
120g (4oz) unsalted butter, softened
a pinch of cayenne pepper
3–4 sage leaves, finely chopped
260g (9oz) Cheshire cheese, finely grated
4–5 tablespoons Fino sherry
30g (1oz) shelled walnuts, chopped
GARNISH
2–3 leaves of sage
a few walnut halves

Blend the butter with the cayenne pepper and the chopped sage. Gradually work in the cheese with the sherry and chopped walnuts until well combined.

Spoon the mixture into a stone pot or jar, or a pottery bowl, and smooth level. Garnish with sage leaves and walnut halves and store in a cold place until required. Serve with warm bread or hot biscuits and celery.

If covered with a thin layer of clarified butter, potted cheese will store in a refrigerator or a cold larder for up to 1 month.

TEA EGGS IN A GREEN NEST

My friend Dr Yan-Kit So, the leading authority on Chinese cooking, has provided the traditional method for preparing quails' eggs.

SERVES 6
24 quails' eggs
1 tablespoon jasmine tea leaves
300ml (½ pint) water
salt
1 tablespoon light soy sauce
1 teaspoon sugar
6 segments of star anise
2.5cm (1in) cinnamon stick
2 tablespoons hazelnut oil
2 tablespoons safflower or sunflower oil
a squeeze of lime or lemon juice
freshly milled coriander seeds and green or white peppercorns
6 handfuls of small young salad leaves or *mesclun*

Place the eggs in a pan and cover with cold water. Bring slowly to the boil and cook for 1 minute. Remove from the heat, tip into a colander and refresh under cold running water – this makes the eggs easier to peel later.

Boil the tea leaves in the water for about 5 minutes to extract the flavour. Strain the tea into a pan large enough to hold the eggs in a single layer. Add a good pinch of salt, the soy sauce, sugar, star anise and cinnamon stick.

Gently crack the shells to create a network of fine cracks. Put the cracked eggs in the pan with the tea infusion and, if necessary, add water to ensure the eggs are covered. Gently bring to the boil, then lower the heat and simmer, covered, for 20–25 minutes. Remove from the heat and leave the eggs in the liquid for about 6 hours or overnight.

When ready to serve, drain the eggs and remove the shells. Make a dressing by mixing the oils with the lime juice, some milled coriander and pepper and a little salt. Gently toss the salad leaves in the dressing and arrange the leaves to resemble a nest on each of 6 small plates. Divide the eggs among the plates, placing them in the centre of each nest. Serve straight away.

TAGLIATELLE WITH TOMATO AND BASIL SALSA

This luscious combination of hot buttery pasta and a cool aromatic sauce is exceptionally good. Serve in generous amounts as a main course or in smaller portions as a preface to a summer meal.

SERVES 4
225g (8oz) plain tagliatelle
225g (8oz) tagliatelle verde
100g (3½oz) unsalted butter
freshly milled black pepper
SALSA
450g (1lb) ripe fleshy tomatoes
1 clove garlic, crushed
100ml (4fl oz) basil flavoured olive oil (see page 164)
a small handful of basil leaves
salt

Prepare the salsa first. Immerse the tomatoes, one at a time, in boiling water and leave for ½ minute. Remove, nick the skin with the point of a knife and then plunge into ice-cold water to prevent the tomato from cooking. Skin and deseed the tomatoes, dice the flesh neatly and place in a nylon sieve to drain.

Mix the garlic in a bowl with the oil and half the basil leaves snipped into shreds. Stir in the diced tomato and season with salt.

Cook the tagliatelle until *al dente*. Drain it and return to the pan with the butter. When the butter has melted, stir until the pasta is evenly coated, then turn on to a hot serving dish. Spoon over the salsa, garnish with basil and season with freshly milled black pepper.

SAFFRON ORZO WITH FRESH BAY LEAVES AND LEMON

Orzo is the rice-shaped pasta from Calabria – the most southern toe of Italy. Orzo is delicious served quite plain, though in this luxurious version the slim oval pasta is cooked with saffron, cream and bay leaves and dressed with lemon juice. It makes a very fine dish that is splendid served on its own or as an accompaniment to grilled meat.

SERVES 6–8
450g (1lb) orzo
salt
30g (1oz) butter
1 tablespoon finely chopped onion
a sliver of garlic, finely chopped
2 generous pinches of high quality saffron threads
2 tablespoons hot water
150ml (¼ pint) double cream
6 fresh bay leaves
finely grated zest and juice of 1 lemon
sprigs of fresh bay leaves, to garnish

Cook the orzo in plenty of boiling salted water for 8–12 minutes until almost tender. Drain, reserving one-quarter of the cooking liquor.

Melt the butter in a pan, add the onion and the garlic and stir over a moderate heat for 4–6 minutes until soft and translucent.

Meanwhile, place the saffron on a saucer and warm in a low oven or under a low grill for 2–3 minutes. Remove from the heat, add the hot water and stir together for 3 minutes until the water starts to take on the distinctive deep yellow colour of saffron.

Add the saffron threads and liquid to the onion with the cream and bay leaves and stir over the heat for 5 minutes. Add the orzo and cook together, stirring, for 5–10 minutes, adding some of the orzo cooking liquid as necessary, until the orzo is tender and has taken on the colour of the saffron. Add salt to taste and discard the bay leaves.

Spoon the orzo on to a hot serving dish. Squeeze lemon juice over the orzo and sprinkle long slim shreds of lemon zest on top. Garnish the dish with fresh bay leaves.

WILD MUSHROOM RISOTTO WITH NASTURTIUM BUTTER

The slightly peppery flavour of nasturtium flower butter seems to have a natural affinity with rice and pasta. Like all herb butters, it can be stored for 1–2 weeks in the refrigerator or for 1–2 months in the freezer.

SERVES 3–4
90g (3oz) butter
1 red onion, chopped
1 clove garlic, chopped
225g (8oz) Italian arborio or risotto rice
150ml (¼ pint) dry white wine
300–450ml (½–¾ pint) chicken or well-flavoured vegetable stock
120–225g (4–8oz) wild mushrooms, trimmed and cleaned
salt and freshly milled black pepper
a little extra wine
1 tablespoon flat-leaf parsley leaves
few extra nasturtium flowers, to garnish
NASTURTIUM BUTTER
30 nasturtium flowers, assorted colours
90g (3oz) butter, softened
lemon juice, to taste

To make the nasturtium butter, inspect the nasturtium flowers for any insects, remove the stalks and use scissors to snip the flowers into small pieces. Blend the butter with the chopped flowers and add lemon juice to taste. Spoon into a small dish and set aside.

Melt half the other butter in a heavy-based pan and cook the onion and garlic until soft. Stir in the rice and when it is translucent, add the wine. Cook, stirring, until all the liquid has been absorbed. Add the stock, a ladleful at a time, and let each addition be absorbed by the rice before adding the next.

Meanwhile, soften the wild mushrooms in the remaining butter. Add to the rice with some salt and pepper and cook the risotto until the rice is tender.

Add a splash of extra wine and stir in the parsley leaves. Turn the risotto on to a hot serving dish and spoon over some of the nasturtium butter. Garnish with nasturtium flowers and serve.

RICOTTA AND OREGANO RAVIOLI WITH WALNUT BUTTER

Eating in San Francisco is invariably a treat. This pasta dish is derived from a fine meal at the Postrio restaurant near Union Square.

SERVES 4
PASTA DOUGH
120–140g (4–5oz) plain unbleached flour
$\frac{1}{4}$ teaspoon salt
1 size-2 egg
1 egg yolk
2 teaspoons olive oil
FILLING
60g (2oz) butter
$\frac{1}{2}$–1 teaspoon finely chopped oregano leaves
340g (12oz) ricotta cheese
1 egg
salt and freshly milled black pepper
30–55g (1–2oz) Parmesan cheese, freshly grated
WALNUT BUTTER
60g (2oz) butter
60g (2oz) walnut halves or pieces

Sift 120g (4oz) of the flour and the salt into a wide, shallow bowl and add the egg beaten with the egg yolk and the olive oil. Mix well, adding just a little extra flour, if necessary, until you have a smooth dough. Shape into a ball and knead on a floured surface for 3–5 minutes until the dough is elastic. Wrap the dough in plastic film and refrigerate for 30 minutes–1 hour.

To make the filling, melt the butter with the oregano and mix into the ricotta with the egg and salt and pepper to taste.

Roll out the dough on a very lightly floured surface until it is very thin. Cut into long narrow strips about 10cm (4in) wide. Fold each strip in half lengthways, then open out again. Place a teaspoon of the filling just below the folded line along the strip every 5cm (2in). Brush the exposed dough lightly with cold water, fold over the strip to enclose the filling and press gently with your fingertips to exclude air from each ravioli pocket. Cut into squares around the mounds of filling using a toothed pasta wheel. Place the filled ravioli on a floured plate or board, cover with a cloth and keep in a cold place until ready to cook.

Poach the ravioli in boiling salted water, in batches, for 4–8 minutes until they rise to the surface. Remove with a slotted spoon and arrange on 4 individual hot gratin dishes. Sprinkle with Parmesan cheese and place under grill until melted.

To make the walnut butter, heat the butter until foaming and stir in the walnuts for 1–2 minutes. Spoon over the ravioli and serve.

OEUFS EN COCOTTE WITH CHIVES AND HAM

This is a slight adaptation of a lovely little dish of baked eggs from the famous Troigros brothers of Roanne.

SERVES 4
4 new-laid eggs
150ml (¼ pint) double cream
salt and freshly milled black pepper
30g (1oz) raw cured ham such as Bayonne or Parma, diced
½ tablespoon finely chopped chives
15g (½oz) butter

Carefully separate the eggs, keeping the yolks whole. Place the whites in a mixing bowl and put each of the yolks in a saucer.

Mix the cream with the egg whites, season with a little salt and beat with a whisk for 30 seconds. Stir in the ham and the chives.

Heat four 75ml (2½fl oz) ovenproof cocotte dishes in a moderately hot oven (200°C, 400°F, gas mark 6) for a few minutes. Divide the butter between them and place the dishes on a baking tray. Pour the cream mixture into the dishes and bake for 1–3 minutes, or until the custard begins to set.

Remove the dishes from the oven and slip an egg yolk into each, season lightly with pepper and bake for a further 2–3 minutes. Remove from the oven – the eggs will continue to cook in the heat of the dish for a few minutes. Serve straight away.

Goat's cheese coated or gently sprinkled with a variety of herbs such as chopped chives, rosemary, marjoram, thyme, garlic or parsley not only looks spectacular but is imbued with a richly aromatic flavour. Greek cooking favours wrapping the cheese in vine leaves, while the French apply charcoal dust, black peppercorns or chestnut leaves for flavour and decorative effect.

GOATS' CHEESE GRILLED IN VINE LEAVES WITH MARJORAM AND THYME FLOWERS

This is a wonderful mid-summer way to eat freshly drained mild-flavoured goats' cheeses. Choose cheese that is 4–6 days old and that is firm enough to withstand the heat of the grill. Serve the hot cheese with a round loaf of good-tasting country bread like a pain de siegle.

SERVES 4
8–12 flowering sprigs of marjoram and thyme (at other times of the year use non-flowering sprigs)
4 round goats' cheeses
salt and freshly milled black pepper
garlic-flavoured olive oil
16–20 young tender vine leaves
crusty bread, to serve

Arrange 2 sprigs of the herbs on each cheese. Season lightly with salt and pepper and dribble some olive oil over each one. Place each cheese on 3–4 overlapping vine leaves and wrap up like a parcel. Leave the cheeses in a cold place until ready to cook.

Cook the vine-wrapped cheeses on a grid over a charcoal grill, allowing 3–5 minutes for each side. The vine leaves may singe in places but that does not matter. Serve the cheese straight away: unwrap the vine leaves, trickle a little more olive oil on top and eat the cheese with the bread. The inner vine leaves are usually tender enough to eat with the cheese, but discard the outer singed ones.

SALADS AND VEGETABLES

*One of the joys of growing your own herbs is to be able to nip out into the garden
to gather a handful of leaves, and to return indoors
to create the freshest, most delectable salad ever.
Rocket leaves, a few sorrel shoots and some sprigs of chervil, fennel and claytonia
are all that you need as a base. For a dressing,
combine a few leaves of tarragon, coriander, basil and lemon balm and snip
some chives and parsley into a garlic-flavoured oil blended with a little
elderflower vinegar. Toss everything together and delight in the end result.
There are times when all cooks need to preserve fresh herbs from the garden
or the market in tip-top condition. Standing the stalks in water
in a cool place works well for 8–12 hours.
For longer storage, wrap the herbs in a damp cloth or place in a roomy plastic bag
and keep in the crisper of the fridge for 1–2 days. Many herbs
will store for up to a week when added, finely chopped, to virgin olive oil, crème fraîche
or yoghurt to make a base for a salad dressing or a sauce for vegetables.
A salad composed entirely of herbs is a fairly exotic mix.
More commonly the herbs are mixed with other young leaves such as lettuce or endive.
And it is, of course, also worthwhile to employ herbs as a
flavouring for cooked vegetable dishes. Try steaming summer vegetables like
baby carrots and sweet peppers on a bed of bay leaves or thyme.
Stuff courgettes and mange-tout peas with a mixture of finely chopped herbs
and freshly drained cheese. Or add their flavour to smooth
vegetable purées and garnish with their attractive leaves. For, as most people discover,
fresh herbs offer an endless source of inspiration to the creative cook.*

PREVIOUS PAGE *left to right* ROSEMARY KEBABS OF CHAR-GRILLED SUMMER VEGETABLES, *page 133;*

AUTUMN SALAD, *page 133;* SUMMER SALAD, *page 133.*

ROSEMARY KEBABS OF CHAR-GRILLED SUMMER VEGETABLES

The slightly woody stems of the rosemary bush make admirable herbal skewers for vegetables, fruit, fish and meat. Grill the vegetables over charcoal for a superb flavour and serve with a spiced rosemary dressing and plenty of freshly baked bread.

SERVES 4–6
a selection of summer vegetables suitable
for grilling, such as courgettes, sweet
peppers, tomatoes, mushrooms, whole
cloves of garlic, red onions
8–12 stiff stems of rosemary with most of
the leaves removed or, alternatively,
wooden skewers
MARINATING DRESSING
2 tablespoons lemon and garlic vinegar
(see page 161)
1 tablespoon water
3 star anise
6 green peppercorns, coarsely ground
1 tablespoon fresh rosemary leaves
150ml (¼ pint) mild olive oil or
sunflower oil

Make the dressing by gently heating the vinegar and water with the star anise, peppercorns and rosemary leaves in a small pan. Bring almost to the boil, then remove from the heat and allow to cool slightly before mixing in the sunflower or olive oil.

Prepare the vegetables by washing and trimming where necessary. Cut the vegetables into similar size pieces, large enough to be threaded on to the skewers. Place the vegetables in a dish, pour over the dressing and toss the ingredients gently together. Leave to marinate for at least 1–2 hours until you are ready to cook.

Thread the vegetables on to the rosemary stems or skewers, alternating the different kinds to create an interesting mixture of colours and textures. Cook over a moderately hot charcoal grill, turning as required, until the vegetables are cooked. Serve with the remaining dressing spooned over.

FOUR SEASONS SALADS

Begone dull salad: for as each of the seasons of the year arrives the fortunate herb gardener is able to prepare unusual and delectable salads that reflect the kaleidoscope of different leaves and flowers harvested from his plants. So that, for example, a spring salad is based on the fresh green and yellow shades of new growth while an autumn salad glows with the claret and burgundy tones of the end of summer. When concocting your own salads, look for colour and flavour harmonies in the leaves and blooms so that each salad has a distinctive character.

A SPRING SALAD

The predominant colours in this salad are green and cream. Arrange the leaves attractively on individual plates and hand the dressing separately. For each person select a handful of tender young leaves from the following: sorrel, both French and Buckler, young spinach leaves, lamb's lettuce or mâche, cooked asparagus tips, blanched baby mangetout peas, sprigs of variegated ginger mint, dill shoots, sprigs of sweet cicely, and the creamy heads of sweet cicely and elderflowers – separated into their separate blooms. For a spring salad dressing; mix together for each person 1 tablespoon hazelnut oil, 1 tablespoon safflower oil and 1 teaspoon dill-flavoured vinegar (see page 161). Season to taste with salt and pepper. Dribble the dressing over the salads and each person can gently toss the leaves to coat them evenly just before eating.

A SUMMER SALAD

A cheerful orange and yellow salad. Arrange each serving of salad with some of the following: bronze-leaved oak-leaf lettuce, fresh coriander leaves, nasturtium leaves – especially the yellow-veined Atlantic varieties, narrow strips of roasted green, red and yellow peppers, red and yellow nasturtium flowers, marigold petals, small sprigs of basil and mint, long thinly shredded zest of lemon. To dress each salad, mix 2 tablespoons garlic olive oil

(see page 164) with 1–2 teaspoons nasturtium and lemon vinegar (see page 161), some finely chopped basil or flat-leaf parsley, according to their availability, and seasoning of salt and freshly milled pepper to taste.

AN AUTUMN SALAD

The russet, red and purple colours of autumn fruits are the key to this salad. Assemble a background to the salad using red radicchio leaves, purple-flushed Continuity or Four Seasons lettuce, perella leaves and red mountain spinach or orache, and garnish with halved and seeded dark red grapes, black olives, sprigs of pink thyme flowers, a few sprigs of bronze fennel and tiny young leaves of red sage. Complete with a few purple hearts-ease pansies (or Johnny jump ups) and some needles of purple chive flowers. Make the dressing for each salad by mixing 1 teaspoon prepared tapenade with 2 tablespoons walnut oil and some hyssop vinegar (see page 161) and season to taste.

A WINTER SALAD

In this pale green, yellow and ochre-coloured salad, several of the ingredients are blanched by covering the plants with an upturned box to exclude the light for 1–2 weeks. This gives a normally bitter-tasting salad plant an agreeable nutty flavour which is most appetizing during the short days of winter. Select the ingredients for the salad from the following: endive frisée, blanched dandelion leaves, blanched escarole or Batavian endive, yellow chives produced by excluding the light from chive shoots for 7–10 days, a few yellow bean sprouts, and spring onions that have been trimmed, shredded lengthways and soaked in iced water for 1 hour. The salad is garnished at the last moment with whole roasted cloves of garlic and garlic croûtons.

For the dressing for each salad, blend 2 tablespoons of olive oil from roasting the garlic cloves with 1–2 teaspoons of thyme vinegar (see page 161) and seasoning of salt and freshly milled pepper to taste. Dress the salad just before serving.

ONION AND LEMON THYME TART

The combination of crisp thyme-flavoured pastry and rich creamy onion filling is very good indeed. Serve the tart straight from the oven while piping hot.

SERVES 6
PASTRY
120g (4oz) plain flour
½ teaspoon lemon thyme leaves, chopped
60g (2oz) butter, softened
2 egg yolks
1 egg white
FILLING
30g (1oz) butter
120g (4oz) peeled, chopped onion
2 tablespoons milk
2 spring onions, chopped
3 eggs
150ml (¼ pint) double cream
a pinch of grated nutmeg
salt
6 small sprigs of lemon thyme

First make the pastry: sift the flour into a bowl and stir in the chopped thyme. Add the butter and egg yolks and rub together until the mixture forms a soft dough. Form into a ball, wrap and chill for 30 minutes.

Roll out the pastry and use to line a buttered 23cm (9in) fluted flan tin. Brush the pastry case with the lightly whisked egg white and prick all over with a fork. Bake in a moderately hot oven (200°C, 400°F, gas mark 6) for 10 minutes or until the pastry is set. Remove from the oven and set aside until needed. (If need be, the pastry case can be made ahead and frozen until required. Simply thaw the pastry at room temperature for 1 hour before adding the filling.)

Melt the butter in a saucepan and stir in the chopped onion. Cook, stirring now and again, for 4–5 minutes without allowing the butter to brown. Add the milk, cover and cook over medium-low heat for 8–12 minutes or until the onion is cooked.

Remove the pan from the heat and stir in the spring onions. Cool slightly, then mix in the eggs lightly beaten with the cream, nutmeg and a little salt. Pour this filling into the pastry case and bake at the same temperature for 20–25 minutes or until set.

Remove from the oven, garnish with the sprigs of lemon thyme and serve straight away, before the tart begins to cool.

POTATO PIE WITH GARLIC AND PARSLEY

This classic dish of the French country kitchen retains its deserved popularity despite every twist of gastronomic fashion.

SERVES 6
450g (1lb) peeled waxy potatoes such as Desiree
2 cloves garlic, finely chopped
2–3 tablespoons chopped flat-leaf parsley
salt and freshly milled black pepper
340g (12oz) puff pastry
1 large egg, beaten
100ml (3½fl oz) crème fraîche or double cream

Slice the potatoes very thinly into a bowl and mix with the garlic, parsley and some salt and freshly milled black pepper.

Roll out just over half the pastry and use to line a 20cm (8in) diameter tart or quiche tin. Layer the seasoned potato slices in the pastry case and cover with the rest of the pastry rolled to fit. Brush the top of the pie with beaten egg, then use a sharp-bladed knife to mark a criss-cross pattern on top. Cut a steam vent in the pastry lid and position a roll of foil or baking paper in the vent to prevent it closing.

Bake the pie in a moderately hot oven (200°C, 400°F, gas mark 6) for 50 minutes.

Remove the pie from the oven. Mix the remaining egg with the crème fraîche and pour into the steam vent. Bake the pie for a further 8–12 minutes, then serve immediately, cut into wedges.

This lovely layered pie (right) is a subtle variation on the tradition of serving the parsley herb with potatoes. It is one of the tastiest ways of serving potatoes.

GRILLED BABY LEEKS

Steamed baby leeks grilled with citrus butter make an excellent hot salad or side dish.

SERVES 3–4
225–340g (8–12oz) baby leeks, trimmed and washed
a handful of bay leaves
60g (2oz) butter
½ teaspoon finely grated lime or orange zest

Steam the baby leeks over a layer of bay leaves in a steaming basket for 5–10 minutes until tender. Arrange the leeks in a single layer on a heat-proof dish.

Melt the butter with the lime or orange zest and brush over the leeks. Place under a very hot grill for 3–5 minutes until starting to brown. Remove from the grill and serve the leeks hot or warm with the citrus butter spooned over them.

BLANCHED VEGETABLE SALAD WITH FRANKFURT GREEN SAUCE

This delicious salad of dressed blanched vegetables looks most attractive when arranged in diagonal rows. The recipe for the famous Green Sauce from Frankfurt, which she describes as 'nice and easy', came from my dear friend Christel Scholpp.

SERVES 6–8
900g-1.4kg (2–3lb) mixed raw vegetables, such as mangetout peas, cauliflower florets, broccoli florets, baby carrots, radishes, baby turnips, baby sweetcorn, French beans, baby courgettes, etc.
salt
a bouquet garni of fresh herbs
(see page 165)
120g (4oz) red and/or yellow cherry tomatoes
sprigs of fresh herbs, to garnish (optional)
DRESSING
6 tablespoons herb-flavoured oil
(see page 164)
1 tablespoon lemon and garlic vinegar
(see page 161)
GREEN SAUCE
6 tablespoons finely chopped fresh herbs, including some or all of the following: sorrel, salad burnet, borage, dill, parsley, chives, chervil, tarragon and lovage
3 hard-boiled eggs, shelled and roughly chopped
150ml (¼ pint) sunflower or olive oil, plain or herb-flavoured
about 2 tablespoons tarragon or dill vinegar
salt and freshly milled pepper
caster sugar
made mustard

Wash and trim the vegetables where necessary. Blanch each vegetable separately until almost cooked either by steaming or in a pan of boiling salted water containing a bouquet garni. Drain the vegetables and place in a large bowl. Add herb oil and vinegar and toss gently until lightly coated with the dressing.

ARMENIAN OKRA SALAD

Okra, or ladies' fingers, cooked with tomatoes makes its own colourful and delicious sauce. Serve the salad as a separate first course or use to accompany cold ham or poultry as a main course for a summer lunch.

SERVES 6–8
450g (1lb) okra
2 tablespoons sunflower oil
1 medium onion, finely chopped
450g (1lb) tomatoes, peeled and roughly chopped
1 teaspoon sugar
salt and freshly milled black pepper
150ml (¼ pint) Greek style goats' or sheeps' milk yoghurt
2–3 tablespoons finely chopped mint
a squeeze of lemon juice

Trim the stalk end of each okra and rinse them in cold water, then drain well.

Heat the oil in a large shallow pan and soften the onion over moderate heat for 5 minutes until golden and translucent. Add the tomatoes, sugar, salt and pepper and cook, stirring, for 4 minutes.

Add the okra and spoon the tomato mixture over them. Cook the mixture over moderate heat for 20–30 minutes, turning over the okra now and again, until well cooked, by which time the tomatoes and onion should have cooked down enough to make a rich red sauce for the okra.

Spoon the mixture on to a shallow dish or plate and allow to cool. Mix the yoghurt with the mint and add lemon juice to taste. As a finishing touch, lightly spoon the yoghurt mixture over the okra and set aside until ready to serve.

Peel the tomatoes by dipping them briefly in boiling water and then in cold water before removing the skins. Spoon some of the oil and vinegar dressing from the vegetables over them and arrange the tomatoes in a neat row, stalk side down, diagonally across the middle of a serving dish. Arrange the rest of the vegetables in rows next to the tomatoes, varying the colours and shapes to make an attractive presentation. If you wish, garnish the dish by placing sprigs of herbs around the rim in a fresh leafy border.

To make the sauce, mix the herbs with the eggs in a food processor to a fairly smooth paste. Alternatively, press the mixture through a fine sieve. Gradually beat in the oil, drop by drop as when making mayonnaise. Mix in vinegar, seasoning, sugar and mustard to taste.

Spoon the sauce into a wooden or pottery bowl and serve with the vegetable salad.

MARINATED SHIITAKE MUSHROOMS

A cold mushroom salad, flavoured with garlic and coriander leaves, this American recipe was inspired by the cooking of Greens, San Francisco's pre-eminent vegetarian restaurant.

SERVES 4
225g (8oz) fresh shiitake mushrooms
2–3 tablespoons olive oil
a few drops of sesame oil
1 clove garlic, halved
**2–3 tablespoons Californian chardonnay
or lime juice**
**1 tablespoon coriander,
roughly chopped leaves**
salt and freshly milled black pepper
a little extra olive oil

Trim a sliver from the stalk end of each mushroom and wipe over with a damp cloth. Heat the olive and sesame oils in a large shallow pan and stir in the garlic. Cook for a short while but do not let the garlic colour.

Add the mushrooms and turn them over in the oil, then cover the pan and cook over a low heat for about 5–10 minutes until they are cooked through.

Transfer the mushrooms to a shallow dish and, if you wish, discard the garlic. Add the white wine or lime juice to the pan and boil the liquid fast for 2–3 minutes until syrupy. Remove from the heat and gradually stir in the coriander leaves, seasoning and additional olive oil. Spoon the mixture over the cooked mushrooms.

Set aside in a cold place to marinate for 2–3 hours, then serve with some sourdough or French bread.

ASPARAGUS WITH LEMON AND TARRAGON MOUSSELINE SAUCE

The asparagus season arrives with the first tender young shoots of tarragon. The combination of the two exquisite flavours is a timeless example of French country cooking.

SERVES 4
700–900g (1½–2lb) fresh asparagus,
preferably a green variety
bay leaves and sprigs of tarragon, to
steam (optional)
SAUCE MOUSSELINE
3 egg yolks
1 tablespoon tarragon vinegar
salt
2–3 green peppercorns, finely crushed
225g (8oz) unsalted butter, creamed with
1 teaspoon finely chopped tarragon
¼ teaspoon finely grated lemon zest
juice of ½–1 lemon
100ml (3½fl oz) crème fraîche

Trim the cut end of each asparagus spear, then tie them in one or several bundles with a length of cotton tape.

Cook the asparagus in 5–7.5cm (2–3in) of lightly salted boiling water, with the cut ends standing in the water and the tips covered with a hood of foil that you tuck inside the pan so that the tips cook in the steam. Alternatively, steam the asparagus in a Chinese steaming basket lined with bay leaves and sprigs of tarragon. Freshly cut asparagus takes 6–12

minutes to cook depending on its size; bought asparagus usually takes a little longer. The asparagus is cooked when the point of a sharp knife goes easily into the cut end of the spear. When cooked, drain the asparagus, arrange on a warm serving dish and keep warm by covering with a clean dry cloth.

To make the sauce, whisk the egg yolks with the vinegar, a little salt and the green peppercorns in a bowl placed over a pan of hot water. Add the butter in small lumps, whisking in each addition. The butter should soften but not melt. If the bowl gets too hot, immediately stand it in a bowl of ice-cold water to cool and then replace it over the hot water. Continue whisking the butter into the sauce, which should mount and thicken like a mayonnaise.

Remove the bowl from the heat and gradually whisk in sufficient lemon juice and the lemon zest to sharpen the flavour agreeably. Fold in the cream, check the seasoning and serve in a bowl with the asparagus.

BAKED SWEET POTATOES WITH CHIVE AND GINGER BUTTER

Two varieties of sweet potatoes are generally available in Europe, both are delicious.

SERVES 4
4 medium-sized sweet potatoes
120g (4oz) butter, softened
a walnut-size piece of fresh root ginger,
peeled and finely grated
2 tablespoons finely chopped chives
salt and freshly milled pepper
a squeeze of lemon juice

Scrub the sweet potatoes, prick their skins and place on a lightly oiled baking sheet. Bake in a moderately hot oven (190°C, 375°F, gas mark 5) for 40–60 minutes, or until cooked.

Meanwhile, cream the butter with the grated ginger and the chopped chives. Season to taste with salt, pepper and lemon juice.

Halve the potatoes lengthways and arrange on a cloth-lined dish or wooden bowl. Serve straight away with the savoury butter.

DESSERTS AND PUDDINGS

*During long winter hours of armchair gardening I sometimes plan a confectionery
border as a kind of annexe to my herb garden. In it I'd grow all the herbs
whose leaves, flowers and seeds are a delight when used in sweet dishes and desserts.
These are the highly perfumed herbs whose scent amplifies the flavours of
a dish in a most bewitching fashion: the flowers and leaves of lavender and
lemon verbena, pineapple sage and angelica,* eau-de-cologne *and
ginger mint, sweet cicely and bergamot. And to these one must add the most
ancient of herbal delights, the rose, the sweet violet and the muscat-scented elderflower.
This chorus of scent would need to be planted near the house,
under a window perhaps, where the perfume could waft indoors.
The most ephemeral plants in the sweet herb border are the edible flowers;
marigolds, nasturtiums and heart's ease pansies, gilly flowers and cottage pinks.
Some of the most charming recipes for using these plants come from
the sixteenth and seventeenth centuries. Small wonder that the sugared flowers
and perfumed preserves that were the products of the still rooms of
Elizabethan houses are no less appealing to the herb gardening cooks of today.
Milk, cream, honey and sugar all readily absorb the volatile oils from aromatic
herbs when gently heated. Simply add the herbs to the liquid
in a heavy based pan or a* bain-marie *and stir over moderate heat until the
mixture is subtly scented. Strain the mixture, discard the herbs
and you have a perfumed preparation for making custards, sorbets and syllabubs.*

PREVIOUS PAGE *left to right* JASMINE TEA CREAM, *page* 147;
NECTARINE AND LEMON VERBENA ICE CREAM, *page* 143;
STUFFED PEACHES WITH PEACH LEAF CUSTARD, *page* 148.

NECTARINE AND LEMON VERBENA ICE CREAM IN ROSE CHOCOLATE CASES

For my daughter's birthday in mid-August I usually devise a new ice cream. This blend of crushed ripe nectarines scented with lemon verbena was especially good. The unusual rose water and chocolate cases work particularly well filled with summer fruit ice-cream.

SERVES 12
6 leaves of lemon verbena
60ml (2fl oz) muscat de Rivesaltes or other sweet white wine
8 ripe nectarines
90–120g (3–4oz) caster sugar
450ml (¾ pint) double cream
2 egg whites
ROSE CHOCOLATE CASES
225g (8oz) plain dessert chocolate, broken into pieces
2 tablespoons double cream
1 teaspoon rose water
12 paper cake cases
12 rose leaves

Chop the leaves of lemon verbena and infuse in the wine over low heat for 3 minutes. Remove from the heat and set aside.

Wash and dry the nectarines and slice the fruit into a food processor, discarding the stones. Purée the fruit with the wine and lemon verbena mixture. Stir in the sugar.

Whisk the cream until thick but still glossy and fold in the nectarine mixture. Whisk the egg whites until stiff and fold into the mixture. Freeze in an electric sorbetière or pour the mixture into a lidded plastic box and still-freeze until almost firm.

To make the chocolate cases, melt the chocolate gently in a pan with the cream. Remove from the heat and stir in the rose water. Place the paper cases in a patty tin and spoon melted chocolate into each one, spreading a thin layer over the bottom and sides of each case. Place the patty tin in the freezer until the chocolate is set. Spoon the remaining chocolate over the underside of each rose leaf and chill until set.

Peel the paper layer from the chocolate cases and the rose leaves from the chocolate leaves, and replace the chocolate cases and leaves in the freezer until you are ready to serve the ice cream.

Spoon ice cream into each chocolate case and decorate with a chocolate leaf. Place the filled cases on a dish and scatter a few fresh rose petals around them.

MUSCAT GRAPE AND ELDERFLOWER TART

The deliciously similar flavours of elderflower and muscat grapes is well exploited in this lovely tart which makes a perfect end to a summer meal.

SERVES 6–8
120g (4oz) sugar
150ml (¼ pint) cold water
3 heads of elderflower
1–2 tablespoons Beaumes de Venise muscat wine
450g (1lb) red or white seedless muscat grapes
90g (3oz) cream cheese
150ml (¼ pint) soured cream
a 23cm (9in) baked pastry tart case

In a medium size pan, dissolve the sugar in the water and bring to the boil. Simmer for 4 minutes, then remove from the heat and cool slightly. Add the elderflower to the syrup and leave to infuse for 3–4 minutes, then discard the heads of the flower.

Stir one or two tablespoons of the Beaumes de Venise muscat wine into the syrup, according to taste, and add the red or white seedless grapes, which you should have already washed and halved. Set aside in a cool place to macerate until ready to fill the tart.

Blend the cream cheese with the soured cream and sweeten to taste with some of the elderflower syrup. Spoon the cream into the pastry case and spread evenly. Arrange the halved grapes in circles on top and spoon a little of the syrup over them. Set aside for no more than 2 hours before serving.

ROSE-PETAL SORBET WITH ROSE-PETAL MERINGUES

This is the kind of charming and romantic dish that I make in a small quantity for a birthday lunch with my daughter or a special friend. Serve the pale pink confection in a fine stemmed glass so that the delicate colour can be appreciated.

SERVES 4
225g (8oz) caster sugar
450ml (¾ pint) cold water
600ml (1 pint) red or pink scented rose petals
a squeeze of lemon juice
rose petals, fresh or crystallized, to serve
MERINGUES
2 egg whites
120g (4oz) rose-scented sugar (see page 167)
1–2 drops of pink food colouring
a little extra caster sugar

Dissolve the sugar in the water over medium heat. Bring to the boil and simmer for 5 minutes. Remove the pan from the heat and stir in the rose petals. Set aside for 2 hours until the syrup has absorbed most of the fragrance.

Strain the syrup into a bowl and add a squeeze of lemon juice to adjust the flavour. Freeze in an electric sorbetière, or still-freeze in the freezer, whisking the mixture every half hour to make a smoother sorbet. Store the sorbet in the freezer until needed.

To make the meringues, whisk the egg whites until stiff, then whisk in half the sugar. Gently fold in the rest of the sugar and, if desired, tint the mixture a very pale pink with food colouring. Spoon or pipe teaspoons of the mixture on to sheets of baking parchment on baking trays. Sprinkle with a little extra sugar to give the meringues a frosted finish.

Bake in a cool oven (100°C, 200°F, gas mark ¼) for 1½–2 hours. Turn off the oven and leave the meringues inside for 3 hours until cold. Carefully remove from the baking paper.

Serve the sorbet in pretty glass dishes accompanied by the meringues.

QUINCE AND APPLE CUSTARD TART WITH SWEET CICELY CREAM

The scented quince effectively perfumes its fellow ingredients with the result that an apple or a pear tart made with an almond pastry reflects a glorious marriage of flavours.

SERVES 6–8
ALMOND PASTRY
120g (4oz) plain flour
60g (2oz) ground almonds
30g (1oz) icing sugar
90g (3oz) butter
2–3 tablespoons milk
FILLING
45g (1½oz) amaretti or almond macaroon crumbs
450g (1lb) ripe Cox's Orange Pippin apples
1 large ripe quince, peeled, sliced and cooked
150ml (¼ pint) double cream
90g (3oz) vanilla-flavoured sugar
2 eggs
SWEET CICELY CREAM
3 leaves of sweet cicely
2 tablespoons muscat or sweet white wine such as a monbazillac
1–2 tablespoons sugar
300ml (½ pint) whipping cream
a few small leaves and flowers of sweet cicely, to decorate

To make the pastry, sift the flour, almonds and sugar into a bowl. Rub in butter and add milk to mix to a dough. Form the dough into a ball, wrap and refrigerate for 30 minutes.

Meanwhile, make the sweet cicely cream. Infuse the 3 leaves in the wine in a small pan over low heat for 5 minutes. Strain into a bowl and stir in the sugar. When cool, add the cream and whip until thick. Spoon into a pretty bowl and decorate with small sprigs and flowers of sweet cicely. Keep in a cool place.

Roll out the dough and use to line a 23cm (9in) pie dish about 5cm (2in) deep. Crimp the edges of the pastry case and spread the amaretti crumbs over the bottom.

Peel, core and slice the apples and arrange in the pastry case with the sliced quince. Lightly whisk the cream with the sugar and eggs and pour over the fruit. Bake in a moderately hot oven (200°C, 400°F, gas mark 6) for 20 minutes, then lower the heat to moderate (180°C, 350°F, gas mark 4) and bake for a further 10–15 minutes until the apples are tender and the custard is set. Remove from the oven and serve warm or cold.

ELDERFLOWER SYLLABUB

This is one of those light-as-air puddings that make the perfect end to a summer meal. A traditional syllabub was made by milking the cow straight into the wine or fruit syrup.

SERVES 4
75g (2½oz) caster sugar
5 tablespoons cold water
3 heads of elderflower
1 tablespoon sweet white wine
300ml (½ pint) double cream
1 egg white
small sprigs of elderflower, candied violets or primroses to decorate

Dissolve the sugar in the water over medium heat. Bring to the boil and simmer for 3 minutes. Remove the syrup from the heat and cool for 2 minutes, then add the elderflower heads and infuse for 2–3 minutes. Strain the syrup into a bowl and stir in the sweet white wine. Cool the syrup.

Place 1 teaspoon of the syrup in the bottom of each of 4 stemmed glasses. Mix the remaining syrup with the cream and whip until stiff but still glossy. Whisk the egg white until stiff and fold into the cream.

Spoon the mixture into the glasses and chill for at least 30 minutes. Decorate the syllabub with elderflower, candied violets or primroses just before serving.

The delicate flavours of elderflower and sweet cicely impart a subtle flavour and a summertime aroma to these dishes.

EXOTIC FRUIT AND FLOWER SALAD IN AN ICE-BOWL

If you have both passion fruit and passion flowers available, then it's a pretty idea to freeze the flowers – which, by the way, are not edible – in the ice-bowl and add the passion fruit to the salad. However, any pretty flowers can be included in the bowl. For a comprehensive list of edible flowers see page 166.

SERVES 6–10
2 handfuls of pretty flowers and petals such as pinks, pansies, borage flowers and rose petals
SALAD
1 ripe Charentais or Galia melon
1 mango
8–12 fresh lychees
1 carambola (star fruit)
1 pawpaw
4 passion fruit
caster sugar or clear honey to taste
a few drops of orange-flower water
edible flowers, to decorate

The ice-bowl can be made several days ahead and stored in the freezer until needed. Half fill a large shallow bowl with cold water. Trim the stems from the flowers and add to the water. Place the bowl on a firm level base in the freezer and leave for 1–2 hours until the water is starting to freeze around the edges. Now place a second, slightly smaller bowl inside the first bowl. Add a small weight to make the bowl float at the right depth and place corks or crumpled foil around the edge to locate the second bowl centrally. Add a few more flowers to the water and freeze until the water has turned to ice.

Remove from the freezer and carefully pour warm water into the smaller bowl to melt the

This exotic fruit and flower salad in an ice-bowl never fails to create a dramatic impression at the dinner table and can easily be made in advance. Borage flowers are here enhanced by the addition of vibrantly-coloured passion flowers.

ice just enough to help you remove the bowl. Turn the ice-bowl upside down and pour warm water over the larger bowl so you can lift it off. Wrap the ice-bowl in freezer film and store carefully in the freezer until needed.

To make the fruit and flower salad, peel and deseed the fruit as required and cut into bite-size pieces. Gently toss together in a mixing bowl with the flesh from the passion fruit. If desired, add a little sugar or honey to sweeten, and flavour with orange flower water. Chill the fruit salad until ready to serve.

Place the ice-bowl on a folded napkin on a platter and fill with the fruit salad. Decorate with the extra edible flowers that you have left over and serve straight away.

JASMINE TEA CREAM

Jasmine tea is a large-leaf black China tea scented with the dried flowers of the highly perfumed white jasmine. This delicately flavoured light cream looks charming decorated with fresh jasmine blooms.

SERVES 6
2 tablespoons jasmine tea leaves
150ml (¼ pint) boiling water
60g (2oz) caster sugar
300ml (½ pint) single cream
2 tablespoons powdered gelatine
2 tablespoons cold water
fresh jasmine flowers, to decorate

Measure the tea in a warmed saucepan, pour over the boiling water and leave to infuse for 1 minute. Add the sugar and cream and slowly bring the mixture to the boil over gentle heat, stirring all the time. Check the taste every so often until the cream is well-flavoured.

Remove from the heat and strain the cream into a bowl. Soften the gelatine in the cold water and heat gently until dissolved. Cool slightly, then pour in a fine stream into the cream, stirring all the time.

Pour the cream into a pretty glass bowl or several small dishes and put aside in a cold place until lightly set. Decorate the tea cream with jasmine blossoms just before serving.

SPRINGTIME ANGEL CAKE WITH SUGARED FLOWERS

This very light white cake, smothered in whipped cream and decorated with sugared spring flowers is pretty enough to serve at Easter or for an anniversary.

SERVES 8–10
90g (3oz) plain flour
15g (½oz) cornflour
175g (6oz) caster sugar
6 size-2 egg whites
1 teaspoon cream of tartar
½ teaspoon vanilla essence
¼ teaspoon almond essence
ALMOND CREAM
300ml (½ pint) whipping cream
60g (2oz) vanilla-flavoured sugar
a few drops of almond essence
1–2 teaspoons peach brandy
SUGARED FLOWERS
1 egg white
caster sugar
fresh violets and primroses

Sift the flour with the cornflour and 120g (4oz) of the caster sugar on to a piece of greaseproof paper. Whisk the egg whites with the cream of tartar in a wide bowl until stiff and fluffy but still a little moist (do not whisk until dry). Sprinkle the remaining sugar over the egg whites and gently whisk in. Fold in the vanilla and almond essences. Sift some of the flour mixture over the egg whites and gradually fold it in. Repeat with the remaining flour mixture. Spoon the mixture into an ungreased non-stick 25cm (10in) ring tin and smooth level.

Bake in a moderate oven (170°C, 325°F, gas mark 3) for 45–55 minutes until the cake is cooked. It will shrink away from the tin slightly when it is ready. Cool in the tin for 5 minutes, then turn the cake out on to a wire rack.

Prepare the sugared flowers (see page 166).

To make the almond cream, whip the cream with the vanilla-flavoured sugar until thick and smooth. Flavour to taste with the almond essence and peach brandy.

Spread the cream all over the cake and decorate with the sugared flowers.

STUFFED PEACHES
WITH PEACH LEAF CUSTARD

*This Italian pudding of peaches stuffed with
amaretti biscuits is a real delight served with
smooth custard flavoured with peach leaves.*

SERVES 8
8 large, ripe peaches
60g (2oz) amaretti biscuits, crushed
60g (2oz) ground almonds
1 tablespoon Amaretti di Sarone liqueur
finely grated zest and juice of 1 orange
300ml (½ pint) medium dry Italian white
wine
1–2 tablespoons caster sugar
CUSTARD
600ml (1 pint) single cream
8 egg yolks
60g (2oz) vanilla-flavoured caster sugar
8 tender young peach leaves

First make the custard. Heat the cream in a
double boiler. Whisk the egg yolks with the
sugar in a bowl. When the cream is almost
boiling, whisk into the egg yolks, then return
to the pan and add the peach leaves.

Cook, stirring all the time, for 5–8 minutes
until the custard thickens sufficiently to coat
the back of the spoon. Do not allow the
custard to boil or the eggs will separate and
spoil the smoothness. Strain the custard into a
pretty glass dish or jug and leave until cool.

Cover one or two peaches at a time with
boiling water and leave for 1–2 minutes, then
cool in cold water and carefully remove the
skins. Halve and stone the fruit.

Mix the biscuit crumbs with the ground
almonds, liqueur and orange zest and add
sufficient juice to bind the mixture together.
Divide the mixture between the peaches,
sandwiching it between the two halves.

Place the peaches in a flameproof dish and
pour the wine over them. Bake in a moderate
oven (180°C, 350°F, gas mark 4) for 15–20
minutes until tender. Remove from the oven
and sprinkle caster sugar over each peach.
Place under a very hot grill until the sugar has
caramelized to a golden brown. Serve warm or
cold with the peach leaf custard.

BANANA, LIME AND
PINEAPPLE SAGE YOGHURT
ICE

*The leaves of pineapple sage have a strong
pineapple scent and flavour which acts as a
delightful foil to the sweetness of bananas.*

SERVES 8
900g (2lb) ripe bananas
finely grated zest and juice of 1 lime
120g (4oz) caster sugar
300ml (½ pint) low-fat natural yoghurt
6 leaves of pineapple sage, chopped
2 egg whites
a small handful of pineapple sage flowers,
to decorate

Peel the bananas and mash until smooth with
the lime zest and juice. Stir in the sugar,
yoghurt and chopped pineapple sage until
well combined. Whisk the egg whites until stiff
and fold into the mixture.

Freeze the mixture in an electric sorbetière
or in a lidded plastic box and still-freeze until
firm. Serve in coupé dishes, decorated with the
scarlet flowers of pineapple sage.

Note: as an alternative to pineapple sage, try
pineapple-scented geranium leaves.

MINTED PEARS
ON CHOCOLATE SHORTBREAD

*The crisp chocolate shortbread can be made
ahead and stored in the freezer or refrigerator until needed.*

SERVES 6
3 almost ripe dessert pears
60g (2oz) caster sugar
150ml (¼ pint) water
2 sprigs of mint
a small strip of lemon peel
85g (3oz) cream cheese
1–2 teaspoons caster sugar
1–2 teaspoons Poire William liqueur
6 sprigs of frosted mint leaves, to decorate
(see page 166)
CHOCOLATE SHORTBREAD
140g (5oz) plain flour
15g (½oz) cocoa powder
a pinch of ground cinnamon
120g (4oz) butter, softened
70g (2½oz) vanilla-flavoured caster sugar

Peel, halve and core the pears. Dissolve the
sugar in the water and bring to the boil. Add
the mint and lemon peel and simmer for 3
minutes. Add the halved pears and poach
gently for 8–12 minutes until almost cooked.

Remove from the heat, cover the pan and
leave for 10–15 minutes to complete the
cooking. Then use a slotted spoon to transfer
the pears to a plate. Discard the mint and the
lemon peel and boil the syrup until reduced to
2–3 tablespoons. Set aside to cool.

To make the shortbread, sift the flour,
cocoa and cinnamon into a bowl. Cream the
butter with the sugar until fluffy, then gradually
work in the flour mixture until you can form
the dough into a ball.

Place a sheet of baking parchment on a
baking tray and pat or roll out the dough on it
to make a round 20cm (8in) in diameter. Pinch
the edge into a fluted shape and prick all over
with the prongs of a fork. Bake in a moderate
oven (180°C, 350°F, gas mark 4) for 25–30
minutes. Cool on the baking tray for 5
minutes, then transfer to a wire rack or flat
serving plate.

Blend the cream cheese with the sugar and flavour with the liqueur. Spread the mixture over the shortbread base. Arrange the pears on top, either whole or sliced, pointing to the centre. Spoon over the pear syrup and garnish with sprigs of frosted mint leaves. This dessert is best served within 2 hours while the shortbread is still crisp.

Pears, mint and chocolate shortbread make a subtle and tangy dessert which is a welcome change from the classic dish of pears in red wine. Other fruit desserts with herbs include Nectarine and Lemon Verbena Ice Cream (see page 143) and Quince and Apple Custard Tart with Sweet Cicely Cream (see page 144).

BREADS, CAKES AND BISCUITS

*In classical Rome, bakers used to place a seedhead of fennel under their loaves as
they slid them into the oven. Chinese cooks have added poppy seeds
to their steamed buns for centuries and today, in Devon and Cornwall, a golden
saffron doughcake studded with dried fruit, a relic of medieval times, is still baked.
After many years of home-baking, my own favourite biscuit remains
a thin pale disc of buttery shortbread flecked and flavoured with
finely chopped leaves of rosemary or lavender.
How beautifully an aromatic herb pervades a pastry or dough during baking.
A few leaves of rose-scented geranium placed in a cake tin,
under the mixture, perfumes a whole cake by the time it is taken from the oven.
Edible herb flowers add a new and unexpected dimension to the tea table:
marigold sandwiches or thinly sliced brioche enclosing sugared rose petals or a
lavender honey wafer are best accompanied by a herb tisane or tea,
ideally prepared with a sprig of fresh rosemary, a handful of lime flowers or some
leaves of lemon balm. Increasingly, people young and old are finding that
herbal tea makes a stimulating yet relaxing drink with none of the disadvantages
of caffeine, while a tisane's digestive properties only adds to its charm.
But baking with herbs is not restricted to sweet dishes.
Timeless baking traditions have produced classic breads that are characterized
by their appropriate herbs. The flat sage breads of Italy,
the thyme-flavoured fougasse of Provence and the English plaited loaf
infused with marjoram – once specially made to celebrate the harvest
– are all enduring yeast-leavened loaves.*

PREVIOUS PAGE CROISSANTS FILLED WITH BRAISED STRAWBERRIES
AND LAVENDER HONEY, *page 153.*

HERB BUTTERS

Butter is one of the most delicious vehicles for the aromatic essential oils in herbs. And there are very few dishes, such as soups and sauces, freshly cooked vegetables or a warm loaf of bread, that are not improved with a pat of a well-flavoured herb butter. The simplest herb butter is no more than a blend of freshly chopped herbs and a sweet unsalted butter. The result stores well in the refrigerator for 2–3 weeks and in the freezer for 2–3 months.

CHIVE AND LEMON BUTTER: blend 120g (4oz) softened butter with the finely grated zest of ¼ lemon, 1 tablespoon finely chopped chives and lemon juice to taste.

TOMATO AND OREGANO BUTTER: blend 120g (4oz) softened butter with 1 teaspoon tomato paste, ¼ teaspoon finely grated orange zest and 1 teaspoon finely chopped oregano or marjoram.

BLACK OLIVE AND HERBES DE PROVENCE BUTTER: blend 120g (4oz) softened butter with 1–2 tablespoons finely chopped sun-ripened black olives and ½–1 teaspoon crushed *herbes de Provence*, add lemon juice to taste.

DILL BUTTER: blend 120g (4oz) softened butter with 2 hard-boiled egg yolks, 1–2 tablespoons finely chopped dill and lemon juice to taste.

HORSERADISH BUTTER: blend 120g (4oz) softened butter with 2–3 teaspoons finely grated horseradish and lemon juice to taste.

TARTARE BUTTER: blend 120g (4oz) softened butter with ½ teaspoon Dijon mustard, ½ teaspoon Worcestershire sauce, ½ teaspoon lemon juice and 1 teaspoon chopped parsley.

MAITRE D'HOTEL BUTTER: blend 120g (4oz) softened butter with 2 tablespoons finely chopped parsley and 1 tablespoon lemon juice; season to taste with salt and freshly milled pepper.

RAVIGOTE BUTTER: blanch 1 finely chopped shallot and 2–3 tablespoons mixed parsley, chervil, tarragon and chive leaves in boiling water, drain well and chop finely, then blend with 120g (4oz) softened butter and lemon juice to taste.

TARRAGON BUTTER: blend 120g (4oz) softened butter with 2–3 teaspoons finely chopped small tender tarragon leaves and 1–2 teaspoons lemon juice; season to taste with salt and freshly milled pepper.

GARLIC BUTTER: blend 120g (4oz) softened butter with 1–2 crushed cloves garlic, 1 tablespoon finely chopped parsley and a squeeze of lemon juice.

CROISSANTS FILLED WITH BRAISED STRAWBERRIES AND LAVENDER HONEY

One summer morning in France, I decided to make something delicious for breakfast. So I combined ripe strawberries and lavender from the garden with fresh croissants from the village baker. The result tastes wonderful.

SERVES 4
4 large croissants
60g (2oz) butter
340–450g (12–16oz) fresh strawberries, hulled and halved
1–2 tablespoons lavender honey
a few individual lavender flowers or finely chopped lavender leaves
about 150ml (¼ pint) crème fraîche

Heat the croissants in a low oven or under the grill. Meanwhile, melt the butter in a wide, shallow pan and add the strawberries. Cook, stirring, over high heat until they give up their juice. Stir in the honey and cook, stirring, for 3–4 minutes until the juice has thickened into a syrup. Add the lavender flowers or leaves and remove from the heat.

Cut each croissant almost in half, spoon some of the strawberry filling into the centre and add a large spoonful of crème fraîche. Serve immediately.

LAVENDER HONEY WAFERS

These delicate wafer biscuits are excellent eaten quite plain with a sorbet or ice-cream. Or for serving at afternoon tea, the wafers are very good filled with a light rose-water cream and some alpine strawberries.

MAKES ABOUT 24
60g (2oz) unsalted butter, softened
90g (3oz) icing sugar
90g (3oz) plain flour
1 egg white, lightly whisked
4 tablespoons clear lavender honey
120g (4oz) alpine or wood strawberries (if available)
a little extra icing sugar
ROSE WATER CREAM
150ml (¼ pint) whipping cream
rose-scented sugar or plain caster sugar and a few drops of rose-water
1 egg white

Cream the butter with the sifted icing sugar, and gradually mix in the sifted flour with the egg white and honey. Place the mixture in teaspoons on a buttered non-stick baking sheet and spread each spoonful level to make a round 5–7.5cm (2–3in) across. You should be able to make 4–6 lavender honey wafers on each baking sheet.

Bake the wafers in a moderate oven (180°C, 350°F, gas mark 4) for 7–10 minutes until the edges of each wafer are golden brown. Remove from the oven and, as soon as you can handle the wafers, take each one and wrap it loosely around the handle of a wooden spoon so that the wafer has a conical shape. Cool on a wire rack for a few minutes, then carefully remove the wooden handle. When cold, store the wafers in an air-tight plastic box until ready to serve with the cream.

Whip the cream until fairly stiff and sweeten to taste with the rose-scented sugar. Fold in the stiffly whisked egg white.

Spoon some cream into the open end of each wafer and add some alpine strawberries. Dust the wafer lightly with a little icing sugar shaken through a sieve. Serve within 30 minutes, before the wafers soften.

An unusual but inspired selection of ingredients in the form of blackberries and other red fruits are complemented by rose geranium cream which produces a taste of summer right through the year. Remember to freeze some berries each summer to tide you over the winter months. Alternatively, the more common red fruits such as raspberries, strawberries and blackcurrants can be bought frozen at any time of year.

FRESH BLACKBERRY CAKE WITH ROSE GERANIUM CREAM

This summer cake with a centre layer of fresh fruit is just as delicious made with raspberries, bilberries or blackcurrants.

SERVES 8

3 size-2 or 4 size-4 eggs
225g (8oz) plain flour
225g (8oz) rose- or vanilla-flavoured caster sugar (see page 167)
225g (8oz) butter, melted
1 teaspoon rose water (optional)
225g (8oz) fresh, dry blackberries
1 tablespoon caster sugar
1 teaspoon cornflour
½ teaspoon finely grated orange or lemon zest

ROSE GERANIUM CREAM

3–4 rose geranium leaves
2–3 tablespoons caster sugar
300ml (½ pint) whipping cream
rose water (optional)
a few small rose geranium leaves, to decorate

Beat the eggs in a bowl and gradually mix in the sifted flour, flavoured sugar, melted butter and rose water. Spoon half the mixture into a greased and lined 23cm (9in) round loose-bottomed cake tin.

Mix the blackberries with the sugar, corn-flour and orange zest and spoon into the tin in an even layer. Carefully spoon the remaining cake mixture over the top and smooth level.

Bake in a moderate oven (180°C, 350°F, gas mark 4) for about 45 minutes until the cake is springy in the middle. Remove from the oven. Cool in the tin for 2 minutes, then transfer to a wire rack.

To make the cream, place the rose geranium leaves in a heavy-based pan and add the sugar. Heat gently over a low heat for about 5 minutes, stirring all the time, until the sugar has absorbed some of the aromatic oils of the leaves. Remove from the heat and discard the leaves. Whip the cream with the sugar until stiff and, if you wish, add a little rose water. Spoon the cream into a dish and garnish with small rose geranium leaves.

Serve the cake warm or cold, cut into wedges, with the cream spooned on top.

ANGELICA AND ALMOND CAKE

The green crystallized stem of the angelica plant gives this cake its unusual and attractive flavour. Good quality French angelica can be used but this tends to be rather expensive and not always easy to find, so why not try making your own candied angelica (see page 167).

SERVES 8–12
120g (4oz) butter, softened
120g (4oz) caster sugar
3 eggs
140g (5oz) self-raising flour
60g (2oz) ground almonds
120g (4oz) candied angelica, chopped
60g (2oz) candied orange peel, chopped
MACAROON LAYER
90g (3oz) caster sugar
90g (3oz) ground almonds
30g (1oz) flaked almonds

Cream the butter with the sugar until light and fluffy. Gradually beat in 2 eggs and the yolk of the third. (Set aside the remaining egg white in a bowl.) Sift the flour with the ground almonds and fold into the mixture with the angelica and orange peel.

Spoon the mixture into a greased and lined 18cm (7in) round loose-bottomed cake tin. Lightly whisk the egg white and mix in the sugar and ground almonds. Spread the mixture over the cake and sprinkle the flaked almonds on top.

Bake in a moderate oven (180°C, 350°F, gas mark 4) for 50–60 minutes until the cake is cooked. Halfway through the cooking, place a layer of foil over the cake to prevent the flaked almonds from browning too much. Cool the cake in the tin for 3 minutes, then transfer to a wire rack to cool completely.

This delightful angelica and almond cake is the most delicious treat for a late-summer afternoon tea. Surprisingly light in texture yet full of sweet herbal flavours, it is perhaps best accompanied by a refreshing pot of mild herbal tea.

PLAITED HERB LOAF

Plaited loaves always look appetizing. This milk-bread flavoured with fresh herbs stays fresh for several days if need be.

MAKES 1 LOAF
2 teaspoons dried yeast
150ml (¼ pint) warm water
450g (1lb) unbleached strong white flour
2 teaspoons salt
150ml (¼ pint) warm milk
2 tablespoons herb-flavoured oil
2–3 teaspoons finely chopped fresh herbs:
chives, thyme, rosemary, hyssop,
marjoram
beaten egg or milk
few extra finely chopped herbs

Sprinkle the yeast on to the water in a small bowl and set aside in a warm place for 10 minutes until frothy.

Sift the flour and salt into a mixing bowl and stir in the yeast mixture, milk, oil and chopped herbs. Mix together to make a soft dough. Turn out on to a floured board and knead for 8–10 minutes until the dough feels elastic. Replace the dough in the mixing bowl and place the bowl in a roomy plastic bag. Leave to rise in a warm place for about 1 hour until the dough has doubled in size.

Place the dough on a floured board and knead for 1 minute. Divide the dough into 3 equal pieces. Roll each piece into a sausage about 30cm (12in) long. Press the pieces together at one end and then plait the dough, taking care not to stretch it too much, and press the ends together.

Place the loaf on a greased baking sheet. Brush with beaten egg or milk and sprinkle with the extra herbs. Leave the baking sheet in a warm place for 30–45 minutes until the dough is swollen and puffy.

Bake in a hot oven (220°C, 425°F, gas mark 7) for 30–35 minutes until golden and crusty. Cool on a wire rack.

Herb butters freeze well and for hot dishes they can be used straight from the freezer.

MARIGOLD AND NASTURTIUM LEAF SANDWICHES

During the sixteenth and seventeenth centuries, marigold petals were known as the poor man's saffron. The yellow and orange petals were used to give a saffron colour to butter, cheese and custards. Marigold leaves taste rather like nasturtium leaves with the same slightly peppery flavour. Both marigold and nasturtium leaves can be used as a filling for sandwiches for afternoon tea.

thinly sliced white or brown bread
young marigold and nasturtium leaves
marigold and nasturtium petals and
flowers, to garnish
MARIGOLD BUTTER
120g (4oz) unsalted butter, softened
2 tablespoons marigold petals
a pinch of ground cinnamon
a squeeze of lemon juice

Blend the butter with the marigold petals and cinnamon and add lemon juice to taste.

Spread the marigold butter on to the thinly sliced bread. Cover with a layer of marigold or nasturtium leaves and place a second layer of buttered bread on top. Press the sandwiches together and cut to shape. A nice variation is to use one slice of brown bread and one of white. Arrange the sandwiches on a serving plate and garnish with marigold petals and nasturtium flowers. Serve straight away.

STORECUPBOARD ESSENTIALS

Both gardeners and cooks have always endeavoured to lengthen the life of the
herb garden beyond the summer. Unless you live in a climate where
your herbs will grow well all year round you will doubtless be keen to investigate
many of the traditional ways of preserving herbs.
The suitable methods extend from drying bunches of midsummer herbs to making
an aromatic purée or a well-flavoured preserve like a herb jelly.
Drying: this is one of the simplest techniques for preserving herbs
and is particularly suitable for the highly scented Mediterranean herbs such as
thyme, rosemary and lavender. The level of essential oils
secreted in the leaves of all herbs is highest just before the plant blooms.
Choose a dry day and pick the herbs in mid-morning before the heat of the sun
makes the leaves limp. Discard any old, tough or discoloured leaves
and strip the lower end of each stalk so that the bunch can be tied together with string.
Hang up in a warm place, preferably away from bright sunlight,
and leave undisturbed until the herb feels paper dry – the drying time depends
upon the level of humidity and the ambient temperature.
Next strip the leaves from the stalks and store in a screwtop jar in a dark cupboard.
The flavour of the dried herbs will be stronger if you store the leaves unbroken.
It's a simple matter of crushing or pounding them to a powder when required.
Herb jellies, sugars and syrups (see pages 161 and 167) are a delight to prepare.
These unusual preserves are indispensable for use in sweet dishes and desserts and the
high quality that you can achieve at home is virtually unobtainable commercially.

PREVIOUS PAGE *left to right, front row* ROSEMARY JELLY, *page* 161; PEACH AND SWEET CICELY CONSERVE, *page* 161;
SAGE JELLY, *page* 161; KUMQUAT AND ANGELICA MARMALADE, *page* 161;
back row FENNEL VINEGAR, *page* 161; ROSEMARY OIL, *page* 164;
THYME OIL, *page* 164; DILL AND GREEN PEPPERCORN VINEGAR, *page* 161.

HERB VINEGARS

Almost all culinary herbs can be used to make a herb flavoured vinegar. The method could not be simpler: take a bottle of white wine vinegar and pour a little into a cup. Add your chosen herb to the bottle, for instance a long sprig of tarragon or a handful of leaves of basil. Pour back the reserved vinegar and seal the bottle tightly. Place the bottle in a warm room and leave for 1–2 weeks or until the vinegar has absorbed the aromatic oil from the herb. Use the herb vinegar as required, but store in a cool, dark place to preserve its flavour.

The principal herbs used for making herb vinegars are basil, bay, chervil, chives, dill, elderflower, fennel, garlic, juniper, lavender, lovage, marjoram, mint, nasturtium flowers, oregano, rosemary, sage, salad burnet, smallage, savory, tarragon and thyme. It is also worth making a herb vinegar by adding several herbs together. For instance, for a Provençal vinegar, add 1–2 cloves of garlic with a sprig each of thyme and rosemary to a bottle of white wine vinegar. In this way the cook can make a range of individual herb vinegars that are an asset in the kitchen.

PEACH AND SWEET CICELY CONSERVE

By adding just a sprig or a few leaves of the right herb you can transform the flavour of a jam, jelly or conserve into something quite exotic. Simply slide the herb into the hot jar of preserve before you seal and label it.

MAKES ABOUT 1kg (2¼lb)
1kg (2¼lb) ripe peaches
450kg (1lb) sugar
2 lemons
1 tablespoon peach brandy (optional)
4–6 sweet cicely leaves

Cover the peaches, 2–3 at a time, with boiling water, then lift out and remove the skins. Slice the fruit into a pan and discard the stones. (If you wish, you can crack a few stones and add the blanched kernels, sliced, to the peaches.)

Add the sugar and lemon juice to the peaches and place over low heat, stirring now and again until the sugar is dissolved. Then bring to the boil and boil until the conserve reaches setting point at 105°C (220°F). Remove from the heat. If desired, add the peach brandy to the conserve.

Place a sweet cicely leaf in the bottom of each of 3–4 small hot dry jars, spoon in the conserve, seal and label.
Note: this conserve does not set firmly. It is ideal for spooning over ice creams or on to a cream-topped scone.

KUMQUAT AND ANGELICA MARMALADE

Small orange kumquats, sliced into circles, make a fine-flavoured marmalade with the added interest of chopped angelica leaves which act as a 'sweetener' to the sharp citrus taste of the fruit.

MAKES ABOUT 1.8kg (4lb)
1kg (2¼lb) kumquats
600ml (1 pint) water
1–1.25kg (2–2½lb) sugar
1–2 fresh angelica leaves, chopped or 15g
(½oz) candied angelica (see page 167), diced

Wash and dry the kumquats. Use a sharp knife to cut each kumquat into thin slices. Remove the pips and place them in a muslin bag. Place the fruit in a pan with the water and bag of pips. Bring to the boil, then simmer for 30–40 minutes or until the peel is tender.

Measure the contents of the pan and add 450g (1lb) of sugar for every 600ml (1 pint) of fruit pulp. Stir over low heat until all of the sugar is dissolved, then raise the heat and boil the mixture until setting temperature of 105°C (220°F) is reached, squeezing the pip bag occasionally.

Remove from the heat and discard the bag of pips. Stir in the fresh angelica leaves or the candied angelica and carefully pour the marmalade into hot, dry jars. Cover straight away or when cold.

HERB JELLIES

Herb jellies are one of the glories of the English store cupboard. A small pot of crystal-clear rosemary jelly is a wonderful partner to roast lamb or cold ham. Or a jar of claret and sage jelly makes an excellent accompaniment to roast pheasant or guinea fowl. The autumn is usually the best time of year to make herb jellies, when there are plenty of windfall apples around.

MAKES ABOUT 450g (1lb)
1–1.8kg (2¼–4lb) apples, washed and quartered
preserving or granulated sugar, warmed
juice of 1 lemon
fresh herbs: rosemary, thyme, chives, mint, marjoram, sage
green vegetable food colouring (optional)

Place the apples in a large pan with cold water to cover. Slowly bring to the boil, and then turn down the heat and allow to simmer for about 1 hour. Gently mash the fruit once or twice during the cooking.

Remove from the heat and cool slightly, then pour the contents of the pan into a jelly cloth or bag suspended above a bowl to catch the drips. Leave for several hours, preferably overnight, until all the juice has dripped through. It is important that you are not tempted to squeeze the bag or the final jelly will be cloudy.

Measure the juice into the clean pan and bring to the boil. For every 600ml (1 pint) of juice add 450g (1lb) of warmed sugar and stir over medium heat until dissolved. Boil until the jelly reaches setting point at 105°C (220°F). Add the lemon juice to the jelly and remove the pan from the heat.

If you wish, you can tint the jelly a pale green with just a drop or two of vegetable food colouring. Fill several small, hot dry jars with the jelly and add the appropriate herbs to each jar. Seal and label the jars.
Claret and sage jelly: replace one third of the strained apple juice with claret and proceed as above; add 3–4 finely chopped sage leaves to each jar of jelly, seal and label.

Mint, a herb commonly used for flavouring lamb, is an essential adjunct to many freshly made drinks – alcoholic as well as non-alcoholic. Whether it is added to a glass of iced tea or placed decoratively in a jug of cool southern mint julep, it provides a strong, refreshing flavour.

ICED TEA
WITH MINT AND LEMON

A frosted glass of iced tea decorated with borage flowers and a sprig of mint is guaranteed to allay the most fearsome thirst on a hot summer's day.

SERVES 6
3 rounded teaspoons Darjeeling tea leaves
4 sprigs of mint
1 litre (1¾ pints) cold water
caster sugar to taste
slices of lemon
borage flowers
a few extra sprigs of mint
borage flower ice cubes, made by placing
a borage flower in each ice cube
compartment before freezing

Measure the tea into a jug, add the sprigs of mint and pour on the cold water. Stir well, then cover and chill for 4–6 hours.

Strain the tea into a chilled serving jug, stir in sugar to taste and garnish with slices of lemon, borage flowers and sprigs of mint. Serve the iced tea in glasses with some of the borage flower ice cubes.

APRICOTS
PRESERVED IN EAU-DE-VIE
WITH LEMON VERBENA

This method of preserving dried fruit works equally well with fresh or dried cherries, dried pears and muscatel raisins.

450g (1lb) ready-to-eat dried apricots
225g (8oz) white sugar
300ml (½ pint) cold water
3 sprigs of lemon verbena
300–425ml (½–¾ pint) eau-de-vie

Check the apricots and remove any stalks or leaves. Place in a litre (2 pint) preserving jar: the fruit should fill just over half the jar.

Dissolve the sugar in the water over low heat, then bring to the boil and simmer for 5 minutes. Tuck the lemon verbena into the preserving jar and pour on the hot sugar syrup. Add eau-de-vie to the rim of the jar, making sure that it covers the fruit. Cover tightly and leave in a cold, dark place for 4–8 weeks before serving.

SOUTHERN MINT JULEP

One of the great classic cooling drinks – at its best served out of doors as the sun goes down. The distinctive flavours of mint and whisky complement each other deliciously.

SERVES 2
2 tablespoons crushed ice
2 cubes of sugar
6 mint leaves, lightly crushed to release
their flavour
2 tots of whisky or more according to
taste
2 sprigs of mint

The easiest way to make the crushed ice is to place ice cubes in a plastic bag on a solid surface and crush with a rolling pin. Divide the crushed ice between 2 whisky glasses. Add the sugar and mint and pour in the whisky. Stir briskly and serve when the glass is frosted, with more ice if liked and garnished with a sprig of mint.

PINK ELDERFLOWER
CHAMPAGNE

Everyone enjoys this traditional English fizzy, yet non-alcoholic, drink. The best time to make elderflower champagne is when the elder tree produces its creamy heads of blossom in late May and June – in fact, in some parts of the country this drink is known as June champagne. In other areas, it is known as Frontinac due to its muscat flavour which resembles the Languedoc wine of the same name. Elderflower champagne should be stored in strong sparkling wine bottles in a cold place for at least 2–3 weeks before opening and drinking.

MAKES 6 × 75cl BOTTLES
3 heads of elderflower in full bloom
300ml (½ pint) blackcurrants, fresh or
thawed
2 tablespoons wine vinegar
680g (1½lb) white sugar
4.6 litres (8 pints) cold water
6 champagne or sparkling wine bottles
plus corks and wires

Cut the large stems from the heads of elderflower and put the blossom in a large bowl or bucket. Add the blackcurrants, the vinegar and the sugar. Pour in the cold water and stir well. Cover the bowl with a cloth and set aside for 24 hours, stirring the mixture from time to time to release the juice from the fruit.

Next day, strain the liquid into bottles, and cork and wire them securely. Store the bottles on their sides in a cool, dark place for 2–3 weeks. The wine is ready when the corks start to rise in the wires. Take care when opening the bottle to point the cork away from any objects or people.

Fresh herbs always impart flavour and decoration to homemade drinks. An ingenious way of using them decoratively is to place them inside an ice cube and drop several cubes into individual drinks. As the ice cube melts it gradually releases a delicate taste of herbs into the drink.

RASPBERRY AND HYSSOP SHRUB

A shrub is a fruit-based cordial similar to the sherbet of the Middle East. For drinking on a hot day, the concentrated syrup is nicest served in thin glasses, and is diluted with plain or carbonated mineral water and ice-cubes.

1kg (2lb 3oz) raspberries
3 sprigs of hyssop
340g (12oz) sugar
juice of 1 lemon
mineral water
ice cubes containing flowers and/or leaves
of hyssop

Slowly bring the raspberries almost to the boil, stirring until the fruit begins to give up its juice. Remove from the heat and strain the fruit juice through a fine nylon or muslin sieve, gently pressing the fruit with a wooden spoon to extract all the juice.

Return the fruit juice to the pan and add the hyssop, sugar and lemon juice. Stir over low heat until the sugar is dissolved. Pour the fruit syrup into a jug and chill until ready to serve.

Discard the sprigs of hyssop and serve the shrub in glasses, diluted with mineral water and chilled with hyssop ice cubes.

PUREE D'AIL

The best garlic for making this very good purée is 2–3 months old with fat, juicy cloves. Serve the purée, at room temperature, with grilled meat.

MAKES ABOUT 600ml (1 pint)
4 large heads of garlic or 450g (1lb) garlic
salt
300ml (½ pint) cold water
2 bay leaves
8 tablespoons fruity olive oil

Peel the cloves of garlic, cut each in half and, if necessary, remove the green growing shoot in the centre. Roughly chop the garlic. Cook, covered, in the salted water with the bay leaves for 8–12 minutes or until tender. Remove from the heat, discard the bay leaves and strain the garlic into a food processor, reserving the cooking liquor and adding it as necessary to make a smooth purée. Then mix in the oil.

Spoon the purée into an airtight lidded jar. Seal tightly, label and store in a cold place until it is needed.

GARLIC PRESERVED IN OLIVE OIL

Whole heads of the new season's garlic are highly delicious preserved in an aromatic olive oil for winter use.

4–6 heads of garlic
600ml (1 pint) olive oil, approximately
a sprig of thyme
a sprig of rosemary
a few bay leaves

Remove the outer papery layers from the garlic until the separate cloves are uncovered, but leave them intact. Brush a sheet of baking parchment or foil with olive oil and place in a roasting tin. Arrange the garlic on top, then wrap the paper or foil securely around to enclose it. Bake the garlic in a moderately hot oven (190°C, 375°F, gas mark 5) for 15–20 minutes or until the cloves are tender.

Transfer the heads of garlic to a wide-necked preserving jar, tuck in the herbs and pour in enough olive oil to cover. Fasten down the lid of the jar and store in a cold place for 1–2 months before using.

The cloves of garlic are superb added to soups and casseroles.

HERB OILS

The magical combination of an aromatic herb with a fine olive oil is as ancient as it is satisfying. A virgin olive oil scented with a handful of basil leaves or a sprig of rosemary transforms the humblest salad into a very special dish. Although herb-flavoured oils have been used cosmetically for centuries, their principal role is in the kitchen.

The method for making them is indeed simple and akin to that for a herb vinegar. Take a bottle of extra virgin olive oil and pour a little into a cup. (Other good vegetable oils like sunflower, safflower, grape seed and groundnut oil can be used as an alternative to olive oil.) Add the herb to the oil, allowing 2–3 sprigs or 1–2 tablespoons of leaves to 300ml (½ pint) oil, and pour in the reserved oil. Seal the bottle and keep in a moderately warm room for 1–2 weeks until the oil has absorbed the flavour of the herb. Then strain the flavoured oil into another bottle and keep in a cold place until required.

HERBS RECOMMENDED FOR FLAVOURING OILS: bay, basil, chervil, dill, fennel, garlic, juniper, lavender, lovage, marjoram, mint, parsley, rosemary, sage, savory and thyme.

BOUQUET GARNI

Making a bouquet garni of fresh herbs is one of the great pleasures of herb gardening. Picking a bay leaf, a sprig of parsley and another of thyme and then tying them neatly with fine string is a task that any cook welcomes. The essential contribution of a fresh bouquet garni to a dish is invaluable and no amount of alternative seasoning can replace the unique flavour of fresh herbs.

The classic bouquet garni of French cooking consists of 2 sprigs of parsley, 1 sprig of thyme and a bay leaf tied together with thread long enough for tying it to the handle of the pan in order that it can be easily removed at the end of the cooking.

Which herbs comprise your bouquet garni is a matter of personal preference. There are, however, some established combinations which work well when cooking particular ingredients:

FOR CHICKEN AND TURKEY: parsley, chives or leek, thyme and a little celery

FOR BEEF: bay, parsley, thyme, 2 cloves and possibly a little orange zest

FOR LAMB: parsley, lemon thyme, bay and celery

FOR PORK: parsley, bay, thyme and lemon zest

FOR VEAL: parsley, bay, marjoram, lemon zest and sage

FOR GAME: parsley, bay, rosemary and 2 juniper berries wrapped in layer of leek

FOR TOMATOES: parsley, bay and basil or tarragon or hyssop

FOR BROAD BEANS: parsley, chives and summer savory

FOR PEAS AND MANGETOUT: parsley, mint and chives

FOR ROOT VEGETABLES: parsley, bay, oregano and thyme

FOR POTATOES: parsley and bay

FROSTED FLOWERS

The English enthusiasm for frosted flowers with their pretty apppearance and sweet taste dates back to Elizabethan cooking and earlier. Most seventeenth-century cookbooks include a wide range of flower recipes for cowslips, roses, violets and calendulas or pot marigolds. Provided that the plants are free from pesticide sprays, edible flowers can be picked and eaten straight from the plant. Frosting is a simple and effective way of preventing an edible flower from wilting and also preserves the bloom for later use.

The flowers of most herbs taste delightful, with a delicate flavour of the herb itself. I recommend basil, bay, bergamot, borage, chamomile, chervil, chive, claytonia, dill, elderflower, fennel, hyssop, lavender, lemon balm, lemon verbena, lovage, marjoram, mint, pineapple sage, purslane, rocket, rosemary, sage, salad burnet, sorrel, sweet cicely, tarragon, tansy, thyme and woodruff.

The following garden plants also have edible flowers: alyssum, anchusa, begonia, carnation, chrysanthemum, clover, coleus, cornflower, cosmos, cowslip, dahlia, daisy, day-lily, forget-me-not, geranium or zonal pelargonium, gladioli, hawthorn blossom, hibiscus, hollyhock, honeysuckle, hop flower, jasmine, lilac, lime flower, mallow, marigold, mesembryanthemum, monarda, nasturtium, hearts-ease pansy, pink, rose, sedum, stock, tiger lily and violets.

egg white
caster sugar

Lightly whisk the egg white and brush gently on to both sides of each flower or petal. Dust the flower all over with caster sugar and shake gently to remove excess sugar, leaving a thin layer. Place the flower on baking parchment on a wire rack in a warm place and leave for 1–3 hours until completely dry.

Store frosted flowers in an air-tight plastic box, although they taste best as soon as they are dry and before their scent evaporates. Use frosted flowers for decorating sorbets, ice-creams, cakes, custards and tartlets.

CANDIED ANGELICA

To make candied angelica, select some narrow tender stems and cut into 7.5cm (3in) lengths. Cook in boiling water until tender. Drain well and remove any tough outer skin, though with young angelica this is not usually necessary.

Weigh the angelica and layer it in a dish with an equal weight of caster sugar. Set aside for 1–2 days until the sugar has liquified. Transfer to a pan and heat gently until the liquid has almost evaporated. Place the pieces of angelica on a wire rack over a plate and leave in a warm place or a low oven for 1–2 days until dry. Store the candied angelica in an air-tight container and use as required.

These dishes of French herbs mixed into dried beans serve two purposes: not only are they decorative and aromatic, but they could also be kept in an airtight jar, placed in the storecupboard and used as a base for making delicious winter-warming soups. Good combinations to try would be chick peas and bay leaves, butter beans and sage or lentils and thyme.

HERB SUGARS

It is most fortunate for the pastry cook that the highly aromatic oil secreted by the leaves of a herb is readily absorbed by a jar of fine sugar. Scented rose petals make a delightful perfumed sugar that is perfect for sprinkling on custards, sponge cakes and biscuits.

Herbs recommended for perfuming sugar include angelica, aniseed, bay, rose geranium and other scented leaf geraniums, hyssop, lavender, lemon balm, lemon verbena, marigold flowers, mint – especially eau-de-cologne and pineapple mint, rose petals, rosemary, sweet cicely and sweet violet.

FOR LAVENDER SUGAR: layer 225g (8oz) of caster sugar with 60g (2oz) spikes of fresh lavender flowers or 30g (1oz) dried lavender flowers in a lidded jar. Leave in a warm place for 1–2 weeks, giving the jar a shake now and again to distribute the scent evenly. When the sugar has absorbed the scent of the lavender, sift the sugar to remove the lavender flowers. Keep the jar tightly sealed and use the lavender sugar as required.

Rose petal sugar is made in the same way. Select dry, highly-scented rose petals and arrange them in layers with caster sugar in a lidded jar. Leave in a warm room for 1–2 weeks and use the sugar as required by shaking it through a sieve to remove the rose petals.

HERB SYRUPS

A herb syrup is a most appealing way of capturing the scent of a herb for use later in the year. Herb syrups are an excellent way of sweetening and flavouring desserts like sorbets, ice creams and custards. Alternatively, a herb syrup can be used hot or cold as a sauce for a steamed pudding or an ice cream: for example, try drizzling a lemon verbena wine syrup over a freshly baked sponge cake just before serving with pouring cream.

The best herbs to use for making a flavoured syrup have a fairly strong scent: they include angelica, aniseed, elderflower, fennel, rose geranium and scented leaf geraniums, hyssop, lavender, lemon balm, lemon verbena, all mints, pineapple sage, rose petals, rosemary, sweet cicely and sweet violet.

Prepare a sugar syrup by dissolving 120g (4oz) caster sugar in 150ml ($\frac{1}{4}$ pint) water over low heat. Bring to the boil and simmer for 3 minutes, then remove from the heat and pour the syrup into a jar. Add 2–3 sprigs of the desired herb. Cover the jar and allow to cool. Discard the herb and use the syrup as required. Herb syrups store in a refrigerator for 2 weeks, or in a freezer for 2 months.

Herb-scented wine syrup is made by replacing half the water in a syrup with a medium dry or sweet white wine.

Part 3

INDOOR HERBAL

In the gardening world few plants are as consistently fragrant as those we describe as herbs. And few sensations stir the memory as forcefully as that of scent. How many of us, at the first hint of the clove-like bouquet of basil or caught in the lee of a gust of air heavy with the perfume of lavender, can prevent long-forgotten images crowding into the mind. And who would want to. Time and again gardens are planted, food is prepared and perfume is rubbed on to skin as a deliberate aromatic evocation of good times remembered.

This power of association in scent is doubtless part of the therapeutic effect of aromatic herbs. Many of the scents, perfumes and smells first identified during our childhood make us feel happy and secure when we come across them later in life. And it is a well-known and scientifically proved fact that people's spirits are lifted by the presence of a fresh, natural scent in a room. However, in the case of herbs, their capacity to alter our moods also depends upon the action of their complex chemical structure upon the body. The exact result depends upon the choice of herb and how it is administered: it might be by mouth as an infusion or tisane, or it might be applied directly as a decoction or in the form of an essential oil smoothed into the skin.

The beneficial effect that herbs have upon the body has been noted and valued since the appearance of the first printed herbals over 2,000 years ago. Yet we are still making important discoveries in this field that point to new ways of treating serious illness and its symptoms.

ABOVE *A twelfth-century drawing showing the herbs cinnamon, balsam, valerian and nard.*

OPPOSITE *Pietro Longhi's (1702–1785) painting* La Bottega della Speziale *features the herbal apothecary at work in his shop.*

And now that, as urged by Eugene Schumacher for over twenty years, we are at last beginning to reassess the true cost and nature of what we term progress, these ancient skills in the use of herbs are being reappraised. Whereas in China, India and many other parts of the world where the medicinal virtues of herbs have never been forgotten, herbal medicine is still widely practised. It is now also the subject of renewed interest in the developed world.

Until two centuries ago in Britain, herbs still played a major role in people's lives. Herbs, far more than expensive spices, were the most common flavouring for food; herbs were the basis for medicine; and herbs contributed to the pleasures of living, from the perfuming of water for washing to the scenting of rooms, clothes, furniture and bed-linen and the making of decorative garlands and posies for celebrating festivities. It is these uses of herbs in the household which are enjoying a timely revival now. Easy to achieve and a joy to behold, the decorative possibilities of herbs are once again inspiring their regular use in the home, and leading to the rediscovery of their numerous useful medicinal applications as well.

In a world that is moving relentlessly towards uniformity it is not a little surprising that many people are choosing to emphasize the individual and personal values in their lives. In the tradition of all devotees of these bewitching plants I advocate that by developing a knowledge and skilled use of herbs, one deepens one's relationship with the natural world and enhances one's own quality of life.

INDOOR HERB GARDENS

Once beguiled by the charm of fresh herbs, most people are understandably reluctant to forego herbal fragrance and flavour for up to half a year when outdoor supplies are unavailable. Consequently few herb lovers exist without a pot or more of their best-loved herb perched on the kitchen windowsill or nestling amongst other houseplants in a porch, hallway or conservatory.

Gardenless gardeners have always been inventive about growing their favourite plants indoors. And gardening cooks who depend upon the vitality and rich variety of flavours that freshly-picked herbs bring to their cooking are naturally keen to extend the season of these plants and, where possible, ensure a year-round supply.

Herbs grown indoors require much the same conditions as most houseplants: adequate light and fresh air, an even temperature of 55–65°F (13–18°C) and a fertile growing medium that is kept moist but not allowed to become sodden. Central heating can make the atmosphere uncomfortably dry for them, so when the heating is on it is wise to put a bowl or saucer of water near the herbs to provide a degree of humidity. A sunny windowsill is an ideal spot for many herbs, and on balmy days they will appreciate a warm breeze (but not a howling draught) from an open window. If you have a garden or balcony where you can put them outside now and again on fine days, or even for the whole summer, so much the better: happy as they are to grow indoors, herbs will grow more vigorously and live longer for the occasional change of air, especially if they generally live in the heavy atmosphere of a kitchen.

Many herbs will thrive indoors if they are given the right amounts of heat, light and food. Their dual nature – at once useful and ornamental – is shown off to best advantage inside the house, where they are not only constantly available for flavouring cooking or scenting the air, but can also be arranged and grouped to make decorative displays, ranging from sparse minimalism to careless profusion.

Almost every herb that can be grown outdoors can be moved under cover providing that the growing requirements are met. Although a herb may have the same appearance as when grown outdoors, the flavour is usually less intense and more delicate. And though you may need more of an indoor-grown herb to obtain the same depth of flavour in a dish, these cossetted plants usually produce leaves that are ideal for salads and for use as year-round garnishes. Growing habits can also subtly alter when herbs are brought indoors: tall herbs such as fennel and lovage that tower above most other herbs in the garden conveniently take on a dwarf form when grown in a container inside.

Tender and less hardy herbs such as lemon verbena and pineapple sage positively flourish in the protected environment of an indoor garden. When grown indoors in a warm, light position even the capricious basil plant can be persuaded to produce its delectable leaves until well after Christmas.

Indoor herb plants should be harvested with discretion to guard against weakening the plant. Pick only a few leaves at a time and pinch out the central stem of fast-growing herbs like chervil, coriander, basil and parsley in order to promote plenty of side shoots and ensure a bushy shape. Pinch out any flowers as they appear, and give the pots a quarter turn every few days to keep their growth even and prevent them from leaning towards the light at too extreme an angle. True enthusiasts might even like to try their hand at indoor topiary. Surprisingly, although it requires a certain amount of planning and care in the early stages, this is much less fussy

ABOVE AND RIGHT *A trough of bushy, low-growing and small-leaved herbs, such as marjoram and balm and different varieties of mint and thyme, can make a delightfully aromatic table decoration, especially if, as here, they are set in a deep layer of moss, which also serves to disguise the trough. Propagating herbs by root division, layering, taking cuttings or harvesting seeds is quite simple, and will ensure a constant supply of small, compact plants which can be grown indoors.*

than it sounds; with the plants under your nose every day it is simple enough to keep them in trim with a snip of the scissors, and it is never difficult to find a use for the clippings. Perennial herbs such as rosemary, bay, lavender, myrtle, santolina and scented-leaved geraniums all make good subjects, for they thrive on constant pruning, and make well-shaped bushes.

The watering and feeding requirements of herbs grown indoors are more demanding than when grown outside. In a hot, dry location watering can be a problem unless you can attend to your plants every day or so. There are, of course, sophisticated watering systems on the market, which may be the best solution if you have regularly to leave your plants unattended. A simple solution is to use terracotta pots, which act as a convenient water reservoir, and bed them on a layer of gravel to provide a damp but not sodden environment. In dry conditions herbs benefit from a fine mist of warm water sprayed over them each day; to avoid scorching the leaves, wait until the sun is no longer on them.

Although herbs may be a little more exacting in their requirements when grown indoors, it is generally easier to notice and respond to the first telltale signs of trouble, such as wilting or yellowing leaves. Pests and diseases tend not to be much of a problem indoors. If you should notice any signs of disease it is probably best to discard the plant and start again. The only pest you are likely to find is greenfly, which is easily dealt with. If there are only a few you can pick them off individually; if they appear in clusters the simplest thing is to hold the pot upside down, anchoring the plant and soil with your fingers, and swish the leaves back and forth in a bowl filled with a mild solution of soapy water.

Container-grown herbs need careful feeding. Either incorporate a slow-release fertilizer in the soil before potting up the plants or apply an organic liquid feed every 1–2 weeks during the growing season to ensure healthy growth.

Creating an indoor herb garden offers almost as many possibilities as an outdoor version. And an even wider range of containers can be utilized (see pages 60–63) since they will be protected from the elements. At the simplest level, clay or plastic pots are fine. I find the 10–12cm (4–5in) size useful for a single herb. If there is enough space, though, I prefer to group herbs in a larger pot or trough. Containers of mixed herbs not only look attractive but they usually grow better due to the micro-climate that they create. A family of coloured sages, for example, red, tri-colour and the usual grey-leaved variety, look attractive planted together and, in a frost-free place, will survive longer than when grown outside.

And herbs do not need to be confined to the kitchen, though it is obviously convenient to keep the most commonly used culinary ones close at hand. Clumps of fragrant herbs make a wonderful welcome to the house if your hall is light enough, or can be placed at the side of staircases or in passageways where people will release the scent as they brush past. A pretty trough of mixed herbs or a group of little pots can make an attractive and aromatic centrepiece for a table setting, and a pot of herbs can go in any spot where you might otherwise put a houseplant or a vase of flowers, always providing that they have enough light and heat. Or you could revive the Elizabethan fondness for planting evergreen aromatic herbs such as rosemary in hanging baskets suspended in a sunny spot, perhaps a brightly lit stairwell or a corner by a window. Trailing nasturtiums are also very effective used in this way.

Herb specialists can still build their particular style of herb garden in an indoor environment, although its size and scope will naturally be dictated by the space available. A scented or culinary herb garden, an edible flower garden, a citrus garden reminiscent of a seventeenth-century French orangery or a topiary garden with clipped plants of bay, juniper, rosemary and myrtle are all delightful indoor herb gardens, even in miniature form.

The easiest way to start is by buying healthy herb plants from a reputable nursery – or if your outdoor herb garden is overstocked, simply pot up some of the surplus plants. Pot the plants in a proprietary potting mixture or mix equal parts of loam, peat, mature compost and gritty sand. Leave the pots outdoors in a sheltered, shady place for 1–2 weeks until established, then take them indoors.

As the plants grow, pot them on so that their roots have room to spread. You can tell when the roots start to get too crowded as they will poke through the drainage holes of the pots. Perennial herbs will benefit from repotting annually in new soil, as the soil quickly becomes exhausted even if you feed regularly. Annuals will need replacing. As buying new plants every time is expensive it makes sense to propagate from existing plants.

Unless you want to keep them for purely decorative effect, most herbs are best harvested for drying just before they come into flower, when their production of aromatic oils is at its peak. After flowering the plant concentrates on reproduction, and its energies are diverted to producing seeds. For the majority of herbs the longest day signals the plant's readiness for harvesting. Once cut, the herbs should be hung to dry in a warm and airy place away from direct sunlight. The herbs need to dry as quickly as possible in order to preserve their properties, but direct heat or sunlight will damage them.

HARVESTING AND PRESERVING HERBS

Every herb has a time of optimum growth when its leaves are highly aromatic and the plant is producing the maximum amount of essential oils. This is the moment that every prudent herb grower anticipates with pleasure, for herbs harvested at this time are in the peak of condition and in the best state for preserving for use later in the year.

It is best to harvest the majority of herbs just before they come into flower. After flowering, the plant concentrates on reproduction and its energies are diverted to producing seeds.

Some herbs flower once a year while others – such as chives – which flower early in the season, can usually be persuaded to produce a second crop of blooms by fairly severe pruning after the first flowering. Similarly, a burst of young tender leaves can be coaxed from herbs like lovage, angelica and chervil, by cutting down their stems by about two thirds in midsummer to promote new growth that has a better flavour for drying or preserving.

The best time of day to harvest herbs is during the morning on a dry day. Gather each herb separately to prevent cross flavours and cut complete stems rather than individual leaves. This helps to keep the herb fresh until you are able to preserve it. Place the herbs in a flat-bottomed basket or box, and in very hot weather, cover the container with a damp cloth.

The simplest method of drying is to make a bunch of each kind of herb and hang it upside down in a warm, airy, sunless place. Mediterranean herbs like rosemary, thyme and marjoram dry beautifully this way. The quicker the herb dries the better its colour and flavour. I usually hang herbs for drying from a beam in the kitchen but a wooden airing rack or a high shelf works equally well. I have found that an electric food dryer or an oven set on low with the door ajar can also give good results.

In central Europe where herbs are dried on a large scale for making tisanes and teas, leaves – such as mint – and flowers, for instance, lime and chamomile, are spread out on large muslin sheets tacked to horizontal frames in well-ventilated drying sheds. A small-scale domestic version can be constructed quite easily at home, even by stretching a net curtain over the legs of an upturned chair. It is essential with this method to provide a fast-moving current of dry air and to turn the herbs regularly to prevent any mildew or off-flavours from developing.

When the herb is paper-dry, it should be stored in an airtight container out of direct light. Leave the leaves attached to the stem and crush them just before use to prevent any loss of flavour.

Herb flowers for drying should be gathered particularly carefully to prevent damage to their petals. Long-stemmed flowers required for decoration can be dried on their stalks. In this case, the simplest method is to hang the blooms upside down, either separately or in loose bunches so that the flowers are not touching. Place in a well-ventilated, dust-free place, out of direct sunlight, in order to preserve the colour of the blooms. Flowers with short stems or no stems – and which may need wiring for decorative purposes – can be dried by supporting each bloom on fine chicken wire. Or use an upturned cardboard box – make a series of holes and thread the stems of the flowers into them until the flower head is resting on the flat surface.

An Elizabethan method of drying flowers is to place them stalk-down in a shallow box of fine, dry silver sand, a thin layer of extra sand is sprinkled over the petals and the box is left in a warm, dark place until the flowers are dry. A modern and more effective alternative to sand is silica gel crystals (obtainable from a chemist or flower-arranging shop). Use the finest grade of crystals spread over the bottom of a cardboard box, place the flowers, stem down, on top and sprinkle a fine layer of crystals over the petals. Leave in a dark, dry place for 2–4 days until the flowers are paper-dry. Carefully remove the blooms, shaking them free of the silica gel crystals.

The best-flavoured herb seeds are harvested after allowing them to ripen on the plant for as long as possible. This calls for careful judgement – if you leave coriander, dill, fennel or parsley seed for too long on the parent plant, the seeds will drop onto the ground before you have time to pick them. In a dry climate it is possible to cover the seed head with a paper bag tied securely around the stem and leave until the seeds rattle when you shake the bag. In a temperate climate it is usually safer to cut the seed head of the herb just as the seed colour starts to turn from green to pale brown. Place the whole head of seed in a roomy paper bag and hang in a warm, dry place for a few weeks until the seeds are dry. They will then separate and fall to the bottom of the bag.

In former centuries drying was virtually the only way of preserving the precious aromas of herbs through the winter. Even though other methods are now possible, such as freezing and microwaving, drying remains the easiest and most picturesque way of keeping herbs. Rosemary, thyme, marjoram and other Mediterranean herbs will dry beautifully if simply tied in bunches and hung upside down in the kitchen. The bunches should be kept small, otherwise there is a danger that the stems in the centre will stay damp and grow mouldy.

WINDOWSILL AND CONSERVATORY HERB GARDENS

Quite the easiest place to create an indoor herb garden is on a windowsill. Since one of the essential requirements of plant life is plenty of light, this is clearly an excellent location as long as you remember to turn the pots round regularly to ensure even growth. A south-facing window is admirably suited to pots of Mediterranean herbs like sage, thyme, myrtle and rosemary, though the leafy, moisture-loving herbs such as sorrel and chives may flag unless shaded during the hottest part of the day. Given a choice, I prefer a wooden windowsill rather than one of stone or tiles because the latter tend to chill the pots during cold weather. One solution is to place a plank of wood or other insulating material under the pots to keep the roots warm and promote growth. Since plants like to grow in groups it makes sense, and often looks more attractive, to plant your herbs in a trough or bowl to create an indoor windowbox. Remember that if you lower a blind or pull curtains across the window at night then the herbs would prefer to be with you in the warmth of the room rather than shut out in the chilly – and possibly drafty – space against the window.

When I lived in a studio-flat with a single, large south-facing window I created the maximum growing space by adding glass shelves to accommodate my windowsill herbs. I utilized every suitable nook and cranny by suspending some of the lighter pots of herbs from large hooks fixed along the lintel above the window. The green tracery of leaves filtered the light into the room and provided an attractive natural screen, making a conventional curtain unnecessary.

Windows that face in other directions than south are best suited to shade-loving herbs or those that scorch easily such as mints and chervil. In a location with poor-quality light consider fitting a couple of horticultural grow-bulbs above the plants to boost their growth.

The term conservatory was first used by John Evelyn at the beginning of the eighteenth century. In Victorian England, Sir Joseph Paxton revolutionized the design of glass buildings. A magnificent example is still to be seen at Chatsworth House, Derbyshire, the home of the Duke of Devonshire. Unlike the more strictly functional glasshouse, a conservatory is intended as an extension of the house, with doors and even windows opening into it. In Victorian conservatories, ferns, palms, aromatic plants and scented flowers were among the plants cultivated. If space permitted, some of these conservatories incorporated curved bays which housed additional seating. The ladies of the house traditionally took tea, read or embroidered in this light, airy space which must have been a welcome haven after the over-furnished drawing rooms of the time. It is hardly surprising that during the last decade, with the introduction of double glazing and more maintenance-free methods of construction, the conservatory has made a widespread reappearance in Britain as well as remaining popular in the United States.

Herbs and aromatic plants are a natural choice for a conservatory. Although it is perfectly easy to simply line up containers of your favourite plants, I think it is worth taking a little trouble to create a proper indoor herb garden. If there is enough space you could construct permanent raised beds of stone, brick or wood. An excellent idea for the back wall of a conservatory comes from my friend, the food writer Sri Owen. In order to grow many different herbs in a small space she has constructed a stepped raised bed by fixing one long plank of wood on its edge at ground level. The space behind is filled with growing compost and then a second plank is placed, edge-down, halfway across to make a narrower, deeper border against the wall.

Traditionally, the back wall of a conservatory has been used for growing highly-scented roses, climbing plants like plumbago with its panicles of heavenly blue flowers or the deservedly popular and intensely-fragrant summer jasmine.

The scented-leaf geranium was an immensely popular Victorian plant, large pots of rose-scented geraniums were used as room fresheners in drawing rooms and halls. I find that the best place to group these lovely plants – and other aromatic herbs – is at an entrance to the conservatory or in a porch.

Unless your conservatory is in continuous shade, it is wise to have blinds or shades fitted. Most conservatories produce a range of temperatures in different parts. Obviously, it is important to grow your plants in the most advantageous positions with, for example, pots of lavender and rosemary in the hotter, sunnier positions and parsley and chervil in the cooler, shadier areas. Many fragrant flowers such as lilies, jasmine and roses prefer to have their roots in shade while their blooms thrive best in the sun.

OPPOSITE AND ABOVE *Where space is at a premium, a single south-facing windowsill can contain enough herbs to satisfy most cooks. All the Mediterranean herbs will enjoy basking in direct sunlight, but those which are shy of direct sunlight, such as mint and chervil, will thrive in a shadier position. A strawberry planter packed with a variety of different herbs is a compact way of making the most of a windowsill, while an ingenious arrangement of pot-holders makes use of vertical as well as horizontal space. Arrangements like this are practical as well as economical, as plants enjoy being grouped together and thrive in each other's company.*

HERBS FOR DECORATION

Using herbs for decoration is one of life's great pleasures. These versatile plants are eminently suited to decorative purposes, imparting their delicious aromas, whether used fresh or dried, in wreaths and garlands, fresh herb flower arrangements and tussie mussies. When making a fresh herb arrangement, be aware of the language of flowers. If you are creating a bouquet for a special occasion, it can be a most delightful and personal way of conveying an important message. In the following pages you will find ideas for creating your own herbal wreaths, seasonal and culinary, decorative posies and table arrangements, as well as information on using herbs for fabric dyes.

HERB WREATHS

Wreaths made of herbs, flowers and aromatic leaves belong to an age-old tradition. In ancient Egypt the Pharaohs wove richly elaborate collars of herbs for placing around the necks of mummified bodies just prior to entombment. Later, in the classical cultures of Greece and Rome, circular wreaths of fresh bay leaves were presented as a mark of honour to writers, statesmen and athletes. The title of Laureate derives from the herb's Latin name *Laurus nobilis* and survives even today in the royal appointment of Britain's Poet Laureate.

The circle is, of course, an early and powerful symbol. Depending upon circumstance it represents not only the sun, the moon and the earth but also the passage of time – a day, a year or a life. Its strong, simple form implies flowing movement and natural

Wreaths and garlands have a long and complex history stretching back to the ancient civilizations of the Persians, the Egyptians, the Chinese and beyond. The potent symbolism of the circle combined with the powers attributed to herbs and flowers have meant that floral and herbal wreaths have remained part of popular western tradition up to the present day. Now we value them as much for their aesthetic qualities: nothing could be prettier than a garland of lavender and delicate pink rosebuds, a chaplet of chive flowers, or an aromatic herbal wreath in muted shades of pewter, silver and grey.

renewal and makes it an appropriate shape for a garland or wreath of living plants such as herbs.

For, on the whole, it is more satisfactory – and certainly more pleasurable – to make a herb wreath with fresh leaves and flowers and then watch it gradually dry, keeping it until its beautiful colour and fragrance fades away completely.

The most suitable frame for a wreath depends upon its intended use. It can be made from a wide range of materials. I find that wire, florist's foam, moss, straw or woven stems of other plants – from grapevines and winter jasmine to basket willow – are all useful when constructing the frame.

Wire-framed wreaths can be made in a variety of sizes. A huge generous circle – up to 60cm (24in) wide – of aromatic bay leaves makes a wonderful present for a cook, or a delightful Christmas wreath. While small, 10–12.5cm (4–5in) wire-frame wreaths look charming slipped over a candlestick on a dining table. Since wire-framed wreaths are generally lightweight, several can be strung together with ribbon to make a spectacular decoration for stretching across a mantlepiece or over a doorway. I have also used wire-framed herb wreaths to decorate the sides of a long buffet supper table by pinning them onto the tablecloth. There are clearly countless ways of displaying herb wreaths.

A WREATH OF BAY LEAVES
Loop 3 to 4 strands of heavy-grade florist's wire into a circle measuring 30–35cm (12–14in) across. Secure the ends of the wire by twisting them around the frame. Then use a short length of thin florist's wire to

secure a 10–15cm (4–6in) sprig of bay leaves to the frame. Place the leaves of the next sprig over the stem of the first and secure in the same way. Continue until the whole frame is covered. Now add shorter sprigs either side of the longer sprigs to widen the wreath, again making sure that the leaves all flow in the same direction. The bay wreath should now be quite dense and form an attractive circle of lustrous leaves. Either leave in this form or fill in the centre of the circle to produce a wide disc-shaped wreath. To do this, thread more wire across the underside of the circular frame to make a network of wire. Next, attach more bay leaves with florist's wire until the centre of the circle is filled. This version of the wreath looks magnificent but it obviously requires an ample supply of fresh bay leaves. Finally add a wire loop to the circular frame for hanging the wreath.

A TABLE WREATH OF FRESH HERBS

I recommend a frame of wet florist's foam for this wreath which, with care, will keep the herbs in a perfect and usable condition for 2–4 weeks. If the wreath is intended to be kept and dried, simply cease to water the foam and place the wreath in a cool, airy and preferably sunless place until the leaves and flowers are paper-dry. I like to make this style of wreath with a 20–22.5cm (8–9in) ring-shaped frame of florist's foam, ideally fitted with a black or green plastic holder so that the wreath can be placed directly on a table. Soak the foam frame in cold water for 1–2 hours until completely wet, then drain off any surplus water and place on a layer of double-thickness newspaper or cloth to absorb any extra water that may drip from it.

Start by placing the background greenery of the wreath around both the outside and inside of the ring, pushing each stem into the foam base. This can be composed of just one kind of foliage or a combination of different types. Grey-green juniper, bright green box or myrtle or even a fine-textured species of *Thuja* work well. The time of year usually dictates the colour theme of each wreath. In early spring or late autumn I like to make a silver, purple and pink wreath; for this I make the background with grey-leaved lavender and curry plant – the dwarf varieties of both herbs create an attractive, dense background and foundation to the wreath.

Then I add several sprigs of the principal herbs, such as red sage, rosemary, hyssop or thyme, and place them evenly. I repeat this process with each extra herb until the frame is completely covered and none of the florist's foam is visible. Finally, I add 3 or 5 specially selected flowers, sprigs of berries or coloured leaves that add a highlight to the whole effect. It is important to vary the shape, texture and colour of the foliage to give the wreath richness. And keep the overall depth of flora as even as possible, to give the wreath a strong shape and to contribute plenty of interest for onlookers and users alike.

I sometimes make such a wreath as a present to my hostess at a dinner party. I find the best way to keep it in good condition during the journey is to place it flat on several layers of wet newspaper, in a large, insulated cool box, resting on its side if necessary. Fresh herb wreaths will keep in immaculate condition this way for up to 48 hours.

A FRAGRANT POT-POURRI WREATH
Naturally, all fresh herb wreaths have fragrance. A scented pot-pourri wreath, though, is made with highly-scented dried flowers and aromatic leaves.

Of course, it is nicer if you are able to pick and dry all the flowers and leaves for the wreath at home (see pages 176–177). But no matter if you have to purchase some or all of the material needed.

The type of base you choose will determine the style of the wreath. A ring of dry florist's foam is lightweight and easy to cover with dried material. A frame of woven branches has an informal, natural appeal. I favour the long whippy growths from winter jasmine, though wisteria and vine prunings are equally attractive. (Note though that the two latter plants should be gathered during the dormant season only, before the sap rises in early spring.) Thick bundles of broom make a dense sage-green base over which the dried flowers and leaves can be scattered rather than massed.

Construct the frame for your wreath by looping or twisting the long growths into a circle or, if you prefer, make a heart shape or a diamond – for a birthday gift I have even made a frame in the shape of someone's initial. Then, if necessary, use wire to keep the base in shape.

Attach your selection of dried flowers and leaves. A background of lavender leaves and flower spikes is always pretty, or try a layer of a silver-leaved variety of artemisia, to which dried pink rosebuds, blue and pink cornflowers and lemon verbena flowers are added. If appropriate, add a ribbon with long streamers to the wreath and, if you feel that the

fragrance needs boosting, sprinkle some drops of rose or lavender oil or other essential oil on the respective flowers.

A CHRISTMAS HERB AND SPICE WREATH
A Christmas wreath is always a joy to make either for your own home or as a gift. The most attractive festive wreath has a colour theme which might be bronze, dark green, burnt umber or orange. Sometimes I make a wreath with a green and gold theme by wrapping the spices in gold foil before adding them to the wreath.

Since a Christmas wreath looks at its best hanging flat against a wall or wooden door, choose a frame which is lightweight and attach the foliage and other material securely. I find that a moss-filled wire frame from a florist makes a first-rate base but, if unavailable, then woven basketwork or a foam base can work quite well.

Fill in the background of the wreath with box, ivy or even holly. Dried bracken gives a pretty, lacy look. Add the culinary herbs which are especially appropriate to Christmas cooking – bay leaves, thyme, rosemary, marjoram, sage, a sprig of fresh green peppercorns, even some small green, red or yellow chilli peppers. Now add Christmas spices – sticks of cinnamon, whole nutmegs, star anise, blades of mace and some tiny kumquats or limes studded with cloves. The spices will need to be wired in order to fix them to the frame.

Wreaths and garlands of fresh or dried plants have always played a part in rites or celebrations to mark the passing of the seasons or momentous stages in individual lives.

BOUQUETS, POSIES AND NOSEGAYS

'Nose-gaies and posies, which are delightful to looke on and pleasant to smell to, speaking nothing of their appropriate vertues.'

GERARD'S HERBALL, 1597

The early herbals gave almost as much prominence to the uplifting effects of herbs as to their medical or culinary virtues. Dioscorides, for example, recommends borage for its mood-altering effects, describing it as a herb that warms the heart and the spirit. The symbolism of plants was an important aspect of their use and by the time of the Elizabethans the association of certain plants with particular qualities or emotions was well established and widely known. Shakespeare makes frequent reference to the connotation of plants, 'I'll set a bank of rue, sour herb of grace'. (Richard II).

The language of flowers came to be used as a kind of code between people – even as today any self-respecting lover gives red roses as a token of his feelings. Up until Victorian times a posy, nosegay or tussie-mussie was often intended as a message, conveying a sentiment not otherwise easily expressed. The language of flowers has now largely fallen into disuse. To revive it is, however, a charming way of giving a traditional and pretty bouquet a hidden meaning (see right).

Herb posies and tussie-mussies can be made in all sizes, though most people find that a small posy that can be held easily in the hand and that measures no more than 10–15cm (4–6in) across is the most charming and simple to create.

Choose and pick the herbs, flowers and leaves that you want to use early in the morning well before the midday heat has destroyed their freshness. Cut each stalk about 12.5–15cm (5–6in) long and detach the lower leaves. If a flower has a weak stem then it is best to strengthen it using florist's wire and a length of flower tape to make it secure.

Now start to assemble the posy by selecting the flower that you wish to place in the centre of the posy – a cottage pink or a rose bud makes a pretty centrepiece – but check that the flower means what you want to say. Now surround the central flower with other flowers or sprigs of leaves, making sure that the combination of colours and textures is harmonious. Then it is usually a good idea to surround the posy with sprigs of feathery soft foliage like rue, salad burnet, or baby's breath to form a pretty frame. If you wish, you can cut a hole in the centre of a small paper doily and then slip it over the stems to give a paper-lace edge to the posy. Finally, starting at the top of the stems, wind flower tape around them, gathering them tightly to give the posy an attractively bunched look, and secure the tape at the bottom of the stems. If the posy is a present, tie a ribbon at the top of the flower stems. To keep the flowers fresh, place the posy in a cold room.

Fresh summer herbs make splendid cut flowers and it always surprises me that more people do not use them as a charming and unpretentious floral decoration. A pitcher of sweet cicely, sprays of elderflower, tansy and angelica is an immediately appealing sight. Or a china teapot of nodding mauve-blue comfrey flowers, bronze fennel and honeysuckle blooms makes a fresh, informal flower arrangement that looks wonderful on a table laid for lunch outside.

Bouquets of dried flowers and herbs have become very popular during the last few years. When in July I am able to be in my house in the Ardèche, I make sure that I join my friends, the Marquet family, for the lavender harvest. Armfuls of the purple, heavily-scented flowers are gathered by cutting the spikes from the plants and tossing them into huge baskets for transporting down the hill to a neighbouring farmer. Here the blooms are added to a metal still that douses the lavender with steam and, after distillation, produces the essential oil of lavender. In rural France lavender oil is still used as an antiseptic for small cuts and grazes, it is often dabbed on the skin as an insect repellent, and is added to a bath as a reviving oil for dispelling tiredness.

Few dried flowers are as appealing as a huge bouquet of dried lavender spikes, neatly cut across the base and tied with a wide mauve ribbon. When large enough, such a bouquet is free-standing and a subtly-hued adornment to a simple wooden table or windowsill. Gradually the flowers fade, the scent disperses and the seed falls. The scent of lavender holds a strong personal charm for me. When a lavender arrangement has come to an end, I add the remaining spikes, a few at a time, to the flames of a wood-fire during the winter and their smoky fragrance evokes the memory of that distant lavender field shimmering in the July heat.

THE LANGUAGE OF FLOWERS

Angelica Inspiration
Basil Love
Bluebell Constancy
Borage Courage
Burnet Gaiety
Chamomile Patience
Chervil Sincerity
Columbine Fickleness
Daisy Innocence
Fennel Flattery
Forget-me-not Loyalty
Heartsease Remembrance
Hollyhock Ambition
Honeysuckle Devotion
Hyssop Sacrifice
Larkspur Infidelity
Lavender Silence
Lily Purity
Marjoram Happiness
Mimosa Sensitivity
Mint Wisdom
Nasturtium Patriotism
Pansy Courtship
Parsley Rejoicing
Pimpernel A meeting
Pink Resignation
Red rose Love
White rose Silence
Yellow rose Infidelity
Rosemary Remembrance
Rue Grace
Sage Esteem
Sweet bay Glory
Violet Faithfulness

ABOVE AND OPPOSITE *With their customary versatility, herbs can be used to make attractive and unusual table and room decorations throughout the year. Homely jugs and pots of feathery dill, white allium flowers, tiny marjoram blooms, bouquets of sulphur-yellow tansy or daisy-like feverfew flowers, or tiny bouquets of hot nasturtiums or cool blue borage flowers all add a welcome note of freshness to the summer table. Later in the year some of the same flowers dried, against a tapestry of green and silver foliage, including santolina, artemisia, sage and box, can be used to make a charming variation on the traditional Christmas tree.*

SEASONAL HERB DECORATIONS

To celebrate Christmas last year my husband, our children and I gathered together in our house in France. We each arrived from a different part of Europe, everyone laden with food, wine and presents. Late on Christmas Eve I realized that in the excitement of reunion I had forgotten to organize a traditional Christmas tree. So on a bright, cold night, I stepped out into the garden and by the light of a torch cut down several large branches from our huge bay tree. Tied together and wedged into a pail of sand, the instant 'tree' looked beautiful – dark green, lustrous and festive. We decorated the herb tree with small wooden toys and golden apples and, according to custom in our family, piled everybody's presents beneath it, ready for Christmas Day. Other shrubby herbs also make fine decorations at Christmas. A rosemary bush, a myrtle or a box are all suitable evergreens for indoor decoration.

A charming alternative to a free-standing herb tree is to use sprigs of herbs pressed into a cone of chicken wire or florist's foam to make a stylized triangular 'tree' for decorating in the usual fashion.

Herb garlands are also simple to make and are most attractive. A length of strong string or garden twine is covered with sprays of greenery and herbs. Depending on the season, it could be decorated with small bunches of herbs such as dried lavender and fresh *bouquets garni*. At Christmas, cut-out shapes of herb shortbread can be tied to the garland with ribbon and given to guests at the end of a party.

Herbs and eggs have always been natural partners. To transport them to market the ancient Egyptians used to pack their eggs among layers of fresh herbs which may well have contributed a subtle and delicious flavour in the same way that a fresh truffle perfumes a bowl of eggs. As the symbol of rebirth, the egg has long been associated with the Christian festival of Easter. So what could be more appropriate for an Easter table decoration than a pretty nest of fresh herbs enclosing a clutch of dyed and decorated hard-boiled eggs.

Long before the arrival of Christianity in Europe, the return of the spring, with its period of regrowth, was celebrated with major rejoicing each year. In rural areas of Britain the ceremony of the Maypole still persists. The pole is garlanded with greenery and ribbons, and danced around by schoolchildren.

May Day celebrations have always been marked by a great display of flowers and greenery: bunches are hung on the doors and gateposts as a good-luck talisman, plaits of herbs and flowers are worn as garlands in the hair and around the waist, and as a decoration for hats. In fact, a herb-decorated hat is a delightful idea for wearing at any time during the summer. One of the oldest remedies for a headache is to bind lavender to the forehead, or more simply, fill a hat with the herb and wear it until the pain abates. I find that a wide-brimmed hat trimmed with sprigs of wormwood, feverfew or tansy acts as a pleasantly scented yet effective insect repellent for wearing outside or when gardening.

The traditional harvest festival at the end of summer offers a wonderful opportunity for a celebration of herbs. Magnificent harvest loaves, shining with a golden crust, plaits of papery garlic and mountains of fruit and vegetables look fabulous in herb-decorated baskets. Thread fresh herb flowers such as purple chive blooms, bright yellow fennel flowers and pink marjoram blossoms, nasturtiums and marigolds around the frame and handle of trugs and flat baskets. Add sprigs of thyme, rosemary and hyssop to the basketwork and line each container with bay leaves. Now arrange the harvest produce in this herbal bower and transport it to the celebration.

HERB DYES

Fabric dyes made from the leaves, flowers and roots of herbs are the oldest form of colouring known to man. The Persians and Pharaonic Egyptians, for instance, used herbal dyes produced from saffron and weld to colour cloth for their dazzling ceremonial robes. By the time of Pliny certain plants were given names that referred to their colouring properties. *Genista tinctoria*, dyer's greenweed and *Isatis tinctoria*, woad, for example employ the Latin *tingere*, meaning to colour.

Dyes made from herbs work best with natural fibres such as wool and silk, unbleached cotton and linen. Dyeing with vegetable colourants is a lengthy but fascinating process which is still used in many parts of the world. The subtle shades and natural variations obtained with herb dyes have always been popular with craftsmen who spin and weave their own unique fabrics.

In the garden of the American Museum at Bath a border of dyer's herbs typical of those grown by the first settlers to North America demonstrates that the plants are attractive and useful, and are sufficiently numerous to comprise an interesting type of herb garden in its own right.

To obtain the dye from a herb the leaves are gathered just before the plant comes into flower; they are then roughly chopped and placed in a muslin bag. The herbs are steeped in warm water overnight and then boiled until the dye reaches the desired strength of colour.

Before placing the fabric in the dye, it is washed and soaked in a bath of mordant which acts as a fixative for the colour. The principal mordants used for dyeing fabrics with herbs are alum, chrome, copper, iron and tin. For some dyes a small quantity of acetic acid, ammonia, salt and cream of tartar are added to the mordant. Each mordant produces a different colour or shade of colour from the dye. Iron for example dulls colour whereas tin brightens it.

The following garden herbs in conjunction with the specified mordant produce the colours listed below and right:

Agrimony, *Agrimonia eupatoria*: the flowering tops used with alum mordant produce creamy yellow.

Alkanet, *Anchusa officinalis*: the root used with acetic acid mordant produce pinky-brown.

Blackberry, *Rubus* species: the young shoots used with alum mordant produce creamy beige.

Bracken, *Pteridium aquilinum*: the young shoots with alum mordant produce yellowy-green.

Comfrey, *Symphytum officinale*: the leaves, with alum mordant, produce yellow.

Dyer's chamomile, *Anthemis tinctoria*: the flowers with alum and cream of tartar mordant produce bright yellow; the flowers with copper and acetic acid mordant produce olive green.

Dyer's greenweed, *Genista tinctoria*: the flowering tops with alum mordant produce yellow.

Elder, *Sambucus nigra*: the leaves with alum and cream of tartar mordant produce greenish yellow; the leaves with copper and acetic acid mordant produce olive green; the berries with alum and salt mordant produce purple.

Heather, *Calluna vulgaris*: the young tips with alum mordant produce yellow; whole branches with alum and iron mordant produce green.

Juniper, *Juniperus communis*: fresh berries with alum mordant produce deep yellow; dried berries with alum, copper and cream of tartar mordant produce olive-brown.

Lady's bedstraw, *Galium verum*: the root with alum mordant produce pinkish-red; the leaves with alum mordant produce yellow.

Madder, *Rubia tinctorum*: the roots with alum and cream of tartar mordant produce bright red.

Marigold, *Calendula officinalis*: the petals with alum and cream of tartar mordant produce pale yellow.

Nettle, *Urtica dioica*: the flowers and leaves with alum mordant produce grey-green.

Onion, *Allium cepa*: the skins with alum mordant produce orange; the skins with copper mordant produce buttercup yellow.

Parsley, *Petroselinum crispum*: the fresh leaves and stems with alum mordant produce cream.

Sorrel, *Rumex acetosa*: the leaves with alum mordant produce buff; the roots with alum mordant produce rose pink.

Tansy, *Tanacetum vulgare*: flowering tops with alum produce mustard yellow.

Weld, *Reseda luteola*: the leaves with alum mordant produce lemon yellow; the leaves with copper mordant produce lime-green.

Woad, *Isatis tinctoria*: the leaves with ammonia and sodium dithionite produce blue.

Yew, *Taxus baccata*: the wood chips with alum mordant produce orange-brown.

AROMATIC HERBS

'I have perfumed my bed with myrrh, aloes and cinnamon. Come, let us take our fill of love until the morning,' wrote the author of Proverbs in the Bible, bearing witness to the potent symbolism and profound significance – mystical, erotic and practical – accorded to aromatic herbs down the ages.

Fragrance is of central importance in the history of herbs and their uses. To the medieval world in which western herb gardens developed it embodied an ideal form of beauty, to be revered and celebrated. A garden hedged round by high walls or hedges and filled with flowery meads, crystal streams and fragrant flowers represented the medieval vision of the earthly paradise. Among the many virtues ascribed to herbs – whether mystical or symbolic, aesthetic or practical, medicinal or culinary – their scent was viewed as paramount, to be treasured above all: in the thirteenth century Peter Crescentius suggested that a herb garden should contain 'a great diversity of medicinal and aromatic herbs which not only please by the odour of their scent, but by the variety of their flowers refresh the sight.'

Every lady of the manor would cultivate perfumed flowers and herbs for a thousand uses. Fresh and dried herbs, and oils, waters and lotions derived from them would be used to sweeten breath and perfume skin and hair, to freshen clothes and to scent the air. Strewing herbs such as lavender and santolina would be tossed over stone flags and placed under rugs where passing feet would crush their leaves and release their fragrance; cushions, pillows and mattresses would be filled with aromatic mixtures of herbs such as lady's bedstraw.

Lavender is the queen of the aromatic herbs. Traditionally it has always been used to scent linen and laundry (its name derives from the Latin for 'to wash'), and it is also greatly prized for its soothing and refreshing qualities. All parts of the plant are intensely aromatic, and it can be used to make oils and lotions, soaps and candles, pot-pourris and pillows. Lavender also has useful insect-repellent qualities.

Bowls of pot-pourri and scented water would be dotted around for idle fingers to toy with, and pomanders of musk or ambergris might be carried from room to room or hung from a convenient piece of furniture. Little bottles containing rosemary, lavender or rosewater were sometimes worn pinned to the clothes and suspended by fine chains or ribbons, and dried herbs would be burned over hot embers to fumigate rooms and permeate the furnishings with their scent. A favourite recipe of Queen Anne involved heating dried rosemary and sugar: perhaps she held to the traditional belief that those who slept between sheets scented with rosemary would not be visited by bad dreams.

Aromatic herbs were also used to treat woodwork, penetrating furniture and floorboards with a long-lasting fragrance. The juice of lemon balm and sweet cicely rubbed into oak panelling or boards imparted not only a delicious scent but also a deep gloss. Sachets and sprigs of sweet-smelling herbs were slipped into linen cupboards and blanket chests, and delicately stitched lavender bags were a popular gift for young brides. And if there was a garden containing bushes or hedges of aromatic herbs, sheets would be spread over them to dry.

The heady fragrances of aromatic herbs have lost none of their power or seductiveness over the centuries: still we love to fill our houses and scent our clothes with lavender and lemon balm, southernwood and roses, and the dozens of other herbs and flowers whose evocative perfume combines present pleasure with gentle nostalgia, setting us dreaming and transporting us back through time.

Fragrant dried petals, leaves, seeds, whole blooms, citrus peel, scented wood shavings and more can be combined to taste to make a surprising variety of different pot-pourris. Flowers that are not in themselves strongly perfumed may be added to give colour and bulk, while spices and essential oils give the mixture a more pungent fragrance. A fixative such as powdered orris root, gum benzoin or common or sea salt needs to be added to stop the pot-pourri losing its perfume when exposed to the air. Recipes are a useful guide, but it is also fun to experiment with different combinations of colour, texture and fragrance.

POT-POURRIS AND POMANDERS

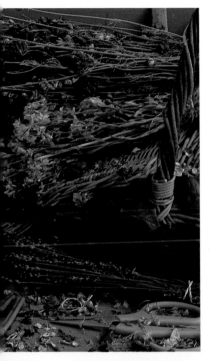

In the highly developed civilizations of ancient Persia and Egypt, the perfume and beauty of flowers and plants was regarded as being of great importance. And in classical Greece fragrance was considered a sign of divinity. Indeed, the word perfume is derived from the Latin *per fumum* meaning through smoke; a reference to the practice of burning aromatics, such as the Egyptian paste *kyphi* made with juniper berries, to perfume the air in temples. The burning of incense in churches is still practised.

When you consider the fleeting nature of scented flowers and leaves, it is comforting to discover that some of a plant's perfumed charm can be preserved in the mixture known as pot-pourri. This blend of dried flowers, petals and leaves is mixed with a fixative such as musk, ambergris or orris root, which helps to retain the natural perfume of a pot-pourri. The perfume can be further enhanced by adding a few drops of an appropriate essential oil.

Attar of roses is the most costly essential oil. It was first distilled from the petals of damask roses by the Persians during the seventeenth century. These days rose geranium oil often replaces attar of roses. Fortunately, though, the essential oils of other scented flowers such as lavender, hyacinth and violet are more affordable, making them useful in home-made pot-pourri.

When preparing your own ingredients for pot-pourri, the flowers and leaves are dried in the usual way (see pages 176–177). Since it may take some weeks to prepare sufficient dried material for your mixture, store completely dried flowers and leaves in a sealed plastic bag or a glass jar, out of direct light, until ready to prepare the recipe.

The following flowers, herbs and aromatic leaves are specially recommended for making pot-pourri: anemone, angelica, bay, borage, box, carnation, catmint, chamomile, cornflower, daisy, eucalyptus, fennel, feverfew, freesia, geranium, hibiscus, holly-hock, honeysuckle, hydrangea, hyssop, iris, jasmine, jonquil, larkspur, lavender, lemon balm, lemon verbena, marjoram, mint, lilac, lily, lunaria, lily of the valley, marigold, nigella, orange blossom, pansy, peony, poppy, rose, rosemary, rue, sage, scented leaved geranium, southernwood, sweet cicely, sweet woodruff, stock, tansy, thyme, wormwood, violet.

These pot-pourri recipes come from my mother who has been preparing scented mixtures for fifty years. Pot-pourri can be made by the moist or dry method. She recommends the dry method since the mixture looks more attractive and it is easier to obtain a greater variety of fragrances. She uses orris root powder as the fixative since it is widely available and is less expensive than its alternatives. However, since scent and fragrance are matters of personal taste, you may wish to adapt a mixture slightly, though try to keep to the same proportions. If you cover your pot-pourri from time to time with a well-fitting lid its scent will last longer and remember to stir the pot-pourri, crushing some of the leaves now and again to release their fragrance. The recipes use a standard cup measuring 300ml, ½ pint or 10fl oz.

COTTAGE HERB GARDEN POT-POURRI

Like a traditional cottage garden, this is a glorious and colourful mixture of flowers and aromatic leaves spiked with powdered spices. Use the recipe simply as a guide and blend the ingredients to your own taste – just as no two cottage gardens are alike, each version of this delightful pot-pourri is subtly different.

3 cups mixed herb garden flowers, dried: cottage pinks, marigolds, pansies, violets, primroses, jasmine, clary sage, etc.
1 cup rose petals, dried
1 cup mixed sweet herb leaves, dried: rosemary, lavender, lemon verbena, hyssop, pineapple sage, sweet cicely, thyme, etc.
25g (1oz) dried lavender flower and seed
25g (1oz) orris root powder
1 teaspoon ground cinnamon
¼ teaspoon ground allspice
5 star anise
¼ vanilla pod, cut into small pieces
2 drops lavender oil
2 drops carnation oil
2 drops honeysuckle oil

Reserve a few of the whole dried flowers to decorate the pot-pourri later. Gently mix together all the remaining ingredients, taking care not to crush the petals and blooms. Cover the bowl with a plastic bag and leave in a warm dark place for 2 weeks. Spoon or tip the pot-pourri into one or several bowls and decorate with the reserved flowers.

LAVENDER AND SWEET HERB POT-POURRI

1 cup lavender flowers and seeds, dried
1 cup sweet herb leaves, dried: bay, lemon
verbena, hyssop, pineapple sage, lemon
balm, lemon thyme, etc.
½ cup chamomile or feverfew flowers,
dried
½ cup violet or heartsease pansy flowers,
dried
1 teaspoon fine shreds of orange peel,
dried
25g (1oz) orris root powder
½ teaspoon grated nutmeg
½ teaspoon cloves, finely crushed
3 drops lavender oil
1 drop rose-geranium oil

Gently mix together all the ingredients, taking care
not to crush the flower heads. Cover tightly and leave
in a warm place for 2–3 weeks until the scents have
blended together. Transfer the pot-pourri into a
shallow bowl, lined basket or pot.

ENGLISH ROSE POT-POURRI

Roses are the easiest of flowers to gather and dry. My
mother gathers rose petals all summer so that by the
autumn she has a good supply of ingredients for this
traditional pot-pourri.

4 cups dried rose petals
2 cups dried lavender flowers
1 cup dried rosemary flowers
1 cup dried rose-geranium leaves
1 cinnamon stick, broken into small pieces
1 tablespoon allspice berries, coarsely
crushed
1 tablespoon cloves, bruised
25g (1oz) orris root powder
3 drops of attar of roses or rose oil
1 drop rosemary oil
1 drop of geranium oil
½ cup dried rosebuds

Measure all the ingredients except the rosebuds into
a large bowl and gently mix together with a wooden
spoon. Cover with cling-film and leave in a warm
place for 1–2 weeks, stirring every day, until the
scents have combined.

Spoon into one large or several smaller pots or
bowls and sprinkle the rosebuds on top.

POMANDERS

Up until 200 years ago the floors of houses in Europe
and North America were strewn with sweet-smelling
herbs and leaves in order to purify the air. As a
protection against infection the wealthy carried
pomanders – balls of sweetly scented unguents –
that they sniffed in order to mask unpleasant odours.
In the time of the plague and other pestilence both
tussie-mussies (see page 187) and pomanders were
considered an essential bactericide to be carried in
public places at all times.

During the affluence of Tudor England many
beautiful silver filigree holders were fashioned for
holding such pomanders. The word itself comes
from *ponum ambre*, apple of amber, and probably
referred to a piece of ambergris or musk which in the
heat of the hand would give off its powerful and
bewitching scent. Some pomanders were made from
a blend of aromatic substances, and the household
books of Elizabethan England give many recipes.

One of the simplest forms was an apple or orange
stuck with cloves and dried. This type of citrus
pomander is easy to make and does indeed sweetly
perfume a room or closet for some months.

Select a sound, firm, preferably thin-skinned
orange, lemon or lime. Wash the outside of the fruit
and dry with a cloth. Secure two lengths of tape
around the fruit, crossing at the top and base – this is
where the ribbon will be tied on the finished
pomander. Now cover the remaining sections of skin
with cloves stuck into the peel, taking care to place
them evenly so as to give an attractive appearance.

Place a teaspoon of orris root powder and the
same amount of ground cinnamon in a paper bag
and add the clove-studded fruit. Seal the bag and
shake to coat evenly with the powder. Hang the bag
in a warm, dark place for 4–6 weeks or until the fruit
has dried. Carefully remove the strips of tape, gently
dust off any surplus powder and reserve it for making
the next pomander. Tie a pretty ribbon around the
pomander and remember to make a hanging loop.

Place the pomander wherever you wish to perfume the air. A wooden bowl of home-made
pomanders mixed with pine fir cones and some
cinnamon bark makes an attractive room freshener.
And even the simplest version of a pomander – strips
of orange and lemon peel studded with cloves and
tied into loops and kept in a warm place until bone
dry – give off a lovely spice and citrus scent.

While bowls of pot-pourri dotted
around the house will impart a
subtle but delicious scent to each
room, pomanders are the
traditional way of scenting
clothes, especially when stored
for the winter. In earlier
centuries they were also carried
or worn hung from neck chains
in order to ward off noxious
fumes and germs. Originally
they were small, apple-shaped
pieces of highly perfumed
ambergris; hence ponum ambre,
apple of amber, the French
name pomme d'ambre, *and*
eventually our word pomander.
The simplest pomanders are
now made of apples or oranges
stuck with cloves and dried, and
more sophisticated china or
porcelain versions can also be
found. A bowlful of papier
mâché pomanders in poster-
paint colours like those opposite
makes a colourful alternative to
a dish of pot-pourri.

Herbs such as lavender, rosemary and especially wild hops have always been valued for their relaxing, sleep-inducing qualities, and their ability to soothe frayed nerves and aching heads. The hectic pace of twentieth-century living makes these natural remedies for tension and sleeplessness doubly welcome. A pot of herbs, conveniently placed on a bedside table so that you can bruise a few leaves with your fingers, will release its calming aromas as you doze off. Sleep pillows, stuffed with dried herbs and slipped inside a soft cover of light material which will allow their fragrance to filter through, are a more traditional and long-lasting approach.

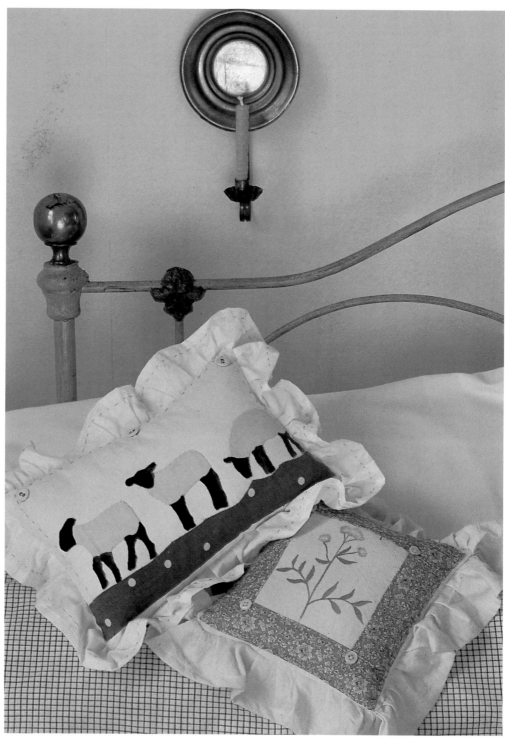

The previous recipes are for what are known as dry pot-pourris. Another, more old-fashioned method accounts for the origin of the name, which translates literally as 'rotten pot'. Originally, partly dried leaves and petals would be packed between layers of salt in a pot to make a *moist* pot-pourri. While dry pot-pourris are put in open bowls, moist ones should ideally be kept in china jars with perforated lids. Moistened with brandy, orange peel or orange or rosewater and topped up regularly, they will remain fragrant for many years. Unlike dry pot-pourris, it is essential to keep moist pot-pourris covered when they are not being used.

OLD-FASHIONED MOIST POT-POURRI
This is essentially a moist version of the English rose pot-pourri, as nothing suits this method so well as the scent of old roses. Remember always to choose the blooms of fragrant, old-fashioned roses, and do not be tempted to let them pass their best before picking them. Flowers and leaves for moist pot-pourris should be left whole and dried until they are leathery, not papery. You can make more or less of this pot-pourri simply by keeping the proportions of flowers, fixative and essential oils constant.

4 cups partly dried roses
2 cups partly dried lavender flowers
1 cup partly dried rosemary flowers
1 cup partly dried rose-geranium leaves
75g (3oz) powdered orris root
6 tablespoons salt
1 teaspoon attar of roses or rose oil
1 teaspoon rosemary oil
brandy, rosewater or orange water to moisten

Measure all the ingredients into a deep, wide-necked jar, preferably with a perforated lid, and mix together gently and thoroughly. Sprinkle with the brandy, rosewater or orange water to moisten, cover and leave for a month. Uncover only for use and top up regularly with brandy, rosewater or orange water.

Moist pot-pourris require whole flowers rather than individual petals. Many people like to add whole flowers to their dry pot-pourris too, as although individual petals keep their fragrance they tend to lose their colour. Pot-pourri mixtures therefore tend to be prettier for the inclusion of a few whole rosebuds, marigolds, borage flowers, violets or other colourful flowers.

Roses in particular need to be gathered with care if they are to be kept whole. Using sharp secateurs, cut only the freshest and prettiest flowers, and lay them gently in a shallow basket or box. It is important that you try to keep them in a single layer if possible, as they are easily bruised and damaged if they are piled on top of one another.

To dry them, cover the bottom of a box with a layer of fine sand or borax, place them carefully upside down on top of this, then gently cover them with more fine sand or borax. Keep the box in a warm, dry place for about a week if you are making a moist pot-pourri, and two weeks if you are making a dry one. Once they are completely dried they can be stored in an airtight container if necessary.

SLEEP PILLOWS AND SACHETS, ROOM FRESHENERS AND CANDLES

In some parts of the world the filling for a mattress or palliasse is still composed of dried grasses, hay or straw which, newly-made, have a sweet meadow scent of their own. It was a simple step, perhaps, to add to the filling the dried leaves of aromatic herbs. The wild herb, lady's bedstraw, *Galium verum*, takes its name from this custom, and sweet wood-ruff, *Galium odoratum*, was also valued due to its perfume of new-mown hay produced by the chemical, coumarin, in its dried leaves.

For centuries the papery blooms of wild hops have been used as a stuffing for pillows due to the relaxing and sleep-inducing effect of the herb. An old-fashioned mixture of dried herbs recommended for stuffing a herbal sleep pillow calls for 1 part hop flowers, 1 part skullcap leaves, 2 parts elderflower and 4 parts catmint leaves and flowers. Naturally, any of the specially fragrant herbs such as rosemary and lavender – the latter is recommended as a treatment for headaches – can also be added to the filling for a pillow or cushion.

Some of the dried pot-pourri mixtures in this chapter also make a wonderfully perfumed filling for a cushion. It is important to gently crush the pot-pourri so that no sharp or tough parts remain, then enclose it in a smaller cloth bag which can be slipped amongst the stuffing.

Small sachets of pot-pourri, made from scraps of pretty fabric, possibly trimmed with ribbons and lace, make delightful 'sweet-bags' for placing among clothes in drawers or in closets. When I was about

A few sprigs of herbs hung among your winter clothes when you put them away for the summer will ward off any hint of mustiness, and some will also act as moth-repellents. The pungent aroma of southernwood, known in France as garderobe, *is particularly effective. Rosemary, santolina, thyme, lavender, sage, woodruff and mint can also be used, either in sprigs or crumbled and put into little muslin moth bags.*

ABOVE *Little sachets of pot-pourri, made with any odds and ends of fabric you happen to have, can be as simple or sophisticated as you care to make them. Patchwork and embroidery give them an air of nostalgia, and extravagantly romantic confections can be put together with scraps of lace and ribbon. Perfect for slipping between sheets in the linen cupboard or among underwear or nightclothes.*

LEFT *Fresh herbs, pine cones or faded pot-pourri smell equally delicious if you cast them on an open fire, following a tradition that goes back many centuries. In the days when noxious odours were more common than sweet ones, rooms would be fumigated with herb mixtures heated over glowing embers, infusing hangings, upholstery and linen with a fragrant mixture of woodsmoke and aromatic perfumes.*

seven years old and keen on sewing, making lavender sachets as presents was a favourite activity.

Similarly in the Ardèche every summer, Brigitte, the young daughter of my friend Madame Marquet, makes charming lavender bottles. The flowering spikes of fresh lavender are bent over and enclosed in their stems which are in turn threaded with narrow satin ribbon to make a bottle shape. You need freshly picked lavender to make a lavender bottle because the stems must be flexible. Interestingly, Dorothy Hartley in her fine book *Food in England*, describes identical lavender bottles which were made in private homes around Mitcham in Surrey where lavender was grown commercially during the eighteenth century. She writes, 'A set of a dozen such lavender batons with loops to hang them together on a hook in the linen cupboard was a dainty small betrothal gift from girl friends.'

Recently, in a London linen shop, I noticed some flat oblong sachets of lavender and pot-pourri for placing between freshly laundered sheets and pillowcases. These would be simple enough to make using remnants of fabric and home-made pot-pourri, a couple of ribbons sewn on at each corner of the sachet to indicate its position in the linen pile.

A scented filling can be used for a wide range of other items such as upholstered chair seats, soft toys, rag dolls and cuddly animals, even the hems of long heavy curtains where the gentle fragrance of dried herbs would be welcome. A traditional plaything for cats is a felt mouse stuffed with dried catmint – the herb that cats are besotted by. I daresay a cat cushion filled with the same herb to fit in the bottom of their basket would also be appreciated.

For centuries housewives have aimed to give their rooms a pleasant scent with fresh and dried herbs spread over the floor to sweeten the air. The custom survives when sprigs of rosemary are placed under rugs and mats so that their perfume is released into the room as people walk over them.

During the summer months I like to fill rooms with vases of fresh herbs and highly scented flowers like lilac or lilies. In winter pots of hyacinths and jonquils, and the indoor climbing jasmine provide a gently pervasive sweet fragrance. Large china bowls of pot-pourri contribute a background scent that in time becomes part of the house, so that visitors invariably enquire about 'that lovely smell' as they enter. Even a small posy of fresh herbs tied to a hook or the back of a chair adds a delightful fragrance to a room. For

hanging amongst clothes and as a protection from moths, include some sprigs of southernwood which indeed in France is known as *garderobe*.

If you grow and dry herbs, bundles of these hanging in a room give off their own fragrance. As well as hanging herbs from hooks in the kitchen and other rooms, I sometimes tie the bunches along the top and sides of an antique mirror in a guest room, where they dry nicely and also perfume the air. Remember, though, that as with pot-pourri, it's necessary to crush some of the leaves in your hand now and again to release their scent.

Most days of the year, on the slightest pretext, I light candles – even in mid-morning on a dark, gloomy winter day. I find their soft light and flickering flames cheer the spirit no end. Quite the nicest kind of candles are scented and burn with a gentle lavender, rose-geranium or other herbal perfume. Subtly scented candles are not always easy to track down in shops so I usually make some of my own using the stubs of other candles.

In a saucepan or a double boiler, over low heat, melt 1–2 handfuls of candle stubs (or use new candles if you prefer). If you want to colour the candles add a child's wax crayon. When the wax has turned to liquid remove the pan from the heat, fish out and discard any used wicks and stir in 1–2 drops of essential oil of your favourite flower or herb. Or add a small bundle of stems of rosemary, mint or another herb and stir for 5–10 minutes until the herb has transferred its scent to the wax. Remove and discard the herb or save as an excellent herbal firelighter. Place a new wick in the centre of a candle mould or a clean plastic cream carton. Pour in the liquid wax and set aside in a cool place until set. Then gently warm the outside of the mould and carefully remove. If necessary trim the wick of the new candle and then light it.

One of the easiest ways of scenting a room is to warm a small amount of perfumed oil, such as lavender or rose, in a dish or metal container placed at the side of a fire or over a night light.

Similarly, I rarely discard old lacklustre pot-pourri. I simply add it to a basket of lavender spikes, small fir cones, dried bay leaves and sprigs of rosemary that is kept next to the log fire in the sitting room. Then when we are settled in front of the fire, reading or sipping tea, I toss on a handful of the faded flowers of summer and they surrender their last vestige of scent as the smoke drifts up the chimney.

Lavender-bag dolls with painted wooden arms, legs and faces and rag dolls stuffed with pot-pourri are a more sophisticated version of pot-pourri sachets. Candles scented with lavender, lemon balm, rose geranium or any other aromatic herb are another way of subtly perfuming the air. Easy to make from the melted-down stubs of old candles, they can be counted on to cheer the spirits on gloomy winter days.

HERBS FOR BEAUTY AND HEALTH

Herbal teas, tisanes and infusions can be made in tremendous variety and have an equally wide range of properties: stimulating or soothing, invigorating or relaxing, they have always been known for their therapeutic and medicinal qualities. They also make a delightful drink simply to enjoy in place of ordinary tea. Take time with these drinks to discover the flavours and strengths you prefer.

Strictly speaking, all teas are herb teas. For the China or India tea familiar to the English tea and breakfast table is simply an infusion of the leaves of the plant, *Camellia sinensis*. Like other members of the camellia family, the tea plant can be grown quite easily in mild regions of the British Isles – though its small white flower is no rival for the beautiful hybrid camellia. In the case of green teas the young leaves of tea plants are hand-picked and dried straight away, whereas black teas are produced by slightly fermenting the leaves before they are dried and graded.

All teas, tisanes and infusions made with edible herbs are green teas; the herb leaves can be used fresh or dried, though the amount used is halved when the herb is dried. I personally prefer the extra aroma produced by fresh leaves; the usual allowance is 2–3 teaspoons fresh herb leaves to 0.6 litre (1 pint) of boiling water. The herb is placed in a warmed teapot and boiling water is poured on top. If your water is highly chlorinated, use a mild-tasting, still mineral water to obtain the true taste of the herb. Leave the tea to brew for 3–5 minutes then pour the liquid through a strainer straight into the cup or glass – though first place a spoon in the glass to prevent it cracking. Add a slice of lemon if you wish and, if a

ABOVE Aficionados will probably have a favourite teapot as part of the ritual: mine is a glass one, which I find both pretty and practical for the purpose.

RIGHT Fresh or dried flowers, leaves, hips and seeds are all suitable for herbal teas, though fresh and dried herbs will give noticeably different nuances and intensities of flavour.

sweetener is needed, stir in clear honey rather than sugar. Milk is not added to herb teas. For the purest flavour it is essential that the teapot is scrupulously clean. I rather like to use a glass teapot for herb teas – it is attractive, easy to clean, and also enables you to look at the colour of the liquid and gauge the strength of the brew more easily.

Traditionally herb teas and tisanes have also been prescribed for the treatment of particular complaints or infections. Some had especially charming names, such as the French *Tisane de Sept Fleurs*, which is prescribed for sleeplessness, or Oswego Tea – the favoured beverage of the Oswego tribe of North American Indians – which became popular throughout the country during the eighteenth century, in the aftermath of the Boston Tea Party.

These days, herb teas are increasingly served as a pleasant-tasting and refreshing alternative to conventional tea or coffee. Herb teas with digestive properties like lime-flower or *tilleul*, and peppermint or *menthe*, have been highly popular in France for generations. They are served after dinner in the evening when the caffeine in black coffee can keep you awake. Though, as with all herbs, it is important to respect the individual properties of each plant. Some herbs produce a surprisingly powerful tisane – the tea *yerba mate*, for example, produces a tea which contains more caffeine than coffee.

When you start to drink herb teas it's a good idea to sample those made with a single herb to discover each individual flavour. Then gradually experiment with two or more herbs in the same pot until you discover a blend of herbs that pleases you.

HERBS FOR TEAS AND TISANES

ANGELICA, *Angelica archangelica*: use the leaves alone or with a strip of lemon zest.

BASIL, *Ocimum basilicum*: use the leaves alone or add 2 to a pot of Assam tea. Basil and sage tea is also very good.

BERGAMOT, *Monarda fistulosa*: the fresh or dried flower heads are used to make a tisane known as Oswego tea. For a milder flavour try adding a few flower heads to a pot of green China tea.

BETONY, *Stachys officinalis*: the leaves make a delicious tea that has a similar flavour to China tea. The addition of a short strip of orange or lemon zest, a piece of cinnamon bark or a few cloves are recommended. Betony tea was popular in the time of Caesar Augustus.

CHAMOMILE, *Chamaemelum nobile*: the flowers produce a pleasant herb tea specially recommended for drinking before retiring.

CARAWAY, *Carum carvi*: the fresh leaves produce a mild-tasting tea, the dried seeds give a stronger version.

CATNIP, *Nepeta cataria*: both the leaves and the flowers are used.

ELDERFLOWER, *Sambucus nigra*: the fresh or dried flowers make a fragrant, mild tea.

FENNEL, *Foeniculum vulgare*: the leaves, flowers and seeds can be used to produce teas of varying strength.

FENUGREEK, *Trigonella foenum-graecum*: use the dried seeds. For a stronger flavour bruise them in a mortar before adding to a pot.

HAWTHORN LEAF, *Crataegus monogyna*: both fresh and dried leaves are used.

HIBISCUS, *Hibiscus syriacus*: use the fresh or dried flowers and add a bruised cardamom pod.

HOLLYHOCK, *Althea rosea*: fresh or dried leaves produce a reddish liquid with a good flavour.

HYSSOP, *Hyssopus officinalis*: best made with fresh leaves and a strip of orange zest.

LAVENDER, *Lavandula* x *intermedia* 'Vera': use fresh or dried leaves or flowers, sweetened if desired.

LEMON BALM, *Melissa officinalis*: a classic herb tea. Use fresh leaves and sweeten with honey.

LEMON VERBENA, *Aloysia triphylla citriodora*: use fresh or dried leaves or flowers. Try adding a sprig of lemon balm to a pot of China tea.

LIMEFLOWER, *Tilia cordata*: one of the best herb teas; use fresh or dried flowers.

MINT, *Mentha* species: all varieties of mint make very fine teas – they are widely drunk in Mediterranean countries – use fresh or dried leaves and serve with thinly sliced lime or lemon.

RASPBERRY LEAF, *Rubus idaeus*: use fresh leaves for the best flavour and serve with a little zest of orange.

ROSE, *Rosa* species: both fresh and dried hips or petals make a classic herb tea which is often popular with young people.

ROSEMARY, *Rosmarinus officinalis*: use fresh or dried leaves; one of the best herb teas.

SAGE, *Salvia officinalis*: use fresh or dried leaves; a highly regarded herb tea – England used to export the dried leaves to China. Use with caution; not at all during pregnancy.

THYME, *Thymus vulgaris*: use fresh or dried leaves, an excellent digestive tea.

TEA RECIPES

ROSE-SCENTED GERANIUM TEA

SERVES 3

2 teaspoons gunpowder tea
3 leaves rose geranium
3 cloves

Place the tea, leaves and cloves in a warmed pot and pour on the boiling water. Stir, allow to infuse for 4–5 minutes, then pour.

DILL TEA

This tisane is a good digestive.

SERVES 3

2 teaspoons fresh or 1 teaspoon dried dill
5 cardamom pods, crushed to split their skins
¼ teaspoon dried mint or 1 teaspoon grated fresh ginger
0.6l (1 pint) boiling water
½ lemon cut in thin slices

Place the dill, cardamom pods and mint or ginger in a teapot and pour on the boiling water. Allow to infuse for 5 minutes, then serve with a slice of lemon for each person.

ICED EARL GREY AND LEMON VERBENA TEA

SERVES 4–6

3 teaspooons Earl Grey tea
3 sprigs lemon verbena
1.2l (2 pints) boiling water
honey to sweeten (optional)
ice cubes made with mineral water and leaves of lemon verbena

Measure the tea and lemon verbena into a heatproof jug and pour on the boiling water. Stir and leave to infuse for 5 minutes then strain into another vessel and allow to cool. Sweeten to taste with honey, if desired, then cover and chill. Serve in stemmed glasses with ice cubes.

Before the days of modern sanitation, sweet waters, oils, essences and creams played an important part in keeping both houses and their occupants fragrant. Scented baths have been the height of pampered luxury since the time of Cleopatra, who is said to have safeguarded her legendary beauty by bathing in asses' milk scented with rose petals. And in seventeenth-century France, the celebrated courtesan Ninon de Lenclos attributed her youthful beauty to steeping herself daily in baths perfumed with a blend of aromatic herbs.

SWEET WATERS AND BATH PREPARATIONS

The work of the still room was an important part of a moderately prosperous Elizabethan housewife's chores. In a large house the still room was usually located somewhere near the kitchen with easy access to the garden. A small fireplace provided a source of heat and a ready supply of spring water enabled the herbal potions and infusions that were almost the only medicines of the time, to be prepared. It was here too that the aromatic leaves and flowers from the garden were dried and preserved for decorating and perfuming the rooms in the house.

The simplest way to perfume a bowl of warm water or a freshly drawn bath is to add a sprig of an aromatic herb such as lavender or rosemary. In fact, a small bunch of fresh or dried herbs tossed into the bath water while the tap is running will give a most refreshing and invigorating effect. Try a posy of lemon thyme, marjoram and rosemary for the head-clearing properties of thymol.

The recipe for a sweet water that can be used all year round, for adding to washing water or a soothing footbath, requires fresh herbs picked just before flowering, when their quantities of essential oils are at a peak.

To make a decoction-based sweet water, cover 360g (12oz) of fresh mixed herbs in a pan with 0.6 litre (1 pint) of soft spring water or still mineral water and heat slowly, stirring now and again. Bring to the

boil, cover and simmer gently for 10 minutes. Remove the pan from the heat and leave until cold then strain the liquid into a bottle. Add 150ml ($\frac{1}{4}$ pint) of eau-de-vie, vodka or brandy and shake to mix well. Use 2–3 tablespoons of the sweet water in a bathful of warm water.

To make a vinegar-based sweet water, place 1–2 handfuls of your favourite herb such as rose geranium leaves, lemon verbena or lavender in a bottle and pour in cider vinegar up to the top. Seal the bottle and leave in a warm place for 1–2 weeks, shaking every day. Strain the vinegar and repeat once. Pour into a smaller bottle, seal and label.

Scented baths have been valued as a relaxing beauty treatment since the time of the ancient Egyptians. Mix together one handful each of dried lavender flowers, dried rosemary leaves, dried rose petals, dried mint leaves and crushed comfrey root and spoon into a muslin bag. Place the bag in a large bowl, pour on boiling water to cover and leave to infuse for 20 minutes. Pour the scented liquid into a bath of warm water just before use.

One of the most luxurious beauty products – especially in areas of hard water – is a naturally-scented bath oil which leaves the skin feeling smooth and silky. Choose a light vegetable oil such as apricot or peach kernel, almond or avocado, and pour some into a lidded glass jar. Add spikes of flowering lavender, rosemary in bloom or lemon verbena flowers and leaves, cramming in as many as possible. Place the jar in a warm place for 2 weeks, stirring the mixture every day. Then strain the scented oil into a smaller container, seal and label. Add 1–2 table-spoons to warm washing water.

An alternative method of making a scented bath oil that does not require fresh herbs is to add a blend of essential oils to a small bottle of your favourite skin oil. To make a spicy floral bath oil add 2–3 teaspoons lavender oil and $\frac{1}{4}$–$\frac{1}{2}$ teaspoon clove oil to 100ml (3fl oz) skin oil. Seal the bottle and shake before use.

Now that scent-free soap is widely available it is easy to make small rose-scented soap balls to place in a guest room. Grate or chop a bar of scent-free soap into a saucepan. Add rosewater to cover and heat gently, stirring now and again, until the soap has completely softened. Remove from the heat and set aside until the mixture begins to thicken. Take a spoonful of the mixture, moisten your hands with rosewater and shape the scented soap into a small ball. Set aside on kitchen paper to dry and harden.

MEDICINAL HERB DIRECTORY

USING HERBAL REMEDIES

How herbs are prepared is very important if they are to have a therapeutic effect. In the Directory you will come across various terms for the ways in which the herbs are to be prepared before using and below are the general instructions for these preparations. Instructions that relate specifically to the remedy are given with the herb referred to, such as the number of teaspoons of herb mixture to water and so on. You will find the uses for the herb listed first in the Directory followed by the uses of its essential oil.

AN INFUSION

The principles are the same as making 'real' tea and apply equally to fresh or dried herbs. Although the measures given are for dried herbs unless otherwise stated, fresh can be substituted – simply double the quantity, infusing two teaspoons of fresh for one of dried. How much of a herb you will need depends on the quality of herb you are using and on the strength of infusion you need. Generally, though, a tablespoon of dried herbs to 0.6 litre (1 pint) or a heaped teaspoon to a cupful of water gives the right dose.

Measure the herbs into a warmed, scrupulously clean teapot, pour on boiling water, cover and leave to infuse for ten minutes before straining. In cases of sweating, such as flu, administering the liquid will be beneficial. Drink the infusion cold when a more diuretic action is required. When in doubt, take the infusion hot. The infusion may be sweetened with honey or brown sugar. It is best to make a cupful at a time when needed.

This method works best for leaves, flowers and green stems. If you want to use bark, roots or seeds, either crush them a little or until they form a powder to enable their goodness to leach into the water. With aromatic herbs, ensure that the teapot lid is a good fit or all the beneficial volatile oils will escape in steam.

Cold infusions can be made when a herb is sensitive to heat or it contains highly volatile oils or its beneficial substances would break down at high temperature. Use the same proportions of herb to water as with the hot infusion, but leave it for six to twelve hours in a well-sealed earthenware teapot. After this time the liquid can be strained and used.

With cold infusions, milk can be used instead of water with the added advantage that its fats help to dissolve the oils of the herbs. A milk-based infusion has a soothing action of its own when used in compresses and poultices. Take care, however, not to use milk in this way if the person to be treated displays any sensitivity or allergy to milk or if a poultice or compress irritates the skin.

A DECOCTION

This method is effective for extracting the healing substances from hard or woody parts of herbs, such as roots, rhizomes or bark and nuts, berries and seeds.

Measure the herbs into a glass, earthenware, ceramic or unchipped enamelled (*never* use aluminium) pan, powdering or breaking up dried herbs into small pieces and cutting fresh herbs into small pieces, then pour the water over them. Bring to the boil and simmer for the time given in the Directory (usually 10–15 minutes). You might find you need more water anyway than for an infusion because of evaporation. If the herb(s) contain volatile oils, place a tight-fitting lid on the pan, and lower the heat. Strain the tea directly after simmering while it is still hot, and then use in the same ways you would an infusion.

If your herbal mixture contains woody *and* soft herbs, prepare an infusion *and* a decoction for each of them, using half the water in each, then combine them to obtain the maximum benefit from both types of herb.

BATHS

Because the body can absorb herbs' healing substances through the skin, this is an excellent way of using herbs as health aids.

Add 0.6 litre (1 pint) of infusion or decoction to a warm bath or this amount can be used to bathe a specific part of the body, such as the feet or the hands.

A COMPRESS

This method is a good way in which to apply a remedy externally to speed up healing.

To make a hot compress, take a clean linen or cotton cloth, piece of gauze or cotton wool and soak it in the hot infusion or decoction prescribed. Then put this on the affected area as hot as the person can bear without too much discomfort (as the heat enhances the healing action of herbs) and either replace it with another once it has cooled or cover the cloth with plastic or waxed paper and lay a hot water bottle over it, refilling the bottle with hot water when it cools.

A POULTICE

This method has the same effect as a compress, but instead of using the herbs in a liquid form, the plants themselves are held against the skin.

The herb used can be fresh or dried. If fresh, bruise the leaves or root and place them directly on to the skin or sandwich them between two layers of thin gauze. If dried, make them into a paste by adding either hot water or apple cider vinegar until it is of a spreadable consistency, but not too wet, and apply this to the skin.

To keep it warm, for the same reason as given for the compress, wrap it in the same way and hold a hot water bottle against jt. If your poultice is not being applied between layers of gauze, first rub a little oil over the area to be covered with the poultice as this protects the skin and makes the poultice easier to remove.

A poultice can either have a warming, stimulating effect or else a soothing, softening effect on the skin, promoting a sense of general well-being.

USING ESSENTIAL OILS
Only buy essential oils from a reputable supplier. The uses for each herb's essential oil follows the uses listed for the herb itself in the Directory. Essential oils should never be applied directly to the skin, but should be diluted in a carrier vegetable oil.

BATHS
Essential oils are more easily absorbed by the skin when added to warm bath water. The heat of the water opens the pores and so they are absorbed more by the skin. As a general rule, add five to ten drops to the bath once it has been run then stir the water vigorously. For foot or hand baths, use the same method but add five drops to the water. Never add neat to a baby's bath.

IN MASSAGE
This is one of the best ways of using the healing properties of the oils. Massaging regularly improves well-being and is either relaxing or stimulating depending on the oils used.

The oils are usually added to a 'base' oil before being massaged into the skin so that they are not too overpowering and go further. When 'vegetable oil' is mentioned in the Directory, choose from almond, apricot kernel, avocado, grapeseed, olive, soya and wheatgerm. You can use the light oils – almond, apricot kernel, grapeseed and soya – on their own or combined. The heavier oils – avocado, olive and wheatgerm – have a strong aroma and are sticky when used on their own, so work best if combined with one of the lighter ones, unless a very rich massage base is needed.

How much essential oil is added to the base oil depends on the strength of the essential oil and the amount needed to have the desired effect, but usually the essential oil(s) makes up about one to three per cent of the mixture. For one massage, a good guide is to pour a little of the chosen vegetable oil into a saucer or small shallow bowl and add just two to three drops of essential oil(s) to this.

TO INHALE
Essential oils can be inhaled to beneficial effect in several ways. Three or four drops on a handkerchief held near the nose every few moments and sniffed is very beneficial.

For congested conditions or skin conditions of the face, a steam inhalation is efficacious. Add five to ten drops to a bowl of very hot water, producing plenty of steam, lean over the bowl so the steam is flowing over your face, put a towel over your head so that it encloses your head and the bowl and inhale the vapours given off for a few minutes. Repeat this two or three times a day.

IN COMPRESSES
For small areas such as spots or insect bites, the essential oil can be applied diluted in a carrier oil, covering it with a piece of cotton wool or warm, damp gauze so that the oil is absorbed into the skin.

Where a larger area is being treated, add 10 drops to 100ml (generous 3fl oz) of hot water, soak a piece of cotton wool in the mixture and then put it (as hot as the person can bear without burning the skin) onto the area being treated. Wrap with plastic or cotton and hold a hot water bottle to it to keep the area warm.

TO FRESHEN A ROOM
Add 10 drops of an appropriate essential oil to a plant mister full of water and spray in the room of an ill person or to freshen a stuffy room any time.

Essential oil burners can be used for this purpose. They operate either by means of a nightlight candle or a tiny electric element that heats a plate onto which the essential oil has been dropped.

A CAUTIONARY NOTE
Herbal remedies have been used for centuries and the remedies given in the Directory have been included because they have been proven effective throughout this time. They must be used carefully. Where an illness is serious or recurs, consult your doctor or a medical herbalist, using the remedy in concert with his or her directions and letting him or her know what you are doing. Also, do not use these remedies over a prolonged time or exceed the doses given. If possible, discuss your particular symptoms with a qualified herbalist, as it is possible to misdiagnose your condition and

another remedy may well suit your particular circumstances better. The Directory is meant to be used as a general guide.

Regarding essential oils, do not take them internally unless you are specifically advised to do so after consultation with a fully qualified aromatherapist.

Bear in mind that they are potentially toxic if used in large doses or over a prolonged period of time. For example, it is wise not to use an oil daily for more than three weeks at a time. Also, some people have an adverse reaction to some oils and if you react in this way, do not use this oil again. As with all herbal remedies, the oils need to be used with caution.

Do *not* use the following oils during pregnancy:

basil	marjoram
camphor	myrrh
caraway	nutmeg
cedar	oreganum
chamomile	pennyroyal
cinnamon	peppermint
clary sage	rosemary
fennel	sage
hyssop	thyme
juniper	wintergreen

Also, never use essential oils on babies. Oils may be burned in children's rooms or used well diluted to not more than one per cent in a massaging oil.

The essential oils of spices – black pepper, cinnamon, clove and citrus fruits – can cause skin irritation so use them well diluted.

It is a good idea to read about any remedies suggested in the Directory in greater detail before using, to be sure it is right for you. A selection of titles is given in the Bibliography.

Allium sativum
Liliaceae
GARLIC

Cloves of garlic contain vitamins A, B and C and the volatile oil contains allium, which converts to allicin when the herb is crushed or sliced. On exposure to the air allicin converts to diallydisulphide, which is a powerful bactericide. Used daily, it contributes greatly to the functioning of the body as no other herb does. It is one of the most effective killers of bacteria and viruses, and so helps in the healing of a variety of ailments.

Garlic is an effective aid to healing when sliced and applied directly to the site of a bite or sting, relieving soreness and reducing the chances of it becoming infected. Raw garlic is prescribed by herbalists as a treatment for a wide range of bacterial and fungal infections, such as catarrh. It will also improve bad circulation – simply incorporate cloves of garlic regularly in your cooking. A few drops of garlic oil, warmed slightly, put onto a piece of cotton wool and placed just inside the opening to the ear will relieve earache. Garlic will also increase your overall resistance to colds and bronchial infections in general.

To reduce chronic hypertension or high blood cholesterol levels, first seek qualified help from a doctor or medical herbalist. One treatment is to eat raw garlic cloves six times a day, but results will not be instant: there may be a lowering of blood pressure and cholesterol levels after a month or so. It is inadvisable (and

possibly dangerous) to come off any drugs prescribed to control blood pressure without qualified supervision.

Take garlic as a general health-promoting exercise, taking more when an infection occurs as it has been found that garlic aids the development of the bacterial flora in the digestive tract while killing harmful bacteria and other micro-organisms. A clove of garlic eaten three times a day, every day, is beneficial; increase consumption when unwell. The effective part of garlic is the part that smells; the odourless capsules do not work.

Anethum graveolens
Umbelliferae
DILL

The active ingredients in dill are found in the leaves, flowers and seeds. The herb's principal medicinal uses are as a digestive and sedative. A decoction of dill seed is a valuable anti-flatulent and a useful gripe mixture can be made to relieve colic in babies.

Infuse one or two teaspoons of gently crushed dill seeds in a cup of boiling water for 10 to 15 minutes, then strain out the seeds and either give a teaspoon of the infusion to the baby in a bottle or from the spoon after a feed. The dill water can also be taken in a dose of one tablespoon to cure indigestion, hiccups, stomach cramps and insomnia. An infusion made from the flowers or seeds is recommended as a treatment for insomnia, headaches and earache. Dill seed tea is a good treatment for insomnia. To make it, infuse two teaspoons of dill seed in a cupful

Artemisia absinthium, **WORMWOOD**

of hot water for 10 minutes. Strain out the seeds, then drink the tea before going to bed to ensure a good night's sleep.

Artemisia absinthium
Compositae
WORMWOOD

Wormwood contains a volatile oil containing thujyl and

absinthol, carotene and vitamin C. The herb has been used as a bitter tonic and to expel worms since the time of Dioscorides.

To restore appetite at any time but especially after a bout of flu or other such debilitating illness, see under HOP for a useful mixture. Wormwood should not be used for self-medication, and should not be taken at all during pregnancy.

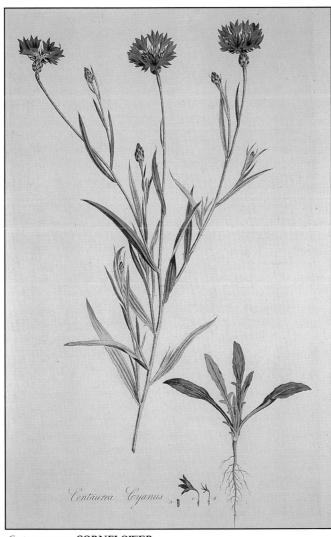

Centaurea cyanus, **CORNFLOWER**

Centaurea cyanus
Compositae
CORNFLOWER

Cornflowers have one of the longest pedigrees of all herbs, being among the forty or so herbs that have been identified, from the remains of wreaths and posies, as having been grown thousands of years ago in the gardens of ancient Egypt.

The flowers of the cornflower contain valuable active ingredients, and a decoction made from fresh or dried flowers is a diuretic.

An infusion can be made using a heaped teaspoon of dried cornflowers to a mugful of boiling water. Leave it for six minutes, then strain it and drink the resulting liquid between meals up to three times a day.

Fragaria vesca
Rosaceae
WILD STRAWBERRY

The wild strawberry contains vitamins A and C and both the leaves and the fruit have been used in herbal medicine for centuries.

An infusion made from the young leaves is beneficial for anaemia and nervousness and as a tonic for the kidneys. It is said that the distinguished eighteenth-century botanist Carl Linnaeus cured himself of gout by administering an infusion of strawberry leaves and a diet of the fresh fruit. Add the fruit to drinks to cool away feverishness. Use strawberry root in a decoction for use as a general tonic and a diuretic.

IMPORTANT
Do *not* try these remedies if you normally have an allergic reaction to strawberries.

Humulus lupulus
Cannabidaceae
HOP

The yellow powder on the cone of the hop flower contains the plant's active ingredient, lupulin. Dried hops should be stored in a cold, dry place and used within three months because they lose their efficacy and healing power after this time.

An infusion of dried hops drunk just before bedtime acts as a mild sedative and is prescribed as a treatment for insomnia. Add the flowers to any tea and the mixture will aid digestion and stimulate the appetite – useful when convalescing after flu. It combines well with valerian, which reduces tension and anxiety, and the leaves of the passion flower. Other good herbs to mix with hops for this purpose are balm, catnip, chamomile, lime flowers, orange blossom, skullcap, vervain and wood betony. A cupful of an infusion of a mixture of some of these herbs, drunk regularly three times a day, should reduce the state of anxiety.

To make a spirit of hops, macerate 20g (¾oz) dried hops in 100ml (3½fl oz) eau-de-vie for three days. Strain into a small, clean glass bottle and store in a cold place. As a treatment for insomnia, take 20 drops of this spirit in a tumbler of warm water or on a cube of sugar before retiring to bed at night.

Hop flowers contain a natural antibiotic, and poultices made from them are used to treat boils.

IMPORTANT
Do *not* take hops internally if you are suffering severely from depression as it could accentuate your condition.

Hyssopus officinalis
Labiatae
HYSSOP

The volatile oil found in hyssop contains pinocamphone, isopinocamphone, pinenes, camphene, terpinene and over 50 other compounds. The herb is powerful, and should only be administered in small doses of 1–2g twice a day.

Hyssop has antibacterial properties and relaxes the tissues of the lungs, so an infusion of hyssop leaves is prescribed as a treatment for a wide range of respiratory disorders, including

Humulus lupulus, **HOP**

Jasminum officinale
Oleaceae
JASMINE

The highly scented essential oil is used in perfumes and aromatherapy. To make jasmine cough linctus, cover 180g (6oz) of freshly-picked jasmine flowers with 570ml (1 pint) boiling water, stir and leave to infuse for 12 hours. Then, strain the liquid into a jug, stir in 225g (8oz) clear honey and pour it into a clean screw-top bottle and keep in a cold place. Administer 1 to 2 tablespoons as required.

Aromatherapists use jasmine essential oil in courses of treatment to cure depression as it has an uplifting effect. A few drops in a warm bath or burned in an essential oil burner would be beneficial.

Jasmine essential oil is also good for respiratory problems and as a tonic for those with sensitive skin.

Lavandula angustifolia
Labiatae
LAVENDER

Lavender flowers have been used for centuries and the plant has a wide range of medicinal uses. The flowers produce a valuable volatile oil that contains linabol, lavandulyl acetate, camphor, pinene and coumarin.

For minor accidents such as bumps, burns and so on, where there is no loss of consciousness or excessive bleeding, lavender essential oil applied to the area of injury is both pain-relieving and healing. For burns, lavender essential oil used liberally and neat soothes, prevents infection

and encourages new skin to grow. It is equally effective for cooling and soothing sunburn, diluted in oil or a cool bath. To relieve the soreness of bites and stings, dab a little lavender essential oil onto and around the site of the bite or sting itself.

Ageing is the natural slowing down of cell division so lavender essential oil, which stimulates healthy cell division, is a useful aid to youthful skin. Either add a few drops to a little vegetable oil and massage all over, or add a couple of drops of the essential oil to a warm bath or a bowl of hot water to steam the face.

Lavender essential oil can be used, too, to relieve some of the side effects of anxiety by relaxing the person through massage or a warm bath – adding two or three drops to a bath or using one drop of lavender with one of basil, geranium, melissa or rose in a saucer of vegetable oil to make a relaxing massaging oil. Lavender essential oil is also soothing and calming in cases of high blood pressure.

For eyestrain, a compress of lavender essential oil can be a great help. Add one drop of lavender or chamomile essential oil to 0.6 litre (1 pint) of cooled, boiled water, stir vigorously, then dip cotton wool into the liquid and gently hold against the eyes. If there is any swelling, let the water go completely cold before mixing. A simpler method is to make a cup of chamomile tea using a teabag as normal, remove the bag and allow to cool before applying to the eyes.

Headaches can be relieved by adding a few drops to a little vegetable oil and massaging it into the temples.

colds, coughs, flu, sore throats, catarrh and bronchitis.

For the common cold, mix hyssop with boneset, elderflower and peppermint, making an infusion from one to two teaspoons of the mixture to a cup of boiling water and drinking it after about 10 to 15 minutes. Take a cup of the infusion three times a day.

For hayfever or hayfever-like symptoms due to allergies to dust, fur and so on, try combining hyssop, echinacea, elderflower and eyebright in equal quantities and make an infusion, using a teaspoon of the mixture to a cup of boiling water, and take three times a day. This will help relieve the symptoms and soothe the irritated mucous membranes, with the added bonus of not making you drowsy.

Also useful for these afflictions is to use two drops of each of the essential oils of hyssop and eucalyptus in a bowl of hot water and inhale the steam.

Melissa officinalis
Labiatae
LEMON BALM

The volatile oil found in lemon balm contains citral, citronella, eugenol acetate, geraniol, polyphenols and rosemarinic acid. The herb has a mild anti-depressant effect and the slightly sedative oils relieve tension and stress so it has long been prescribed as a treatment for depression, insomnia, neuralgia and nervous headaches. Make lemon balm tea by infusing a cup of boiling water with a teaspoon of dried lemon balm or four to six fresh leaves and leaving it for ten minutes or so, keeping it well covered so that it remains hot. Drink a cup three times a day. The liquid has a tonic effect on the heart and circulation, lowers high blood pressure and is also beneficial in the treatment of flu. An infusion of fresh lemon balm leaves is also an excellent digestive for drinking after meals, as it stimulates the digestive system and relaxes the stomach.

Mentha × piperita
Labiatae
PEPPERMINT

Peppermint's volatile oil contains menthol, menthone and menthylacetate. Menthol is antibacterial and antiparisitic and has a wide range of uses.

Mint tea is recommended as a digestive after rich meals, a decongestant and as a reviving drink in cases of giddiness. A handful of crushed fresh leaves held pressed against the forehead relieves headaches. Mixed with balm, meadowsweet, rosemary and vervain, it makes another good treatment for headaches. Add a heaped teaspoon of the mixture to a cup of boiling water and drink a cup every few hours.

For a mouthwash and gargle, infuse 30g (1oz) fresh or 15g (½oz) dried mint leaves in a mugful of boiling water for 10 minutes. Strain and allow to cool before using.

A mixture of peppermint, elderflower and yarrow makes a good decongestant, eliminates the toxins and stimulates the body, so is useful in treating colds. Make an infusion and drink a cupful three times a day. If it is a feverish cold, add boneset to this mixture and if the throat is sore, add red sage. Add freshly grated ginger to any of these mixtures for a comforting, warming effect.

For sunburn, make a cooling infusion using peppermint, chickweed and nettle to drink as tea or leave to cool and bathe parts of the skin that feel hot.

Rosa species
Rosaceae
ROSE

Rosehips are rich in vitamin C and the essential oil of the rose contains nocotinamide and organic acids. A tea made with rosehips is a treatment for debility and a preventative therapy against colds. Rose oil – attar of roses – is valuable in aromatherapy.

A beneficial anti-ageing lotion is a few drops each of rose, neroli, frankincense and sandalwood added to a light vegetable oil. Massage the mixture into the skin or add a few drops of the essential oil mixture to a bowl of hot water for a facial sauna.

Rose added to a little vegetable oil and massaged into the temples, or the whole body, is a very pleasant way to relieve a headache, as is soaking in a warm bath to which a few drops of rose have been added. For a migraine, try adding a few drops of rose to a little almond oil and massaging it into the temples.

To make a mouthwash from rose petals, pour 150ml (¼ pint) white wine vinegar over 300ml (½ pint) freshly picked, scented rose petals and mash together for five minutes. Cover and leave in a warm place for two days, then strain and dilute 1 tablespoon with 200ml (7fl oz) water.

Rose-scented honey is a soothing anti-tussive treatment. Fill a jar with fresh, dry rose petals and clear honey. Cover and leave in a warm place for one week then strain. Sip a teaspoonful as required.

Rosmarinus officinalis
Labiatae
ROSEMARY

The volatile oil in rosemary contains monoterpene hydrocarbons, cineole, camphor, diosmin and phenolic acids.

Rosemary is recommended for headaches, flatulence, heartburn and poor circulation. Rosemary tea is a good digestive, made by placing a 10cm (4in) sprig of fresh rosemary in a cup, adding boiling water to cover and leaving it to infuse for three minutes. Then, discard the herb and drink the tea slowly. See under FEVERFEW for a mixture that is taken as an infusion to relieve migraine.

The oil is valuable in aromatherapy where it is prescribed as a treatment for fatigue, muscular pains and respiratory problems. See under PEPPERMINT for a mixture useful in relieving cold symptoms and under

Mentha x *piperita*, **PEPPERMINT**

Rosa canina, **DOG ROSE**

LAVENDER for a pick-me-up after illness.

A hangover cure that is a great deal more pleasant than most is to add a drop each of rosemary, basil, grapefruit and juniper oils to a warm bath or to add a couple of drops of each to a little vegetable oil and use it for a body massage.

For a headache, add a drop or two to a little vegetable oil and massage into the temples or the whole body or add a few drops to a warm bath.

Rosa x *damascena bifera,* **DAMASK ROSE**

Symphytum officinale
Boraginaceae
COMFREY

Fresh comfrey leaves are rich in vitamins A, B12 and C and in the minerals calcium, phosphorous and potassium. Comfrey also has a higher protein content than any other vegetable.

The herb is at present the subject of extensive scientific research, and until conclusive evidence is available comfrey should only be used externally.

Dried comfrey leaves used to be used to make an infusion that was recommended for soothing away coughs and bronchitis. As comfrey tea stimulates healthy cell division, it was traditionally a health drink for older people, though it should be drunk for a short time only, rather than an indefinite period, and always under medical supervision. A week infusion of comfrey is also prescribed for bathing minor burns and scalds as it helps to heal the skin.

Comfrey was once known as 'knitbone' or 'boneset' due to the herb's reputation for healing bone fractures. An infusion made from the leaves can be used to bathe the site of a fracture provided the skin is not broken. You can also buy or make comfrey ointment and apply it as with the infusion. For sprained or sore muscles, make an infusion of comfrey, soaking a clean cloth in the resulting liquid and applying it to the sore area as a compress. A tablespoon each of comfrey, marigold, witchhazel and yarrow, steeped in 0.6 litre (1 pint) of water and used in a compress over a bruise is both a soothing and a healing medicinal remedy.

Tanacetum parthenium
Compositae
FEVERFEW

The active ingredients, sesquiterpene lactones, and volatile oils are found in the leaves. Use fresh or frozen leaves if possible. The flowers have also been used in the past and preparing them as an infusion was said to cure poor circulation.

Feverfew leaves have always been taken to cure headaches, but recently their beneficial effects on migraine have been proven. In a clinical experiment, seven out of ten sufferers found that their headaches reduced in frequency or severity when they ate a feverfew leaf three times a day. It is important to give this remedy time to work as its effect is cumulative and may take about six months before you get a positive result. A combination of feverfew, balm, meadowsweet and rosemary used to make an infusion that is drunk a cupful at a time, three times a day is also beneficial for mild or infrequent migraine. If you know that nervous tension is a contributing factor to your headache, add skullcap to this mixture.

Feverfew combined with ash, celery seed, cornsilk, devil's claw, meadowsweet, prickly ash and white willow and made into an infusion drunk three times a day for a month to six weeks, will reduce the inflammation and pain of arthritis. If damp weather makes the symptoms worse, add bogbean to the above mixture and this should help.

IMPORTANT
Be warned, however, *not* to take feverfew if you are pregnant as it has a stimulant effect on the womb so may induce labour.

Tanacetum vulgare
Compositae
TANSY

Tansy produces a volatile oil that contains up to 70 per cent thujone, bitter glycosides, pyrethrins, tannin, vitamin C and citric acid.

Traditionally tansy has been used as a strewing herb to deter insects and also for treating parasites. A strong decoction made by steeping 25g (¾oz) each of tansy leaves and poke root in 0.6 litre (1 pint) of boiling water can be used in a compress to bring relief to rheumatic joints, bruises and sprains. Tansy should be used only under the supervision of a medical herbalist, and not in pregnancy.

Thymus species
Labiatae
THYME

The volatile oil produced by thyme contains phenol, thymol and carvacrol and is strongly antiseptic. The two latter components are antibacterial and antifungal. An infusion of thyme can be used to bathe infected wounds, to clean them and promote healing.

As first aid for toothache, make a strong infusion of three teaspoons of equal parts thyme, marshmallow and sage and use it as a mouthwash. For mouth ulcers, use an infusion of thyme as a mouthwash.

For a sore throat and irritable coughs, add two drops each of thyme, lemon and sage essential oils to vodka and add a few drops of this mixture to a cup of warm water: use as a gargle.

Tilia cordata
Tiliaceae
LIME

The volatile oil of lime flowers contains farnesol, flavonoid glycosides, saponins and condensed tannins. An infusion made from the dried flowers has been used to reduce fevers for centuries. Lime tea is also prescribed as a treatment for nervous tension, high blood pressure, insomnia and indigestion. For mild cases of hypertension lime flowers can be mixed with hawthorn, mistletoe and yarrow to make an infusion using a heaped teaspoon of the herb mixture to one cup of boiling water. Leave it to stand for ten minutes before straining it and drinking. Sip a cup of the infusion twice a day for up to six weeks. If you are taking drugs to reduce your blood pressure check with a qualified herbalist before taking any herbal treatment to make sure that it is compatible with the drugs you have been prescribed.

To treat anxiety, combine some of the following: lime, balm, catnip, chamomile, hops, orange blossom, passion flower, scullcap, valerian, vervain and wood betony and use them to make an infusion; drink a cup of the liquid three times a day. For sleeplessness, try mixing lime flowers with balm, chamomile, orange blossom and passiflora to make a relaxing drink before going to bed.

Valeriana officinalis
Valerianaceae
VALERIAN

The herb valerian contains the active ingredients valepotriates and esters of acetic, tuyric and isovalerianic acids and the oil contains limonene, sesquiterpene, valerian camphor, alkaloids, chatinine, and tannins.

Valeriana officinalis, **VALERIAN**

Viola odorata, **SWEET VIOLET**

Use an infusion solely of valerian root to reduce anxiety and tension, making it with one to two teaspoons of the root to a cupful of boiling water, leave it for 10 to 15 minutes and then drink it whenever it is needed. Because of its sedative qualities use this infusion, too, for insomnia. The infusion will also bring some relief in cases of migraine or rheumatism.

See under LIME for a mixture given to alleviate insomnia and add valerian to it if sleep is not coming due to pain. Note, however, that this herb is not suitable for everyone and it can also become habit forming, so do not use it more often than is strictly necessary.

Viola odorata
Violaceae
SWEET VIOLET

The violet has long been used as a remedy for coughs, especially bronchitis and catarrh in the upper respiratory tract. It is also very beneficial for skin conditions like eczema and for the long-term treatment of rheumatism. A more recent discovery has been its anti-cancer properties and it definitely has a future role to play in a holistic treatment of this difficult disease.

An infusion of violet leaves acts as a diuretic, an expectorant and an anti-inflammatory, and works to gradually restore healthy normal functioning and vitality. To make it, add a teaspoon of sweet violet to a cup of boiling water and let it infuse for ten minutes or so. Drink a cupful three times a day. Use the flowers for coughs, bronchitis, headaches, insomnia and for soothing tension; the leaves or root for catarrh and bronchitis.

To make a mixture that will soothe headaches and sore throats, pour a mugful of boiling water over 15g (½oz) freshly picked violet flowers, stir well and leave to infuse for 15 minutes. Strain the liquid into a jar and take two tablespoons three times a day.

CULTIVATION CHART

HERB	FAMILY	TYPE	SIZE	SITE	SOIL	SUITABILITY
Angelica, *Angelica archangelica*	*Umbelliferae*	Biennial	1–2m	Light shade	Rich, damp	Specimen, back border
Aniseed, *Pimpinella anisum*	*Umbelliferae*	Half-hardy annual	40cm	Full sun	Rich, well-drained	Mid border
Basil, *Ocimum basilicum*	*Labiatae*	Tender annual	20–45cm	Full sun	Rich, damp	Front-mid border
Bay, *Laurus nobilis*	*Lauraceae*	Semi-hardy evergreen	up to 8m	Sun, light shade	Rich, well-drained	Specimen tree
Bergamot, *Monarda didyma*	*Labiatae*	Hardy perennial	up to 1m	Full sun	Rich, well-drained	Mid border
Betony, *Stachys officinalis*	*Labiatae*	Hardy perennial	4.5–6cm	Light shade	Rich, well-drained	Mid border
Borage, *Borago officinalis*	*Boraginaceae*	Hardy annual	45–75cm	Sun, light shade	Rich, well-drained	Mid-back border
Caraway, *Carum carvi*	*Umbelliferae*	Biennial	25–45cm	Full sun	Rich, damp	Front-mid border
Catmint, *Nepeta cataria*	*Labiatae*	Hardy perennial	0.5–1m	Full sun	Well-drained poor	Edge, front-mid border
Chamomile, *Chamaemelum nobile*	*Compositae*	Hardy evergreen	20–30cm	Full sun	Light, well-drained	Edge, paths, lawn
Chervil, *Anthriscus cerefolium*	*Umbelliferae*	Hardy annual	20–30cm	Light shade	Loamy, well-drained	Front-mid border
Chives, *Allium schoenoprasum*	*Liliaceae*	Hardy perennial	15–75cm	Sun, light shade	Rich, well-drained	Edge-front border
Clary, *Salvia horminum*	*Labiatae*	Hardy annual	30–45cm	Full sun	Moderately rich	Front-mid border
Claytonia, *Claytonia perfoliata*	*Portulacaceae*	Hardy annual	15cm	Light shade	Rich, damp	Front border
Comfrey, *Symphytum officinale*	*Boraginaceae*	Hardy perennial	1m	Sun, light shade	Rich, well-drained	Mid-back border
Coriander, *Coriandrum sativum*	*Umbelliferae*	Half-hardy annual	30–45cm	Full sun	Rich, light	Front-mid border
Cornflower, *Centaurea cyanus*	*Compositae*	Hardy annual	60–90cm	Full sun	Medium, well-drained	Mid-border
Curry plant, *Helichrysum italicum*	*Compositae*	Half-hardy evergreen	45cm	Full sun	Poor, well-drained	Low hedge, front-mid border
Dill, *Anethum graveolens*	*Umbelliferae*	Hardy annual	45–90cm	Full sun	Rich, well-drained	Front-mid border
Elder, *Sambucus nigra*	*Caprifoliaceae*	Deciduous	3–5m	Sun, light shade	Moderately rich, damp	Specimen tree
Fennel, *Foeniculum vulgare*	*Umbelliferae*	Hardy herbaceous perennial	2m	Sun	Poor, light	Back border
Fenugreek, *Trigonella foenum-graecum*	*Leguminosae*	Tender annual	30–60cm	Sun	Rich, well-drained	Mid border
Feverfew, *Tanacetum parthenium*	*Compositae*	Hardy perennial	45–60cm	Full sun	Medium, light	Mid border
Garlic, *Allium sativum*	*Liliaceae*	Hardy perennial	30–45cm	Full sun	Medium, well-drained	Front-mid border
Geranium, *Pelargonium* species	*Geraniaceae*	Tender evergreen perennial	30cm–1m	Sun, light shade	Medium, gritty	Container, mid border
Hop, *Humulus lupulus*	*Cannabidaceae*	Hardy deciduous perennial climber	up to 7m	Full sun	Rich, deep	On a wall or support
Horseradish, *Amoracia rusticana*	*Cruciferae*	Hardy perennial	45–60cm	Light shade	Rich, damp	Mid-back, separate border
Hyssop, *Hyssopus officinalis*	*Labiatae*	Hardy evergreen perennial	30–60cm	Full sun	Medium, light	Low hedge, front border
Jasmine, *Jasminum officinale*	*Oleaceae*	Hardy, deciduous climber	up to 6m	Sun, light shade	Rich, deep	On a wall or support
Juniper, *Juniperus communis*	*Cupressaceae*	Hardy evergreen shrub	1–3m	Full sun	Well-drained, alkaline	Specimen, hedge
Lavender, *Lavandula angustifolia*	*Labiatae*	Hardy evergreen perennial	30–75cm	Full sun	Poor, light	Low hedge or edging
Lemon balm, *Melissa officinalis*	*Labiatae*	Hardy herbaceous perennial	1m	Sun, light shade	Poor, damp	Mid border
Lemon verbena, *Aloysia triphylla*	*Verbenaceae*	Half-hardy perennial	50cm	Full sun, sheltered	Poor, light	Front border
Lime, *Tilia cordata*	*Tiliaceae*	Deciduous perennial	10m	Sun, light shade	Deep, damp	Specimen
Lovage, *Levisticum officinalis*	*Umbelliferae*	Hardy herbaceous perennial	2m	Sun, light shade	Rich, damp	Mid-back border
Marigold, *Calendula officinalis*	*Compositae*	Hardy annual	30–50cm	Full sun	Rich, damp	Front

HERB	FAMILY	TYPE	SIZE	SITE	SOIL	SUITABILITY
Marjoram, *Origanum* species	*Labiatae*	Hardy herbaceous perennial	15–30cm	Full sun	Poor, light	Edge, front border
Mint, *Mentha* species	*Labiatae*	Hardy herbaceous perennial	1cm–1m	Sun, light shade	Rich, damp	Separate border
Musk mallow, *Malva moschata*	*Malvaceae*	Semi-evergreen perennial	60cm–1m	Full sun	Poor, well-drained	Back border
Myrtle, *Myrtus communis*	*Myrtaceae*	Half-hardy evergreen perennial	2–3m	Full sun	Rich, well-drained	Container, specimen
Nasturtium, *Tropaeolum majus*	*Tropaeolaceae*	Hardy annual	15–30cm	Full sun	Poor, well-drained	Front border
Parsley, *Petroselinum crispum*	*Umbelliferae*	Hardy biennial	25–45cm	Sun, light shade	Rich, damp	Edge, front border
Pineapple sage, *Salvia rutilans*	*Labiatae*	Half-hardy annual	30cm	Sun, light shade	Rich, damp	Front border
Purslane, *Portulaca oleracea*	*Portulacaceae*	Half-hardy annual	15cm	Sun, light shade	Rich, damp	Front border
Rocket, *Eruca vesicaria sativa*	*Cruciferae*	Half-hardy annual	60cm	Sun, light shade	Rich, damp	Mid border
Rose, *Rosa* species	*Rosaceae*	Hardy deciduous perennial	up to 2m	Full sun	Medium, well-drained	Specimen, middle-back border
Rosemary, *Rosmarinus officinalis*	*Labiatae*	Hardy evergreen shrub	30cm–2m	Sun, sheltered	Light, alkaline	Hedge, specimen, back border
Rue, *Ruta graveolens*	*Rutaceae*	Hardy evergreen perennial	30–60cm	Full sun	Poor, light	Edge, container, front border
Sage, *Salvia officinalis*	*Labiatae*	Hardy evergreen perennial	30–75cm	Full sun	Medium, well-drained	Hedge, mid border
Clary sage, *Salvia sclarea*	*Labiatae*	Hardy biennial	up to 1m	Full sun	Poor, light	Mid-back border
Salad burnet, *Sanguisorba minor*	*Rosaceae*	Hardy herbaceous perennial	10–40cm	Sun, light shade	Poor, alkaline	Front-mid border
Santolina, *Santolina chamaecyparissus*	*Compositae*	Hardy evergreen perennial	20–45cm	Full sun	Poor, light	Edge, front border
Smallage, *Apium graveolens*	*Umbelliferae*	Hardy herbaceous perennial	30cm	Light shade	Rich, damp	Mid-border
Sorrel, *Rumex acetosa*	*Polygonaceae*	Half-hardy perennial	25cm	Light shade	Rich, damp	Front-mid border
Southernwood, *Artemisia abrotanum*	*Compositae*	Hardy semi-evergreen	60cm–1m	Full sun	Medium, well-drained	Hedge, mid border
Summer savory, *Satureja hortensis*	*Labiatae*	Hardy annual	15cm	Full sun	Rich, damp	Edge, front
Sweet cicely, *Myrrhis odorata*	*Umbelliferae*	Hardy herbaceous perennial	60cm	Sun, light shade	Rich, damp	Mid border
Sweet violet, *Viola odorata*	*Violaceae*	Hardy deciduous perennial	10–15cm	Light shade	Rich, damp	Front border
Sweet woodruff, *Galium odoratum*	*Rubiaceae*	Hardy perennial	30cm	Light shade	Rich, deep	Front-mid border
Tansy, *Tanacetum vulgare*	*Compositae*	Hardy herbaceous perennial	up to 1.25m	Sun, light shade	Medium, light	Mid border
Tarragon, *Artemisia dracunculus*	*Compositae*	Half-hardy perennial	30–60cm	Full sun	Rich, well-drained	Mid border
Thyme, *Thymus* species	*Labiatae*	Hardy evergreen perennial	2–30cm	Full sun	Well-drained, alkaline	Edge, front border
Wall germander, *Teucrium chamaedrys*	*Labiatae*	Hardy evergreen perennial	10–20cm	Full sun	Medium, well-drained	Edge, front border
Wild strawberry, *Fragaria vesca*	*Rosaceae*	Hardy evergreen perennial	15cm	Light shade, sheltered	Well-drained, peaty	Edge, front border
Winter savory, *Satureja montana*	*Labiatae*	Hardy evergreen perennial	30cm	Full sun	Well-drained, alkaline	Edge, front border
Wormwood, *Artemisia absinthium*	*Compositae*	Hardy, deciduous	60–90cm	Full sun	Light, well-drained	Mid-border
Valerian, *Valeriana officinalis*	*Valerianaceae*	Hardy herbaceous perennial	60cm–1.5m	Full sun	Poor, well-drained	Wall, mid border

USEFUL ADDRESSES

HERB GARDENS

ABBEY DORE COURT,
Abbey Dore, Herefordshire

ABBEY HOUSE MUSEUM,
Leeds, West Yorkshire

ACORN BANK,
The National Trust, Cumbria

ALDERLEY GRANGE,
Alderley, Gloucestershire

ARLEY HALL AND GARDENS,
near Northwick, Cheshire

BARNSLEY HOUSE,
near Cirencester,
Gloucestershire

BATEMAN'S,
National Trust,
Burwash, East Sussex

BRAIDJULE,
Broughshane,
Ballymena, Northern Ireland

CAMBRIDGE BOTANIC GARDENS,
University Botanic Garden,
Cambridge

CAPEL MANOR,
Institute of Horticultural
Field Studies,
Waltham Cross, Hertfordshire

CASTLE DROGO,
near Chagford, Devon

CHELSEA PHYSIC GARDEN,
Chelsea, London

CHENIES MANOR HOUSE,
near Amersham,
Buckinghamshire

CLAVERTON MANOR
AMERICAN MUSEUM,
near Bath, Avon

CRANBORNE MANOR,
near Wimborne, Dorset

DARTINGTON HALL,
Totnes, Devon

DENMAN'S,
Fontwell, West Sussex

DOWER HOUSE (THE),
Badminton, Avon

ELLY HILL HERBS,
Elly Hill House, Barmpton,
Darlington, Durham

EMMANUEL COLLEGE,
Cambridge

EYHORNE MANOR,
Hollingborne, Kent

FELBRIGG HALL,
The National Trust,
Felbrigg, Norfolk

FULHAM PALACE,
Hammersmith, London SW6

GAULDEN MANOR,
Tolland,
near Taunton, Somerset

GLASGOW BOTANIC GARDENS,
Great Western Road,
Glasgow,
Strathclyde, Scotland

GUNBY HALL,
The National Trust,
Burgh-le-Marsh,
near Spilsbury, Lincolnshire

HALL'S CROFT,
Old Town,
Stratford-upon-Avon,
Warwickshire

HARDWICK HALL,
Chesterfield, Derbyshire

HARLOW CAR GARDENS,
Harrogate, Yorkshire

HATFIELD HOUSE,
Hatfield, Hertfordshire

HESTERCOMBE HOUSE,
near Taunton, Somerset

HOLME PIERREPOINT HALL,
Nottinghamshire

HOPETOUN HOUSE,
South Queensferry,
Lothian, Scotland

IDEN CROFT NURSERIES AND
HERB FARM, Staplehurst, Kent

IZAAK WALTON COTTAGE,
Shugborough, near Stafford

KNEBWORTH HOUSE,
Knebworth, Hertfordshire

KNOLE,
The National Trust,
Sevenoaks, Kent

LACKHAM COLLEGE OF
AGRICULTURE,
Lacock, Chippenham, Wiltshire

LINCOLN CATHEDRAL,
Lincoln

LITTLE MORETON HALL,

The National Trust,
Congleton, Cheshire

LYTES CARY MANOR,
Ilchester, Somerset

MALLORY COURT,
Leamington Spa, Warwickshire

MARLE PLACE,
Marle Place Plants,
Brenchley,
near Tonbridge, Kent

MAWLEY HALL,
Cleobury Mortimer, Shropshire

MICHELHAMPTON PRIORY,
Upper Dicker, East Sussex

MOSELY OLD HALL,
Wolverhampton, West Midlands

MOUNT STEWART GARDENS,
Newtonards,
County Down, Northern Ireland

NESS GARDENS,
University of Liverpool Botanic
Gardens,
Ness Neston,
Wirral, Cheshire

NETHERBYRES,
Eyemouth, Borders, Scotland

NEW PLACE,
Chapel Street,
Stratford-upon-Avon,
Warwickshire

NOSEGAY GARDEN (THE),
Royal Botanic Gardens,
Kew, Surrey

OLD BARN (THE),
Fremington,
near Barnstable, Devon

OLD RECTORY (THE),
Burghfield,
near Reading, Berkshire

OXBURGH HALL,
The National Trust,
Oxburgh,
near Swaffham, Norfolk

PETERBOROUGH CATHEDRAL,
Peterborough, Cambridgeshire

PRIORWOOD GARDEN,
The National Trust for Scotland,
Melrose, Borders, Scotland

QUEEN'S GARDEN (THE),
Kew Palace,

Royal Botanic Gardens,
Kew, Surrey

ROYAL BOTANIC GARDEN,
Inverleith Road,
Edinburgh, Scotland

ROYAL HORTICULTURAL SOCIETY
GARDEN,
Wisley,
near Woking, Surrey

ST MICHAEL'S MOUNT,
Penzance, Cornwall

SHAKESPEARE GARDENS:
Anne Hathaway's Cottage,
Shottery,
Stratford-upon-Avon,
Warwickshire

BIRTHPLACE GARDEN,
Henley Street,
Stratford-upon-Avon,
Warwickshire

SCOTNEY CASTLE,
Lamberhurst, Kent

SISSINGHURST CASTLE,
Sissinghurst, Kent

SPRINGHILL,
The National Trust,
Moneymore,
County Londonderry,
Northern Ireland

STOCKFIELD PARK,
Wetherby, North Yorkshire

STONE COTTAGE,
Hambleton,
Oakham, Leicestershire

SUTTON MANOR,
Sutton Scotney,
near Winchester, Hampshire

THORNBY HERBS,
Thornby Hall Gardens,
Thornby, Northamptonshire

THREAVE GARDEN,
The National Trust for Scotland,
Castle Douglas,
Dumfries and Galloway,
Scotland

TRADESCANT GARDEN,
The Museum of Garden History,
Lambeth, London

TUDOR HOUSE (THE),
Southampton, Hampshire

BIBLIOGRAPHY

WELSH FOLK MUSEUM,
National Museum of Wales,
St Fagans Castle
Cardiff, Wales
WEST GREEN HOUSE,
Hartley Witney, Hampshire
WESTMINSTER ABBEY HERB GARDEN,
Westminster Abbey,
London SW1
WHITTLESEA MUSEUM,
Market Street,
Whittlesey, Cambridgeshire
YORK GATE,
Back Church Lane,
Adel, Leeds

HERB SUPPLIERS AND NURSERIES

CHILTERN HERBS,
Bortree Stile,
Ulverston, Cumbria LA12 7PB
CORNISH HERBS,
Trelow Cottage,
Mawgan-in-Meneage,
Cornwall
HERITAGE SEEDS,
Henry Doubleday Research
Association,
Ryton Gardens,
Ryton on Dunsmore,
Coventry CV8 3LG
HOLLINGTON NURSERIES LTD,
Woolton Hill,
Newbury,
Berkshire RG15 9XT
NETHERFIELD HERBS,
37 Nether Street,
Rougham,
Suffolk IP30 9LW
ROBIN HERB GARDENS,
Spring Acre Farm,
Thorpe-in-Balne,
Doncaster,
South Yorkshire DN6 0DZ
SUFFOLK HERBS LTD.
Sawyers Farm,
Little Cornard,
Sudbury,
Suffolk CO10 0NY

HERB GARDENING

Bardswell, Frances A., *The Herb Garden*, A.C. Black, 1911
Bremness, Lesley, *The Complete Book of Herbs*, Dorling Kindersley, 1988
Cooper, Guy; Taylor, Gordon; Bournsell, Clive, *English Herb Gardens*, Weidenfeld and Nicolson, 1986
Garland, Sarah, *The Herb Garden*, Windward, 1984
Grieve, Mrs M., *A Modern Herbal*, Penguin Handbooks, 1980
Hadfield, Miles, *A History of British Gardening*, Hutchinson and Company, 1960
Harvey, John, *Medieval Gardens*, B.T. Batsford Ltd, 1981
Holt, Geraldene, *The Gourmet Garden*, Pavilion/Little, Brown and Company, 1990
—*Recipes from a French Herb Garden*, Conran Octopus/Simon & Schuster, 1989
Hopkinson, Simon and Judith, *Herbs, their care and cultivation*, Cassell, 1990
Larkcom, Joy, *The Salad Garden*, Frances Lincoln/Windward, 1984
Le Rougetel, Hazel, *The Chelsea Gardener, Philip Miller 1691–1771*, Natural History Museum, 1990
Lowenfeld, Claire, *Herb Gardening*, Faber and Faber, 1964
McLean, Teresa, *Medieval English Gardens*, William Collins, 1981
Masefield, G.B., Wallis, M., Harrison, S.G., Nicholson, B.E., *The Oxford Book of Food Plants*, Oxford University Press, 1969
Paterson, Allen, *Herbs in the Garden*, J.M. Dent and Sons Ltd., 1985
Peplow, Elizabeth and Reginald, *Herbs and Herb Gardens*, Webb and Bower, 1984
Phillips, Roger and Foy, Nicky, *Herbs*, Pan Original, 1990
Thacker, Christopher, *The History of Gardens*, Croom Helm Ltd., 1979

A TASTE OF HERBS

A Book of Fruits and Flowers, introduction by C. Anne Wilson, reprint of 1653 edition by Prospect Books, 1984
Boulestin, X. Marcel and Hill, Jason, *Herbs, Salads and Seasonings*, William Heinemann, 1930
The Compleat Cook and *A Queen's Delight*, reprint of 1655 edition by Prospect Books, 1984
Couplan, Francois, *Mangez vos soucis!*, Editions Alternatives, 1983
Culpeper Nicholas, *Complete Herbal*, reprint of 1826 edition by Harvey Sales, 1981
Eales's, Mrs. Mary, *Receipts*, reprint of 1733 edition by Prospect Books, 1985
Evelyn, John, *Acetaria*, reprint of 1699 edition by Prospect Books, 1982
Gerarde, John, *The Herball*, reprint of 1636 edition by Bracken Books, 1985
Glasses, Hannah, *The Art of Cookery made Plain and Easy*, reprint of 1747 edition by Prospect Books, 1983
Grieve, Mrs M., *Culinary Herbs and Condiments*, William Heinemann, 1933
Holt, Geraldene, *French Country Kitchen*, Penguin, 1985, Simon & Schuster 1990
Japanese Herbs and their Uses, Brooklyn Botanic Record, 1968
Launert, Edmund, *Edible and Medicinal Plants of Britain and Northern Europe*, Hamlyn Publishing Group Limited, 1981
Lowenfeld Claire, Back Philippa, *The Complete Book of Herbs and Spices*, David and Charles, 1974
Plat, Sir Hugh, *Delights for Ladies*, reprint of 1609 edition by Crosby Lockwood and Son Ltd, 1948

INDOOR HERBAL

Arber, Agnes, *Herbals*, reprint of 1938 edition by Cambridge University Press, 1988
Blunt, Wilfrid, Raphael, Sandra, *The Illustrated Herbal*, Frances Lincoln/Weidenfeld and Nicolson, 1979
Curtis, Susan, Fraser, Romy, Kohler, Irene, *Natural Remedies*, Arkana, 1988
Garden Lore of Ancient Athens, American School of Classical Studies, 1963
Grigson, Geoffrey, *A Herbal of Sorts*, Phoenix House Limited, 1962
—*Gardening*, Routledge & Kegan Paul, 1952
Herbal Review, the quarterly journal of The Herb Society
Heriteau Jacqueline, *Potpourris and Other Fragrant Delights*, Simon and Schuster, 1973
Jaubert, Jean-Noel, *Les Aromes Alimentaires*, Presses Universitaires de France, 1983
Leyel, Mrs C.F., *Compassionate herbs*, Faber and Faber, 1946
—*Elixirs of Life*, Faber and Faber, 1948
—*The Magic of Herbs*, Jonathan Cape, 1932
—*The Truth about Herbs*, Andrew Dakers, 1943
Mabey, Richard, *New Herbal*, Gaia Books, 1988
Manniche, Lisa, *An Ancient Egyptian Herbal*, British Museum Publications, 1989
Meunier, Christiane, *Lavandes & Lavandins*, Edisud, 1985
Palaiseul, Jean, *Grandmother's Secrets*, Barrie and Jenkins, 1973
Prihoda, Antonin, *The Healing Powers of Nature*, Hamlyn, 1989
Quelch, Mary Thorne, *Herbs for Daily Use*, Faber and Faber, 1941
— *Herbs and how to know them*, Faber and Faber, 1946
Rohde, Eleanour Sinclair, *A Garden of Herbs*, Herbert Jenkins, 1920

INDEX

ACKNOWLEDGMENTS

AUTHOR'S ACKNOWLEDGMENTS

Years before I had agreed to write a book about herbs I was well aware of the daunting size of the subject and its considerable literature. No group of plants can have been better documented, or for longer. This book, though, makes no claims to be encyclopaedic; it is simply a personal view of the herbs I grow and the pleasure they give me.

While working on the book I have received much kindness and generosity from many gardeners, cooks and herbalists. The staff of both the Lindley Library and Wisley Gardens of the Royal Horticultural Society have been patient and helpful. I should particularly like to acknowledge the valuable assistance of several friends. They have photographed gardens, obtained books and recipes and even sent parcels of fresh herbs from as far as Australia, Cyprus, North America, France and Scotland. I thank them all most warmly: Myrtle and Dorinna Allen, Elizabeth Baker, Rosemary Barron, Anna Best, Claire Clifton, Colin Capon, Jeannette and Suzanne Doize, Lisa Kalaydjian, Efterpi Kyriacou, Patsy Guyer, Nevin Halici, Richard Hoskins, Laura Hudson, Allen Lacy, Janette Marshall, Sri Owen, Maro Pambou, Christalla Pantelides, Claudia Roden, Cherry Ripe, Lazaros Sparsis and Julie Toll. Finally my affection and gratitude goes to my husband and children who tirelessly collected information, seeds and plants.

PUBLISHER'S ACKNOWLEDGMENTS

The publisher would like to thank the following people for their help in preparing this book:

Michael and Denny Wickham, Clock House, Coleshill, Nr. Swindon, Wiltshire; Simon Hopkinson of Hollington Nurseries; Mr and Mrs A.J. Radcliffe, Essebourne Manor, Berkshire; Ragna Tischler Goddard; Hollington Herbs, Woolton Hill, Newbury, Berkshire; Mr and Mrs M. Hale; Jane Croswell-Jones of The Grange, Whatley Vineyard, Whatley, Frome, Somerset; Lynne Robinson; Richard Lowther; Lin and David Lobb, Hayford Hall.

Special thanks to the following people for providing props for special photography:

Melanie Williams, 79 Barret House, Benedict Road, Brixton, London SW9 0UN for the pomanders, sleep pillows and herb dolls on pages 199–202; The Hop Shop, Castle Farm, Shoreham, Sevenoaks, Kent; Stitches & Daughters, 5–7 Tranquil Vale, Blackheath Village, London SE3; Gallery of Antique Costume & Textiles, 2 Church Street, London NW8; Tobias & The Angel, 68 White Hart Lane, Barnes, London SW13; The Shaker Shop, 25 Harcourt Street, London W1; Enigma (stand 22), Persiflage (stand 25), Chenil Galleries, 181–183 Kings Road, London SW3; Perfect Glass, 5 Park Walk, London SW10; Ashill Colour Studio, Clovers, Church Street, Alcombe, Minehead, Somerset.

And special thanks also to all those people in England and France who very kindly permitted photography to take place in their homes and gardens.

PICTURE ACKNOWLEDGMENTS

1 Jerry Harpur (Essebourne Manor, Berkshire); 8 Georges Lévêque; 10–11 Clay Perry; 14 Angelo Hornak; 15 Royal Botanic Gardens, Kew; 16–17 Private Collection/Bridgeman Art Library; 18 Jacqui Hurst/Boys Syndication; 19 Heather Angel (designer: Tim Martin); 20–1 Jerry Harpur (designer: Jane Fernley-Wittingstall); 21 right Jacqui Hurst/Boys Syndication; 23 Georges Lévêque; 24–5 Stephen Robson/National Trust Picture Library; 25 right Georges Lévêque (Etta de Haes, The Netherlands); 26 Michele Lamontagne; 27 Jerry Pavia/Garden Picture Library; 28 Tania Midgley; 29 Clive Boursnell/Garden Picture Library; 30–1 Jerry Pavia/Garden Picture Library; 33 Georges Lévêque (Chilcombe House); 34 above S. & O. Mathews; 34 below Brigitte Thomas (Denmans); 35 Karen Bussolini; 38 Karen Bussolini; 40–1 Gary Rogers; 41 right Andrew Lawson; 41 below Jacqui Hurst/Boys Syndication; 42 Michele Lamontagne; 43 Georges Leveque (Samares Manor, Jersey); 44–6 Jerry Harpur (Mr & Mrs A.J. Radcliffe); 48–50 Brigitte Thomas (Haseley Court); 52–4 Karen Bussolini (designer: Ragna Tischler Goddard); 56–8 Jerry Harpur (Essebourne Manor, Berkshire); 68–87 Angelo Hornak (Courtesy of the collections of The Lindley Library, Vincent Square and the Royal Botanic Gardens, Kew); 94 Mike Busselle; 96 left Christian Sarramon; 96 right Yves Duronsoy; 99 Alex Dufort/Impact Photos; 100 Barque/Jerrican; 104 Campagne, Campagne/J.C. Roudil; 109 left John Garrett/Insight Picture Library; 109 right Campagne, Campagne/J.L. Garcia; 112 Mike Busselle; 114 above S. & O. Mathews; 114 centre Barrie Smith; 114 below Mike Busselle; 117 right Mike Busselle; 118 Pictures Colour Library/Tim Clinch; 122 Mike Busselle; 124 Michelle Garrett/Insight Picture Library; 127 Jean-Pierre Godeaut; 128 left Denis Hughes-Gilbey; 128 centre La Maison de Marie Claire/Blochlaine/Saulnier); 132 John Heseltine; 134 Jean-Pierre Godeaut; 136 John Heseltine; 138 left Mike Busselle; 142 John Garrett/Insight Picture Library; 148 Martin Breese/Retrograph Archive; 154 below Karen Bussolini; 157 right Tessa Traeger; 160 Denis Hughes-Gilbey; 162 Martin Breese/Retrograph Archive; 163 left Yves Duronsoy; 164 right S. & O. Mathews; 170 Scala; 171 Mary Evans Picture Library; 172 Pia Tryde; 174 Fritz von der Schulenburg (Ken Turner); 176 Paul Ryan/J.B. Visual Press; 178 La Maison de Marie Claire/Godeaut/Lebeau; 179 Di Lewis/Elizabeth Whiting and Associates; 182 Yves Duronsoy; 184–5 Michelle Garrett/Insight Picture Library; 187 Yves Duronsoy; 194 Pix/Gauthier; 195 Marie Claire Beautes/Le Mene; 196 above and below left Michelle Garrett/Insight Picture Library; 198 Yves Duronsoy; 200 left Yves Duronsoy; 201 Yves Duronsoy; 207 Camera Press; 212 Courtesy of The RHS Library; 213–4 Angelo Hornak (Courtesy of the collection of The Lindley Library); 215 Octopus Publishing Group Ltd./Angelo Hornak; 216 Angelo Hornak (Courtesy of the collection of The Lindley Library); 217 left Courtesy of The Lindley Library; 217 centre Octopus Publishing Group Ltd./Angelo Hornak; 217 right Angelo Hornak (Courtesy of the collections of The Lindley Library).

The following photographs were specially taken for Conran Octopus by Debbie Patterson: 2–3, 5, 6–7, 12–3, 22, 32, 36–7, 60–1, 62, 63, 66–7, 88–90, 92–3, 97–8, 101–3, 106–8, 110–1, 115, 116–7, 119–121, 125–6, 128–131, 135, 137, 138–141, 144–6, 149–152, 154 above, 155–7, 158–9, 163 right, 164 left, 165–9, 173–6, 180–1, 183, 186, 188–9, 190–1, 196 below right, 192–3, 199, 200 right, 202, 204–5, 206, 208–9.